TRUE TO TYPE

TRUE
TO
TYPE

Ruari McLean

OAK KNOLL PRESS
&
WERNER SHAW

2000

First published in the United States of America in 2000 by
OAK KNOLL PRESS
310 Delaware Street
New Castle
DE 19720
USA

Published in the UK by
WERNER SHAW
Suite F22
Park Hall Estate
40 Martell Road
West Dulwich
London SE21 8EN

Library of Congress Cataloging-in-Publication Data
   McLean, Ruari
     True to type : an autobiography of Ruari McLean.
       p.   cm.
     Includes bibliographical references (p.   ) and index.
     ISBN 1-884718-96-5
     1. McLean, Ruari. 2. Typographers—Great Britain Biography.
   3. Book designers—Great Britain Biography. 4. Graphic design
(Typography)—Great Britain—History—20th century.   I. Title
Z116.A44M385—2000
686.2′2′092—dc21
   [B]   99–22457
                                                         CIP

British Library Cataloguing-in-Publication Data
A CIP Record is available from The British Library

ISBN 1-884718-96-5 (Oak Knoll)
ISBN 0-907961-11-8 (Werner Shaw)

Designed and typeset by Nicholas Jones and David McLean
at Strathmore Publishing Services, London N7
in John Hudson's 'Manticore' typeface
   (initial capitals in Matthew Carter's 'Galliard')

Printed in the United States of America by Thomson-Shore, Dexter, Michigan

Contents

continued

For Tony
who was valiant for truth

Note on captions

Dimensions, where stated, are depth followed by width.

Acknowledgements

I am very grateful to Nic Jones and David McLean for producing this book in London, using technologies quite different from those I used all my life (not all that different from Caxton's) before my wife and I moved north first to Dollar on the Ochils in 1973, and then to the Isle of Mull in 1981. She died in Glasgow in 1995.

I am also indebted to my Edinburgh agent Barbara McLean for introducing my manuscript to Oak Knoll in Delaware. Also to my daughter-in-law Mary McLean for typing the manuscript in the first place. Also to the various photographers who have given us permission to reproduce their work. When photographs did not have the photographer's name on the back, it was sometimes impossible to identify the taker, in which case our apologies for non-acknowledgement.

A note from the typesetters about Manticore

In a book about a typographer, it seems appropriate to use a distinctive typeface.

This book has been produced, writes Ruari McLean in his Acknowledgements, 'using technologies quite different from those I used all my life.' Manticore is a typeface which reflects these technologies. It was designed in 1996 by John Hudson, the Canadian type designer. It can be classified as a Venetian design. Though sharing some characteristics with Nicholas Jenson's Roman, William Morris's Golden Type, and even Frederic Goudy's Italian Oldstyle, it is not a historical revival, but an attempt to capture the aesthetic and calming balance between black type and cream paper achieved by the Renaissance printers in the early years of printing.

Whereas most typefaces of the last hundred years have been designed with pencil and paper by one person, and then interpreted and strongly influenced by a punch-cutter using hand-carved punches or pantographs, Hudson has designed and produced the letterforms on computer, able to polish and revise the shape of each letter – with a degree of personal control that pre-computer designers did not have – until he achieved the harmonious inter-relationship he wanted. Designing the font and making the font became one act.

NJ / DMCL

x

Foreword

The long dominance of books without pictures is an aberration of history drawn out by the limitations of letterpress printing. With the ready availability of offset lithography and now other forms of visual record, the walls between word and picture have fallen. Who pushed them? Ruari McLean did his bit.

I was too old to be one of the millions of children who read weekly the *Eagle*, *Girl*, *Swift* and *Robin*; comics with an ethical intent that McLean helped shape. I thought in any event they were for a less subversive caste of society than mine; when I was eleven I was into 'Dennis the Menace' and 'The Bash Street Kids' and welcomed a packet of sherbet and a liquorice straw stuck into the inside cover of *Beano*. So I did not make the acquaintance of the amiable McLean until four years after the *Eagle* hatched.

In 1952 when looking for a job I found myself in the studio of Holden's advertising agency, an agency that was unique in doing the kind of thing I wanted to do. I did not get a job but around Mr McLean's desk were the 'About Britain' series of pocket touring guides. They combined text and illustrations to complement each other rather than stating the same thing twice. They were different, the itineraries were set out in a dia-grammatic way; this lit in me an enthusiasm for *information design* which saw me and my partner, John Miles, through thirty years of art editing the publications of the Consumers' Association.

Part of the production of *Which?* magazine was handled by the Shenval Press, and this brought me into contact and then near conflict with Mr McLean. Miles and I wrote an article for Shenval's magazine *Motif*. It was a mirror reflecting art in illustration, in architecture and in the visually pleasurable artefacts of life. McLean then asked me for 'photographs of Coventry'. I had access to a rich portfolio of prints of the City and people who lived there: he said, 'I don't want those – I need photos of the bloody Cathedral.' His lady partner's dog sensed which way the interview was unfolding, left cover from beneath her desk, and caught hold of my ankle. I think this cemented an empathy between me and the master.

Later I married Geoffrey Grigson's eldest daughter. Grigson was central to the doings of Rainbird, McLean Ltd in the 1950s, so I had an intimate retrospective of how they drove a vision of well-illustrated books that was at that time beyond the wit of established publishers to do themselves. Once when job hunting at one of the biggest, most patronising establishments, I found the 'Design & Production' department dressed in a brown apron behind a green baize door. R, McL Ltd had to bear the sneer of 'Coffee table books', but they more than anyone forced the book trade to respect and pay for design: not easy!

For me this book is an album of a London which was opening to me in the 1950s and 60s. McLean peoples a stage on which the curtain has fallen. He tells us who his actors were, what they were like, and where they – unpredictably – came from. They were for the most part people who would fit awkwardly into today's corporate mega-productions; God stand up for mavericks. He breathes their words and hopes for the rationality and hence moral sense intrinsic to good design. People do not talk like that any more – let us hope they will again – but to read this book is to revisit yesterday's future.

COLIN BANKS
Blackheath, March 2000

xii

Author's Preface: what is a typographer?

You are looking at type. Type is only a tool. It is one method of communication. Typography is the art, or skill, of using that tool in the most useful way for the purpose intended. The typographer is the person who exercises that art, or skill.

The first thing the typographer must have is words – which themselves are also only tools. He starts with words, which he may, and sometimes must, write himself; and his job is to get them, or their sense, transferred through the medium of his type into other people's minds. He will have been successful if it can be said of him, as Belloc hoped it would be said of himself, 'His sins were scarlet, but his books were read'.

The words do not necessarily have to be read easily, but they have to be read unmistakably, and in the right frame of mind, by the right people.

It is the unique fascination of the typographer's problem that it involves both design and literature. The designer who has no feeling for words will never make a good typographer.

There is no such thing as abstract typography. Type may be put into abstract patterns, but that is not typography. Typography is concerned only with the conveying of messages, expressed in words and figures, and composed in type for duplication by printing. It is, and can only be, the servant of those words, or the ideas behind them.

A piece of typography may be 'beautiful': that is to say, pleasing to the eye. But to whose eye? If it is not pleasing to the eye of the customers it is intended to please, it is not a well-designed job.

It is of course often impossible to define, within any useful limits, the sort of people for whom a given job is intended: for example, a novel. Obviously the audience for a popular novel contains people of many different kinds. Endless arguments sometimes take place between client and designer when both think they know what will please that entirely indefinable mass of diversity, the public, and both have opposite opinions. Either may be right. Very often they compromise, and then both are wrong.

Arguments about taste can be interminable, but two things are certain. One is that design is necessary. Design is the alternative, not to bad design, but to no design, which leads to chaos. If a thing is being made, it has to be made on some plan, with some intention; and the question is what degree of skill and design is required. In our modern, highly competitive and design-conscious civilisation, an increasingly high degree of skill and design is required in the production of all printed matter if it is to be read.

The second thing certain is that, at least in typography, there are some fixed standards and rules. These have not been changed by modern technology.

There are four main fields in which typography is practised today. These are books, periodicals (including newspapers), advertising, and jobbing printing. These all present different problems, but the basic tool in all of them is the same alphabet. The best introduction to all forms of typography is the design of books. It was in book printing that the shapes of our letters were finally established and the rules for using them developed; in books, the least ephemeral kind of printing, may be most conveniently studied those rules which in other fields of typography (e.g. advertising, and newspapers) may not apply. In any sport, it is wise to learn the rules before breaking them.

The word 'typographer' can mean many different things. The 'typographer' is no more and no less than the person, man or woman, professional or amateur, who practises typography. The growing complexity of the modern printing trade has made it necessary, since about 1930, for typography to exist as a distinct career, and a most interesting one it is, leading to so many other activities besides typography and printing. But it concerns many other people beside those who practise it as a career.

The design of printed matter affects, in one way or another, everyone, whether they can read or not. The appreciation of it may give pleasure, the more it is understood, to every educated person; it affects, powerfully and commercially, every business man besides those whose province it most directly is, printers and publishers. To put it at its simplest, nearly everyone in civilized countries must at some time in his or her life be concerned with the production of some piece of printed matter. The art of printing, which is the same as that of typography, is no longer a mystery: it is largely a matter of common sense; what is involved can be appreciated by anyone. Typography, like architecture, surrounds all of us: we should look at it critically, not ignore it.

I may appropriately end this introduction by quoting some words of Daniel Berkeley Updike, a great American printer, published in 1922 and still true today: 'The practice of typography, if it be followed faithfully, is hard work – full of detail, full of petty restrictions, full of drudgery, and not greatly rewarded as men now count rewards. There are times when we need to bring to it all the history and art and feeling that we can, to make it bearable. But in the light of history, and of art, and of knowledge and of man's achievement, it is as interesting a work as exists – a broad and humanizing employment which can indeed be followed merely as a trade, but which if perfected into an art, or even broadened into a profession, will perpetually open new horizons to our eyes and new opportunities to our hands.'

When I explained to a friend, 'This is a typographical autobiography, and there are no women in it' (not quite true), he replied, 'What else is there to write about?' That made me think.

RUARI MCLEAN
Sanquhar, Spring 2000

The 'Challand' motor-car, 1921, with father, mother, and author, in Galloway.

1. Galloway to Oxford

HEROUNCROFT was a small house on the edge of moors outside Newton Stewart in Galloway – in the Lowlands of Scotland, but more like the Highlands in its wild and lonely hills. It was as good a place as any to be born in. My parents loved it. How they met I never discovered. My mother was a history graduate of Edinburgh University, whose life up till marriage had been very much among intellectuals. My father was born in Stranraer, where his father was the shoemaker. He and his brother were walking out with the daughters of a local farmer, but one day his brother went out with the wrong girl and came back engaged to her, which left my father free, in his opinion, to look elsewhere. He had been Dux (head boy) of Stranraer Academy: the silver medal on a blue ribbon that went with it (did he ever have to wear it?) is now in the Museum of Childhood in Edinburgh. He joined the Civil Service, studied at the Imperial College in South Kensington, and became a Customs and Excise Officer. A friend of his once said that he would have been happier as a shepherd or the Curator of a small country museum.

We were therefore not rich. The only member of the family who might have become a millionaire was my uncle John Ireland. He was an engineer who was invalided out of the Royal Engineers after the Somme, with a Military Cross. and rather less of one leg than he had started with. He then went into partnership with a man called Challoner to make motor cars. I do not know how many they made – possibly only one – when Challoner decamped with whatever money was in the kitty, leaving uncle John to pay all the debts, which eventually he did. They had called the car the 'Challand', and gave the first one to my mother and father. I remember clearly the day our wooden garage caught fire. At least I think I do. I was 3 at the time. My parents and I were having tea with friends nearby. A neighbour came rushing round to tell us, and we hurried back. The car had been pulled out of the garage and was safe. 'Damn!' said my mother (it was probably the only swear word she knew, until I learned to swear) because she hoped it had been destroyed. It was probably the worst car ever made; among other things it lacked was a differential. Perhaps each partner thought the other had put it in.

John Thomson McLean,
author's father, *c.* 1920.

Isabel Mary McLean,
author's mother, and
author, *c.* 1920.

In 1921, when I was four, my father was posted to, of all places, Oxford —

Towery city and branchy between towers;
Cuckoo-echoing, bell-swarméd, lark-charméd, rook-racked, river-rounded.

We started off in the Banbury Road, but after a couple of years we bought 1 Park Crescent, a house with a dark basement and four floors above it, and a minute triangular garden; I could walk from it to the Dragon School where I was now entered.

One of the masters, J. B. Brown, and his wife Helen, had been friends of my mother in Edinburgh. I started, aged six, in the Baby School, in the form of Daisy Pratt: when I last heard of her, sixty years later, she was riding her bicycle in the Banbury Road with a white walking-stick across the handle-bars.

I soon needed a bike to get to school. Everyone else had one. Mine had three gears, not eighteen, as today. It also had a milometer and a basket to carry school-books and, at intervals, copies of the *Strand, Windsor, Queen*, and *Punch* magazines, to be delivered to my mother's friends and their magazine club.

At school I fought regularly, on the floor, with another small boy called Charles Wrong. Charles bled easily, not only from fighting but also from falling off walls, trees and bicycles; but it was usually blamed on me. 'Why do you hate Ruari McLean so much?' asked his mother, wielding a sponge. 'I don't *hate* him,' answered Charles, 'I only wish he were dead.' Today, in 2000, Charles is my oldest and closest friend.

The Dragon School had about 300 boys and 30 girls, most of these sisters of the boys. With that number, and the staff to look after them, there was something for everybody, not only the clever ones. For example, gardening was both taught and encouraged as a hobby. Poetry was one of the ingredients in this marvellous school, partly through the school's own hymnbook devised by Hum, the headmaster, and the informal Sunday morning services, and partly through the English teaching all through the school. Every Spring term the top English form put on a Shakespeare play, for which the boys were properly made up by masters' wives; and costumes and properties arrived in wicker hampers from Drury Lane.

In due course I took part (acted would hardly be the right word) in three plays: *Hamlet* (I was a Switzer who ran once across the stage); *Macbeth* (I was Donalbain, with two lines to speak); and *Richard II*, when at last, as Bushy, I had a noticeable speaking part. But I ruined it by losing my memory and omitting half the scene, which greatly upset my colleagues on the stage.

I never took part (being judged insufficiently musical) in the Gilbert and Sullivan operas which were performed at the end of every winter term. These were produced by J. B. 'Bruno' Brown with orchestra of staff and friends, but all the parts were played by boys and girls. They were rapturously enjoyed every year by school, parents, staff and friends.

The man whose virtues and eccentricity made the school a unique institution, which enriched for life those children lucky enough to be sent there, was C. C. Lynam. Known as The Skipper, he was the elder brother of the aforementioned 'Hum', A. E. Lynam, my headmaster. The Skipper, with a weather-beaten face, a white walrus moustache, a blue kerchief round his neck and often a parrot on his shoulder, spent his summers sailing a yacht, *Blue Dragon*, to Scotland and Norway, often with Dragon boys and girls as crew. One of his dicta was 'A boy will never learn to use time unless he is allowed to waste it; and he will never learn self-control unless he has the opportunity of getting into mischief.'

Almost every master had a nickname, used by the boys to his face (followed, with luck, by 'Sir'): Hum, Cheese, Joc, Tubby, Fuzz, Straddles, Pug, Bruno, Rats, Ma Dirt, Jacko, etc. One master, Gerald Haynes, actually had three nicknames: Spitter, because he dribbled down his pipe, Tortoise, because of the way he pushed his baldish head and neck out of his clothes, and Dada, because, I suppose, the boys loved him like a father, even when he caned them. He taught practically everything, including rugger, which he had never played. He instilled in many of us a love of wild flowers (he also taught gardening, out of school, and many boys had their own gardens), and a love of architecture, especially French cathedrals. Through him I came to enjoy the stories of W. W. Jacobs and Bret Harte. He was one of the older masters: the younger ones had mostly fought in the war and bore the marks of it. Small boys like me did not realise just how short a time ago those men had been in the trenches. One master with shell-shock occasionally threw a boy through the folding partition into another classroom, and no one seemed to mind, except possibly the boy.

A master I much admired, who surprisingly had no nickname, was Giles Dixey, who had sailed before the mast as a merchant seaman, and was very good at drawing. I once saw him pick up a boy by the hair of his head, who had spat on the floor in the hall during early morning hymn, and deposit him outside in a friendly sort of way. Giles later took up etching, with a pin, and wood-engraving, and after the war I was able to find him supplies of suitable paper when it was difficult to obtain.

The war was kept in our minds. Every November the whole school went down to the granite war memorial cross above the river Cherwell, heard a boy read out the names of all the Dragons who had been killed, and then sang 'At the going down of the sun, and in the morning, we will remember them' and 'O valiant hearts, who to your glory came ...'.

The Skipper used to award prizes for summer holiday diaries. I believe that everyone who sent in any diary at all got some kind of prize. My mother forced me to keep a diary every summer from the time I could write. So keep a diary I must, whatever tears I shed because I wanted to do something else, which was often. The diaries were illustrated with photographs (by my father), pressed seaweed and wild flowers (by my mother, usually), my own drawings, spilt blood, and any other ephemera that came to hand. By the time I left the Dragon School I had acquired the diary habit, and enjoyed trying to record those moments of my life whose memories I wished to save. I never kept a pedantic day-to-day diary, but continually jotted down conversations or descriptions of things I had enjoyed; at one period I even made lists of girls I had kissed or failed to kiss. I also made a note, for many years, of nearly every book I read, often with comments or excerpts. Altogether the diary habit became part of life. Eventually I found that writing came easier to me than drawing.

Another stimulus to writing and drawing was *The Draconian*. This remarkable school magazine was produced three times a year by a master, and contained articles, poems, drawings and photographs, often by distinguished Old Dragons, which any leading paper would have been glad to publish. Verses by O.D.s J. B. Poynton and Frank Sidgwick were certainly 'good enough for *Punch*' – as we used to say in those days.

When I was a small boy, I believed that my father knew everything. He read me stories at night (the first was *Coral Island*), and I watched him practising his drawing, painting, calligraphy, photography, model-making, and gardening. He would make beautiful manuscripts, with Edward Johnston's *Writing & Illuminating, & Lettering* open on the table, with a quill pen poised and tender gold leaf and gypsum ready for the illuminated initials. Then there were all the bottles and trays for developing his photographs (this was in the 1920s) and a lot of complicated apparatus for making enlargements. The resultant views of

Galloway lochs and hills, and then family groups on the banks of the river Cherwell or in the Cotswold hills, usually had my father posed nonchalantly in the background holding a piece of black thread, which you couldn't see, from his finger to the shutter. He made a superb railway station and signal-box for my Hornby train, and then made stations for all my friends. The miniature colour-printed posters were bought in packets, but the magazines on the bookstalls were all meticulously drawn and coloured by him.

Bookplate drawn by author's father for author's mother, *c.* 1913.

In his early days, already working in the Customs and Excise service in Galloway, he had twice failed to pass an exam, which at that time permanently prevented him from getting promotion. When he was posted to Oxford, he had very little to do except take readings of specific gravity in Oxford Brewery once or twice a week. One day the university authorities realised that they had a Customs and Excise Officer right there, and promptly arranged for parcels of dinosaur eggs and other priceless items from overseas to be opened in their presence by my father, instead of being broken (as they were consistently complaining) by ham-fisted Customs officers in Dover. That immediately gave my father friends among the dons. When he died, after the Second World War, I realised that in many ways he was a saint. I do not believe that he ever did a mean thing in his life, or was hard or unkind to anyone.

By the time I was a teenager I found that in some ways I had out-grown him. He was a very simple man. He was no teetotaller, but I doubt if he ever went into a pub by himself, and rarely with others. My own upbringing was totally different from his, and began to separate us. I loved him, but was never intimate with him. It was my mother with whom I was close.

He was dark-haired. My mother had golden hair, an amiable face, a sense of humour (which my father also had), and a sardonic wit. From the age of four till the time I was twelve, she was my main teacher and influ-ence, since I was ill in bed for more days than I was up. This was entirely due to wrong advice taken by my parents that I should have my tonsils removed before we left Scotland, and two incompetent surgeons who tried to take them out, but left them in and infected. The third surgeon, who finally removed them in the Acland Hospital in Oxford, told my mother that he had 'dug them out of a cess-pool'. I have hardly ever been ill since.

I therefore spent a lot of time reading. At first it was *Chick's Own* and other children's papers – to my mother's strong disapproval. She tried to make me read Walter Scott, which put me off enjoying him until I was forty. When it came to books I much preferred the *Just William* stories by Richmal Crompton. When I was eight, my form at school started on Greek, and my mother had to buy a Greek grammar and stay one chap-ter ahead of me. We also possessed Arthur Mee's *My Magazine* and the *Children's Encyclopaedia*, which were wide-ranging and pleasantly varied in their contents and included poetry. An odd moment came when I was about ten, lying on the floor with an anthology which contained poems by Tennyson. Something mysterious actually clicked in my mind, and I suddenly found that poetry had become magic. Words, it didn't seem to matter much what they meant, were intoxicating me. I began copying out poems in a little note-book bound in half red leather which my father had once used for notes in the Government laboratories. My first poem was 'Crossing the bar'. The second was 'The Eagle':

> *He clasps the crag with crooked hands;*
> *Close to the sun in lonely lands,*
> *Ring'd with the azure world, he stands.*
>
> *The wrinkled sea beneath him crawls;*
> *He watches from his mountain walls,*
> *And like a thunderbolt he falls.*

I repeat this poem to myself nearly every day of my old age, when I drive down the steep hill to Carsaig, on the coast of Mull, and look at the cliffs where eagles live, and the sea crawls beneath. I do wonder occasionally if Tennyson was thinking of gannets.

In 1933 I had spent the first fourteen years of my life living with my parents. I believe that my genes, and the particularly happy life I had lived with my father and mother, had now made me. There had been no quarrels or unhappiness that I can remember, but a continual quiet guidance that I never consciously noticed. For the rest of my life, I believe that everything I did was conditioned by my genes and that circumstance. I cannot now see why I should be praised for anything I did later that appeared good, or clever, or brave: I was always doing just what seemed natural and was my inevitable choice. If I did something wrong, or bad, as I must often have done, I might partly blame my poor old genes, but mostly it had to be my own fault. I believe that a horrible childhood would have made me a very different person.

In their early years of marriage, both my father and mother had articles accepted by the *Glasgow Herald* and several other Scottish papers. My father's creativity then went into his photography and painting, and my mother's into training children. A miscarriage prevented her having another child after me, but she kept a flow of children in the house whose parents were abroad, in order that I should never think I was the only pebble on the beach. Then, in 1945 she began a new career, reading and editing for publishers. It began with about a dozen books for her friend Basil Blackwell in Oxford; she then approached London publishers and was soon very busy indeed. She read or edited over six hundred books, some of them very difficult and important, translated over a dozen French texts, and wrote a dictionary for children, published by

Linocut by author,
Christmas 1936.

Frederick Warne in 1954 as *Words: a simple dictionary for boys and girls*. She died in 1958, aged 75; my father died in 1962, aged 82.

From the Dragon I went to Eastbourne College, on the sea in Sussex, and was very happy. In my third year I got into the rugger first fifteen, which beat all the schools we played, including Radley and St Edwards, at that time the best school rugger teams in the country. In my first match for the fifteen, against Christ's Hospital School, one of the opposing team was carried off the field. 'Who tackled that man?' murmured our captain. 'I did', I whispered guiltily. 'Well done!' hissed the captain.

I was taught English and writing by Diarmid Noel-Paton; elementary maths (so well that I once incredibly got 90% in an exam), by Stephen Foot, who had left a high position in Shell Oil Co. to become a schoolmaster in Eastbourne, and who asked me to design the jacket for his autobiography *Three Lives* – but I was not ready for that honour, and my design was not used; I forget what by the headmaster, Gordon Carey, who had been a rugger blue and a Syndic for Cambridge University Press, and had the hymn numbers in the school chapel designed by Stanley Morison; and art by 'Gas' (G. A. Stevens), who did not try to

9

teach art but let it happen. But I failed to get the classical scholarship I was expected to get to Oxford University, and which was financially necessary to my parents. In those days, especially for people living in Oxford, no other university but Oxford was admitted to exist. I blamed my failure on the experience of having had to read one Greek play twelve times, instead of twelve Greek plays once.

So, at the age of eighteen and a half, I had no future. I had already decided against becoming a doctor (they were bad news); the Law was obviously boring; a schoolmaster? You must be joking! What I really wanted to do was ride horses in South America. My parents were not enthusiastic about that. So I must look for a job....

The Diarist

What is he doing there in the dark hour,
The cold hour his bed, laid back, begrudges;
Covering the foolscap to its corners
With a slant hand reflection never smudges?

He is racing the remembrance of a day
To its far end, that sleep would sponge away.

But does he think to rescue what no man
Possesses? It was not his own to save.
One of a hundred million bleak sunrises.
One of oblivion's blanks. A bubble, a wave.

He does not find it so. He loves too well
What passes not to pick it from time's hell.

Fool, if he thinks one coming will comprehend.
His pearl will be a pebble, grey and small,
That men will kick before them down the path
Repeated, with none wiser after all.

He does not race with others. He is rare
And lonely. Leave him, lordamercy, there.

Mark Van Doren, Windmill

10

2. The Shakespeare Head Press

There's something about a soldier
that is fine, fine, fine:
The military chest
seems to suit the ladies best ...

sang Cicely Courtneige in 1936. But I was a pacifist and I was in love with both Carole Lombard and Myrna Loy. I was also aged eighteen and looking for a job – 1936 was not a good time for jobs.

My friend Richard Blackwell's father, the Oxford bookseller and publisher Basil Blackwell, knew that I could read, and that I could draw, two useful qualifications in his world. He suggested to my parents that I might be interested in printing, and if so I could start the following Monday morning in the Shakespeare Head Press in St Aldate's, which he owned. I knew nothing about printing, except that it was presumably a sedentary occupation indoors, exactly what I did not have in mind. However, at 8 a.m. on a Monday in January 1936, I set out on my bicycle to go to work, humming to myself a poem I had just read in the *London Mercury* by Mark Tait:

> *Men on their way to work*
> *The shadows still unwithered*
> > *by the relentless sun;*
> *All things still possible,*
> > *unhampered by the details*
> > *of accomplishment;*
> *Nothing, as yet, left irretrievably*
> *undone.*

The Shakespeare Head Press had been founded in Stratford-on-Avon in 1904 by A. H. Bullen, a Shakespearean scholar, who claimed that he had been told in a dream to print the works of Shakespeare in the poet's birthplace. He actually succeeded in doing just that: the Stratford Town Shakespeare in ten volumes was completed in 1907. He also printed *The Collected Works of William Butler Yeats*, two important volumes on the

Elizabethan playhouse, and among other items, a series of six charming booklets each of 32 pages, which included Shakespeare's *Songs* and *The Nutbrown Maid*.

But when he died in 1919, the press was more or less bankrupt. It was bought by Basil Blackwell and some friends, and handed over to Bernard Newdigate, then aged 51, to direct. In 1930 the press was moved to Oxford, not to a gracious old building which would have been appropriate, but to the first floor of an extremely unromantic yellow brick building in St Aldate's, a poor area close to Folly Bridge over the River Thames.

I doubt if there was anything in the Press that William Caxton would not have instantly recognized if he had dropped in, except the telephone. All composition of type was by hand: machine setting by Monotype, when required, was placed with other printers. The composing-room was presided over by Bill, a middle-aged man with a walrus moustache, and Fred, a young man who may still have been in his apprenticeship. Beyond the composing-room was the machine-room, containing an iron hand-press which had once belonged to William Morris, and an ancient Wharfedale cylinder machine which went 'Tosh-tosh, tosh-tosh, tosh-tosh' when it was printing literature. There were two machine-minders. There must have been some place intended to store paper supplies, printed and unprinted, but I just remember piles of paper lying about on the floor. There was no bindery; Blackwells owned a bindery elsewhere in Oxford.

Mr Newdigate sat in a glass-walled sanctum where he spent most of the day correcting proofs. There was a smaller office which housed the manager, Mr Kendrick, who kept the place ticking, or tried to, and Freda, the secretary, a nice girl against whom I was warned on the day I arrived by one of the other directors: 'Don't try anything on Freda, she packs a pretty punch'. Newdigate would have been shocked if he had heard that.

The Press had two basic functions. The first was to design and print fine limited editions for any publisher in that line of business. For example, in 1923 they had printed *The Player's Shakespeare*, in seven folio volumes, with colour illustrations in collotype and black and white line by artists such as Thomas Lowinsky, Charles Ricketts, Albert Rutherston and Paul Nash, for Benn Brothers; *The Pilgrim's Progress* in 1928, illustrated by Blair Hughes-Stanton and Gertrude Hermes; and *Paradise Lost*, 1930, illustrated by D. Galanis, both for Cresset Press;

and *The Confessions of an English Opium-Eater*, 1930, illustrated with lithographs by Zhenya Gay, for the Limited Editions Club of New York. They were all designed by Newdigate. Manchester University owns a collection of Shakespeare Head Press books, listed in *Books Printed at The Shakespeare Head Press*, edited by Ian Rogerson, 1988.

The second function of the Press was to act as general printer for Oxford citizens. This included, Oxford being what it is, or was, books of verse for well-off undergraduates and others who could not get into print unless they paid for it themselves.

I was introduced to Mr Newdigate, who knew nothing about me except that Basil Blackwell had asked him to take me in as a learner, probably the first he had ever had. After a few kindly words I was given a chair and some proofs to correct: it was assumed that I could at least read. I stared at the proofs for a quarter of an hour and then noticed a sheet of paper on a shelf beside me, written in an elegant kind of hand-writing I had not seen before and rather liked. It was my first sight of the italic hand; the letter was from Stanley Morison (of whom I had never heard) to Bernard Newdigate. My real education was beginning.

For the first three days I did not hear any of the men utter a single swear-word, to my disappointment. I therefore assumed that constant association with great literature, like Jane Austen and the Brontës, had purified their minds. On the fourth day, Bill, with the walrus mous-tache, who spent most of his time planing type with a wooden mallet, hit his thumb and said 'Bugger!' There was a hush, and they all looked at me. I did not faint, and the ice was broken. It transpired that up till then they had refrained from swearing in deference to my supposed innoc-ence. When I showed no shock, their language returned to normal. Far from being elevated by the literature they were handling, they hated it, and I gradually discovered that, sadly, they despised Newdigate too.

Newdigate was then aged 67. He did not allow himself to be photographed, apparently because there was something about his chin of which he was ashamed. I remember it only as deeply dimpled. He was fairly tall, had crumpled clothes and a crumpled weather-beaten face. He looked like what I imagined an Elizabethan sailor might have looked like. His brother Francis, as I learned later, was a senior captain in the Merchant Navy who was awarded the naval Distinguished Service Cross in 1942.

Bernard was a devout Roman Catholic, a scholar in Elizabethan liter-ature, and one of the two or three most distinguished book designers in the Europe of his day. He was also a very kindly man, but not a teacher.

The men in the Press despised him (if that is not too strong a word) because in his search for perfection he was always altering things. One of the books going through the Press while I was there was an edition of the poems of Ben Jonson. It was not only designed by Newdigate but was also edited by him, a fatal combination. Poor Mr Kendrick could never get Newdigate to pass a sheet for press. One day, after a sheet had actually been printed, I watched Kendrick and Freda altering every copy in pen and ink, because a letter had been received that morning from an American scholar which had caused Newdigate to decide to alter a colon to semi-colon.

Newdigate was also absent-minded. He had more than once got into the wrong car and driven it away before realising that it was not his. It was said that he had dictated a letter for twenty minutes without knowing that he was standing on Freda's foot. I know that when my mother invited him to lunch, he arrived on the wrong day – but she gave him lunch without saying anything. He was a man of the utmost integrity and indeed nobility of character.

Newdigate was a doer rather than a teacher. When he came out of the army in 1918 (where he had been a disastrous motorcyclist) he had, for a time, been a consultant to Harold Curwen at the Curwen Press in Plaistow. Joseph Thorp, in his memoir of Newdigate, quotes Harold Curwen, himself a great printer, as saying 'At that time there was of course no general interest in decent printing and moral support such as he gave was as valuable as the actual theories he expounded. Actually his teaching was rather vague and the practical "comps" were always asking for formulae and measurements in place of his feeling little grunts. His head was above the clouds but that was just why I felt he could be useful to us whose noses were on the grindstone. I have the warmest feelings of gratitude for my brief contact with him and the peace that always surrounded him ...'.

I remember those 'feeling little grunts' . He showed me (and lent me) finely printed books, and smiled, and his grunts and hints conveyed that close spacing ('thins, not muttons') was essential, and black ink should be black, not grey, and so on. He certainly never went into any of the finer points, like letter-spacing, that I imbibed after the war from Jan Tschichold. And I assiduously began to practise writing in italic.

One day I was encouraged to try setting type by hand. They gave me a 'modern' poem, which had no capital letters or punctuation, so it

THE SHAKESPEARE HEAD PRESS
Founded 1904 at Stratford-upon-Avon
by the late Arthur Henry Bullen

Telephone 4072

33 Saint Aldates Oxford

January 24th, 1938

Ruari McLean was attached to the Shakespeare Head Press
for a period of four months as a student of printing, with
a view to taking up printing as his trade. Since then he
has had experience of printing in Germany and later went
through a year's course at the Heriot-Watt College Printing
School in Edinburgh. He is now spending a year as pupil in
Waterlow's factory at Dunstable. He showed both keenness
and assiduity while working here. He is a practical
draughtsman with good artistic tastes and a wide outlook
on the various methods and crafts related to printing. He
is aged 21 and is widely read. He was educated at the Dragon
School, Oxford, and at Eastbourne College. While working here
he won the good opinion of all those with whom he worked. I
can cordially recommend him for any post in which his undoubted
abilities and good taste in the graphic arts will find scope;
and I am confident that, given the opportunity, he will do
brilliant work in the sphere which he has chosen.

for the Shakespeare Head Press, Limited,

Bernard H. Newdigate

Director.

A letter of reference from Bernard Newdigate, January 1938.

would be easier for this poor novice to set. I set it and was then allowed to proof it on the hand press, a great step forward. I took my proofs home to show my parents. To my intense satisfaction I had at last found a subject about which I knew a little more than they did. Things were looking up.

It is pleasing to remember that one of the last things Newdigate did was to design the works of Shakespeare in one volume for Basil Black-well. In order to sell it at six shillings Blackwell had to print an edition of 50,000 copies. This was in 1935, and the book made 1,260 pages, set in two columns in 9 point Plantin, yet 'through Newdigate's wizardry' (wrote Blackwell) 'it was easy and pleasant to read. The work was driven through', he continued, 'at a pace which forbade "fidgeting" with the proofs (Blackwell knew what the problem was), the public fulfilled our hopes, and in two years there was a reprint'.

3. Germany

AFTER I had been in the Shakespeare Head Press for a few months, Newdigate received a letter from Anna Simons in Germany (the translator of Edward Johnston's *Writing & Illuminating, & Lettering*) asking him if he could find a young man to exchange with the son of a friend of hers who wanted to come and study in England. The German boy's father, a professor in Bonn University, owned a small book-printing firm in Weimar. So I went, and the young German came to stay with my parents in Oxford.

My time in Germany should be described in poetry, but I cannot do it. In particular it would be love poetry, for love – I think, real love, for the first time from a woman not my mother – touched me in Berlin.

I started in the house of the professor, in Bad Godesburg on the Rhine. The professor had his breakfast (strawberries and white wine) on a little balcony overlooking the Rhine, served by his wife, who did not sit down with him. I was amazed when a lady visitor, the wife of a professor of law in Berlin, with whom I later stayed, had breakfast with my professor on his balcony, still served by his wife who did not join them.

They had a daughter, Irmgard, aged about sixteen, who I was also amazed to find considered it her duty to look after me, which she did, much more than her mother. I expect I bored her; I was not at all like her brother's friends who came to see her, svelt, good-looking young Nazis. She was genuinely kind; but she couldn't teach me German, though she tried. For this, I attended a course for foreigners in Bonn University: girls and young men from various countries, including a girl called Elaine Arapoff who lived in Paris, of whom I at first disapproved and then found she was simple and sweet, and always dropping her possessions on the floor. Four years later I was astonished to find a full-page photograph of Elaine's handsome face, in profile, in an issue of *Lilliput*.

The professor owned a little holiday cottage in the 'Sieben Gebirge' hills above Bad Godesburg. I was allowed to stay there for a week by myself, which I enjoyed hugely and dreamed of Irmgard, who was away that week in Stralsund. The smell of pine woods and new-mown hay drifted in through the window above my bed, as I lay reading *Claudius the God*. There were fabulous views to the south and east: little pointed hills across the foreground, then the winding Rhine, and a flat plain stretching to infinity beyond.

Sadly, I never met Anna Simons; but before I went to the Press in Weimar, I was invited to Berlin to stay with Dodo Husserl, the lady who had visited us in Bad Godesburg, whose husband, himself a professor, was the son of a famous German legal authority. He was Jewish; a large part of his face had been removed by a shell in the First World War. The Nazis falsely accused the Jews of never fighting for Germany, but they could not say this of him, and allowed him to visit America to look for a job, which he did.

I walked around Berlin with a succession of charming girls on my arm, all, it seemed, in the middle of distracting love affairs 'because he isn't writing'. Language was a bit of a problem: 'Your eyes speak, but your tongue doesn't', said one of them kindly to me. German was easier to understand than to speak. At breakfast one morning, my hostess sent her husband to get the marmalade for me. He returned with strawberry jam and a cucumber (Gurke) the size and form of a young python. 'Ach, die verkehrte Marmelade', cried his wife, 'The wrong marmalade!' 'Aber die richtige Gurke', replied Gerhardt Husserl soothingly, 'The right cucumber'. He then put it round his neck and said such things were only made to order.

My friends in Berlin never discussed the Nazis in my presence. I have no idea how much of the future they foresaw in 1936; but one evening on the roof garden, when we were playing Mozart, my hostess said of the Nazis that of course they had hurt her, her husband being a Jew, but she could also look at the situation dispassionately, and she *hated* it – all the high-sounding words and trumpets – she *hated* it. No more was said.

In July I went to Weimar. It was a place in some ways like Oxford, with its beautiful park and atmosphere of scholarship emanating from Goethe and Schiller, whose statue in Weimar was known as 'Die Gebrüder Schmidt', 'the Smith brothers'.

The people in the press were very kind to me. I was taught how to operate a platen and feed paper into it; and after work they tried to teach me how to drink beer, of which I already had some idea. What impressed me most in the press was that in every room there was a washbasin with running water and a towel, and every workman was issued with a cake of soap and a pumice stone, which had to be used before handling a sheet of paper. The Germans were proud of being printers: after all, it was, as they all knew, a German invention.

In August I travelled from Weimar, via Frankfurt, to Paris. The worrying tensions of Nazi Germany evaporated as we crossed the border into France. But I had also learned, for the rest of my life, a little about the poetry, music, and natural loveliness of that great country.

I had been invited to stay a few nights in Paris with the parents of a French boy who had stayed with my parents in Oxford for a month to learn English. Paul had arrived while I was away, and had charmed my parents by singing and chatting to them in French, showing no signs of wanting to learn English or explore the world of pubs and girls. When I arrived back for Paul's last week, we looked guardedly at each other; but suddenly we made good friends. When he returned to France we exchanged precious clothes: he took my school rugby scarf, and I kept two of his white shirts with nicotine stains where he had breathed downwards hard to hide cigarette smoke in class.

The highlight of my visit was to be shown round the Ministry of Finance, followed by an aperitif with the Minister, Paul's father Vincent Auriol. What exotic, totally unfamiliar and exciting potation would we be offered? The large Ministry rooms, all white and gold, had magnificent carpets and ceilings. On a silver tray in the Minister's ante-room stood two bottles of good old English Sandeman's port, white and red, with sweet biscuits.

The next time I saw Paul in Paris, after the war, his father was President of the French Republic.

"aber die richtige Gurke"

Drawing from author's diary, 1936.

4. *The Art of the Book*

I now saw that printing, in one form or another, was going to be my future. I must begin to study it seriously.

'Printing' could lead to publishing, or editing, or typography (whatever that was), or type-designing, or even illustration. Did 'typography' mean 'designing with type'? If so, that alarmed me: did I have the necessary inventive ability? Of course at this early moment in a new career, I didn't. Gradually I found that it was not really a problem. 'Invention' does not come only from magic, but out of the images gradually stored in one's mind; the more one studies examples of printing, with enjoyment and gradually with discrimination, and criticism, the richer becomes the background from which typographic solutions are produced. As, presumably, with all creative activities.

At that time I had not yet seen clearly enough that there were two kinds of graphic design: in books, with words already written, which may not be changed; and advertising, which combines words which may be changed, or entirely omitted, and images, to be created for the occasion.

I went to Edinburgh School of Printing, which was then the only printing school in Britain that accepted people for a year, as opposed to London, which took people only for three years. Edinburgh's real activity was to teach day-release apprentices from local printing firms; but when I joined, I found two other full-time students besides myself. One was a young Indian going out to Madras to run a Monotype composing-room; the other, it soon became clear, had no interest in printing at all, but his father (a Scottish Master Printer) had insisted that he go.

The Principal of the school, Frank Restall, was an able designer from Oxford University Press, but he was not a teacher. The best part of the school for me was a collection of pages or books by Gutenberg , Fust and Schoeffer, Jenson, Aldus Manutius, Estienne, Tory, Plantin, and so on, they were all there – in glass-topped cases in one of the corridors. They had been collected by William Maxwell, the great Managing director of the famous Edinburgh book printers R. & R. Clark. I had very little to do at the school, apart from acquiring a City and Guilds Certificate which no one has ever asked for. I spent my time more profitably in the Advocates' Library, reading Updike, Morison, and in particular, *The Fleuron,* a 'journal' (in fact a series of seven sumptuous volumes) which began in 1923 and ended in 1930, devoted to typography.

The Fleuron was magnificent, a delight, an inspiration for typographers everywhere. But was it 'forward-looking'? It did not need to be. It expressed the views on printing and typography of a small group of men, but essentially two: Oliver Simon, who edited the first four volumes, all printed at the Curwen Press; and Stanley Morison, who contributed to all seven and edited the last three, printed at the Cambridge University Press. Volume 7 contains an index (by A. F .Johnson) which does not contain the words: offset, photo-litho-offset or photography, let alone any such names as, for example, Bauhaus, Bayer, Lissitzky, Tschichold or Picasso. However, the first *Fleuron* contains an article by Bernard Newdigate (a man considerably older than the editors), which actually mentions photo-litho-offset and the fact that photo-typesetting was on the way and likely to be a threat to conventional typefounders. I believe that this may be the only reference to photography in all seven volumes.

We look in vain, in *The Fleuron,* for any sign of what was going on in the art world at this time, but we do find an illustration by McKnight Kauffer in volume 2, and two by Ceri Richards in volume 6, both among the end pages, not as main features; and in a main article in volume 6, Dwiggins is recognised by Beatrice Warde as a 'deliberate modernist'. But the real answer to the 'forward-looking' question lies in the Editor's Postscript at the end of volume 7. Here, one feels, Morison is speaking from the heart: 'It has taken nearly eight years to bring THE FLEURON to its scheduled end. Nobody ever made a penny profit from it. The staff has not at any time been more than two and a secretary; and, as the one member who has contributed an article and reviews to every number, I may be pardoned for congratulating myself upon release from a task which, originally light, made during the last five years heavy demands upon the editorial leisure and means.' He continues with Morisonian severity to lay down his laws: 'There is need for obedience to the simplest possible conventions.... It is not for the printer to assess the literary value of a text. Clearness in printing makes demands upon the printer's intelligence rather than upon his emotions, upon conscientiousness rather than enthusiasm Hence the supreme requirement, in a book which may circulate in the future as well as the present, is intelligibility.' And finally, the utterly false statement: '*Beauty is desirable – and beauty will come if unsought.*' Did Bruce Rogers, or Francis Meynell, or Frederic Warde, or Oliver Simon, or Jan Tschichold, or any other great designer of books believe that?

Then, a contemptuous dismissal of the 'new typography' – Morison of course knew all about it, but could not accept it: 'The apostles of the "machine age" will be wise to address their disciples in a standard old face – they can flourish their concrete banner in sans-serif on title-pages and perhaps in a running headline.' He ends by saying that the justification for the *Fleuron's* 1500 pages is: 'Its disposition to enquire and its conviction that the teaching and example of its predecessors of the English private press movement left typography, as THE FLEURON leaves it, matter for further argument.'

Fine. God be thanked for a man who knew what he wanted, and who would have died to defend his beliefs. But Morison did not allow time (in print) for any arguments on crucial subjects on which he had long ago made up his mind.

While typographers in Britain could buy successive numbers of *The Fleuron* for a guinea (the limited editions on hand-made paper, with editorial insets, cost 3 or 4 guineas), they could get *The Monotype Recorder*, six issues a year, free. The purpose of the *Recorder* was of course to promote the sale of Monotype keyboards and casting machines, but from January 1922 onwards it contained articles by Morison and must often have been designed by him or under his direction. From 1927 it was edited by Beatrice Warde. The *Recorder*, although always the same page size (about 11 × 9 ins), had a pleasing variety of appearance and 'feel', since every issue was printed by a different printer (always, of course, a Monotype customer); and the increasingly frequent special issues, containing long, profusely illustrated monographs by S. M. or Beatrice Warde, were nothing short of magnificent. Britain was indeed fortunate.

It became for me a valuable growing-up year. Living in comfortable digs, I could, for the first time in my life, do more or less what I liked when I liked. In the process of becoming myself, I digested what had happened to me in Germany, and tried to make up my mind about my future. 'You won't become a business man, will you, Ruari?' a German girl had asked me anxiously, and no, I thought, a business man is exactly what I intend not to be: a decision which was probably correct, but made in complete ignorance of what 'business' actually was. In fact, I knew one or two business men whom I liked very much. One was a friend of my uncle's, who owned a big shop in Princes Street and spent the mornings in a Princes Street coffee-shop buying and selling ship cargoes in Leith with a group of cronies.

There were also several of my mother's friends and contemporaries in the city who gave me kind hospitality if I wanted it. I had some friends of my own: one, the wife of Sheriff Jameson, a notable Edinburgh character in those days, was the sister of Rosalind Wrong, the mother of my oldest Oxford friend, Charles. She was, like her sister, beautiful and clever, and had two charming daughters, but they were at school most of the time. Four years later, when in naval uniform, I called on the Jamesons to say hullo (hoping the daughters would be in). The Sheriff insisted on offering me sherry, and dashing down to the cellar came up with a brimming glass on a silver tray. When I sipped it, I was alarmed to find it was neat whisky.

There was Edinburgh and its environs to walk round, in all weathers, often in blizzards blowing up from the borders, and snowdrifts deep over roads and railways and even houses – often with magnificent views of murky roofs and smoke, silhouetted against fiery sunsets. And all the Edinburgh bookshops ... One day I found a copy of Haldane McFall's *The Book of Lovat*, about the illustrator Claud Lovat Fraser, of whom I had never heard. His drawings intoxicated me for three days, and longer. I was deeply moved by photographs of this handsome young man who wrote poetry, drew entrancingly, went through Ypres and Loos, was gassed, and died in 1921 aged only 31. The patterned papers he designed for the Curwen Press were still available in a few shops, as were the broadsheets of poems with his illustrations for the Poetry Bookshop.

One May morning I went up Arthur's Seat with a crowd of others to see in the dawn and drink the dew, and that moved me enough to write a description of it which was printed in the *Scotsman* newspaper, and became my first published (and paid) article. Thank you, *Scotsman*.

When I left Edinburgh, I was extremely lucky to be given the chance to go through all the departments of Waterlow & Sons, a great old printing firm in Dunstable, about 50 miles north of London, and to be paid £2 a week for doing so.

The £2 a week that I was paid were my first official earnings. On receiving my first pay packet, I lithographed a drawing of a young man holding the money, torn between sending it to his aged mother (pictured right) or spending it on the ladies of the town (pictured left). My mother got the lithograph (not the money) and enjoyed it, but I was warned not to show it to some of the old men in the press, who might be shocked. I gained useful experience in the lithography and collotype rooms, and even did corrections on railway posters. More strictly regulated firms would not have allowed me to touch type.

When my Dunstable year was up, it so happened that Bernard Newdigate was engaged in preparing a volume called *The Art of the Book* for The Studio, a publishing firm founded in London in 1893 by Charles Holme. The firm had had an immediate and extraordinary success, due partly to its timing: the nineties public was increasingly design-conscious, and this was the first magazine to discuss and illustrate domestic objects as well as painting, sculpture and architecture. It was also now able to exploit the new photographic reproduction processes which replaced drawings reproduced by wood-engraving and lithography. Apart from the monthly magazine, The Studio was soon producing a marvellous series of art books, called 'Special Numbers', which are still worth collecting today. (See *The Studio: a Bibliography. The First Fifty Years 1893–1943*, introduced by Brian Holme; Sims & Reed, 1978.)

By the late 1930s, The Studio was no longer the dominating art-publishing firm that it had been. The Studio's book department was now headed by William Gaunt, an excellent author: his assistant, being paid, as I learned, £3 a week, had just been appointed assistant editor of the *Queen* magazine. His imminent departure created a vacancy for which, on Newdigate's recommendation, I was interviewed and appointed – at £5 a week. The Studio did not dare tell Newdigate what they had been paying my predecessor, who was both older and abler than me.

The Art of the Book was written, compiled, and designed by Newdigate. All the illustrations for the book passed through my hands, and some I was allowed to choose myself. Newdigate also allowed me to design both the cloth binding and the jacket, and it says much for his generosity that he accepted my designs – my first ever to be used – since I cannot believe that he cared for them. My jacket design was based on a striking Underground Railway poster then on the London hoardings, consisting of two panels, blue and yellow, with sanserif type. I have never discovered who designed that poster; whoever it was deserved my apology.

At the same time we were also producing *The Studio Year Book of Decorative Art*, an annual concerned mainly with house interiors and furniture, illustrated entirely with photographs. I had seen some drawings in an architectural magazine which I admired, signed 'Casson', and asked the artist to come and see us. A slight young man came in, in a shabby raincoat, and showed me his work. He would have been delighted to do some for us at £1 a drawing, but the Studio management was too mean to pay this – photographs came in free – and the young man went away disappointed, as I was. Hugh Casson was knighted in 1951 for his work for the Festival of Britain, and later became President of the Royal Academy.

As soon as *The Art of the Book* was finished, I was sent for by the Managing director of The Studio and sacked. I was slow, I was not well organised, I did not know enough. All true of course, but what he really resented was paying me £5 a week. After I had gone, he gave the job to my secretary (whom I had been teaching what little I knew about book production), at, I suspected, £2 a week.

Bernard Newdigate died in 1944. Stanley Morison wrote that he was 'the most underrated of typographers'. It may well still be true, but he was not underrated by those who knew him. He was the subject of two memoirs which must be among the finest tributes to a dead friend ever written. The first, by Basil Blackwell in *The Times*, said 'No one who knew him would hesitate to say "Here was a gentleman". Those worthy to judge in these high matters might use a greater title'. The second is in Joseph Thorp's short book on Newdigate, published by Blackwell in 1950, with 32 pages of reproductions of some of Newdigate's finest pages. Thorp wrote 'I knew him well for more than fifty years and I have never known a more flawless character. I have never heard from him a malicious word or a complacent piece of self-praise, which we can most of us bring into our conversation with more or less art or discretion.... The integrity of his work was but a reflection of his integrity of character. Nor was there any flabbiness or lack of virility. Always tolerant, he was staunch in defence of his personal ideals and of his faith – if challenged'. Thorp also quotes Harold Curwen's summing-up of Newdigate: 'I thought his work was fine and right and very masculine. A giant among typographers'.

When I joined the Navy and went to say good-bye to Newdigate, he was pained to find that I had never read Thomas à Kempis, and sent me a little pocket edition of *De Imitatione Christi*, in Latin and English, which he had designed and printed and, as I later discovered, had also edited and translated from the Latin. I have it still. I never saw him again. In 1943 I wrote to tell him that I had become engaged to be married; when I returned from the Far East in late 1944, I found that he had died early in that year. I also found that he had put aside his own copy of Updike's *Printing Types*, the seven volumes of *The Fleuron*, and a pile of other precious typographical works, for my wedding present.

5. Black Lion Lane

I N Germany I had made the interesting discovery that some girls attracted me while others didn't. Sex appeal could apparently vary. An English girl with whom I played tennis had none: a Romanian girl with whom I danced had plenty. Back in London my education in such matters now passed into the care of Edward Young.

Early in 1938 I wrote to Penguin Books to ask for a job. A Penguin, in those days, meant a book in red and white paper covers costing sixpence. Penguins had started in 1935.

I got a letter back regretting that the writer already had the only job in the firm that would interest me, but if I could come and have tea with him sometime he might be able to suggest something – signed 'Edward Young, Production Manager'.

I went out to the new Penguin offices on the Bath Road, Harmondsworth, opposite Heathrow Airport, and had tea with this production manager, who turned out to be a pleasant fellow a few years older than me. He had an American secretary, Kay, a baby-faced brunette who acted tough because she was training herself to become a journalist. They were very kind, and said 'Do come again any time you like, we're only allowed to smoke if we have a visitor'. Young gave me some useful introductions, including, for example, to Beatrice Warde, Publicity Manager of the Monotype Corporation.

Some weeks later I was astonished to receive a letter from him saying that he had just moved into a small flat in Hammersmith and needed someone with whom to share it: would I be interested? I was happy in my digs in the London suburb of Highgate. I had never thought of sharing with anybody, and did not wish to lose my independence. After prolonged hesitation I accepted, and entered the most hilarious period of my life.

Black Lion Lane was a narrow street running down to the River Thames. 65a was a small terraced house on three floors; the ground floor was occupied by a sculptor and wood-engraver, Gertrude Hermes, already a friend of Edward's. On the first floor (we had our own front door and stairs) Edward had a large L-shaped room with a double bed and elegant Alvar Aalto chairs and table from Finland and a long bookshelf along one wall. On the end of the bookshelf stood an original bronze head by Jacob Epstein (on loan from Gert downstairs), of

Conrad Nöel, the communist vicar of Thaxted. At the back was a small kitchen and bathroom. Upstairs was my bedroom (single bed) and a spare room. At the end of Black Lion Lane was the Black Lion pub, with a skittle alley, and then Hammersmith Terrace, most of which seemed to belong to A. P Herbert, backing on the river. There were two pubs closer to us than the Black Lion: the nearest was used when we needed a drink urgently, but the one further away had better beer. Nearly opposite us was Mr Dalton's grocery shop. Mr Dalton was an ally to whom we gave our keys when leaving the flat for any period. He could provide most of the sustenances of life at almost any time of day or night, including on Sundays.

Edward had had even less training in typography than I had. He had gone straight from school to the Bodley Head publishing firm as office-boy; one of his jobs there was to keep the firm's book of cuttings, and he had done this so artistically that it had caught the eye of Allen Lane, the firm's young Managing Director. Allen was then gestating the idea of paperback books at sixpence. The Bodley Head was losing money and Lane offered his idea to his fellow directors to save the firm. They turned him down, so he left and started his own firm. He took Edward with him to design and produce the new series. After much debate it was decided to call them Penguins, and Edward was sent to the zoo to study pen-guins in the flesh before drawing what became a famous symbol.

When I joined Edward in Black Lion Lane, Penguins, now three years old, were on the crest of a wave – a wave that never collapsed but rolled on, getting bigger and bigger. Edward was responsible for the firm's publicity as well as the production and design; the friendly informal note he struck in their advertisements and leaflets which he wrote was exactly right.

Every month or so Allen Lane held a high-level lunch in the West End, with guests like H. G. Wells and Bernard Shaw, which went on into the evening. Quite regularly Edward staggered back into the flat, white-faced and cross-eyed, at midnight, having fallen asleep in the tube from Piccadilly and been carried out to the end of the line at Uxbridge before waking up. Sometimes Allen Lane and his two brothers came to the flat and discussed the firm's future into the small hours. One brother was to take entire charge of paper, the other to travel the world for export orders, and so on. Allen, like Edward, was a charmer: in both men iron determination was hidden under a thick layer of velvet.

* * *

Edward's chief girl-friend came for the night at week-ends, but always played hard to get. From my solitary room at the top I could hear a verbal battle going on as they came up the stairs, then stamping up and down in the living-room. Her last act of defiance was to run her hand along behind the books on the shelves. When I heard the books crashing onto the floor along the entire length of the room, I knew that everything was going to be all right. In the morning they often insisted on my bringing them early-morning tea in bed, in the hopes of embarrassing me. I would then pick up the books, many of which were mine, under the unblinking eyes of Conrad Nöel.

In the flat below, Gertrude Hermes was much loved. When she trod on a gramophone record and said 'Bugger!', I fell for her. She was the first woman I had met who could swear like a man without it jarring, and without losing any of her femininity. She had a friend, Francis Watson, whom we saw occasionally; it was not until he had left for India that I read the books he had written: a marvellous novel The Virgin King, a book about Rabelais, and Art Lies Bleeding, discussing how artists could and actually did live in this country in conditions which stifled art. At Bristol, for example, the City Art Gallery's only acquisition of contemporary painting made for years was two paintings of kittens 'at their engaging sports' presented by the artist, Miss Augusta Tallboys. I wished fervently that I had been able to get to know him while he was around.

I had two other friends in London, both spinsters, who were very kind to me; Margaret Wrong, an aunt of my friend Charles Wrong, and Margaret Read. Both women had made Africa and the education of Africans the chief occupation of their lives. Both had spent much time living there, Margaret Read as a doctor of medicine. They were of the generation whose men had been lost in the First World War. They kept open house for young Africans on grants to learn English in London. I remember listening with awe to an animated discussion on what was the opposite of the word 'incipient' in Zulu, to the strains of Beethoven's Seventh, and, with Mozart in the background, what was the longest word in the English language. 'Antidisestablishmentarianism', replied Margaret Read instantly. I also remember that after a visit to Basel I was telling them about seeing a marvellous painting of Erasmus' friend and printer, Froben, painted by Holbein, and how Froben's face was not unlike Margaret Read's. 'Yes', she said quietly, 'I believe my family is descended from him'.

Edward and I were both interested in the history of printing. There were many books about almost every aspect of it, but we could not find any general and complete history. We decided to write it. Edward mentioned this to Allen Lane, who immediately gave us a contract and an advance payment. We set to work. The immense amount of reading required was enjoyable, but of course it had to take second place after our jobs and various other activities. After Munich in 1938 these included preparations for the war that was obviously impending. Edward, who had done some week-end sailing, wanted to join the Navy. He discovered that if he obtained a Master Mariner's Certificate – which could be done by attending evening classes and some swotting – he could go straight into the Navy with a commission. So the history of printing gave way to longitude, latitude, and the rule of the road at sea, and we did half an hour together every evening on a Morse buzzer. I was soon sending about 11 words a minute and receiving about 6, but sending and receiving about 12–14 was required.

When I got the sack from the Studio, I went as trainee art director to the J. Walter Thompson Advertising Agency, then in Bush House in the Strand. I found that art directors in this leading American-owned firm were less important people than the copy-writers. I was put in a small room occupied by a young man recently out of Glasgow School of Art, with tousled black hair, and eyes that looked half asleep. He was Alexander McKendrick, who later directed *Whisky Galore, The Man in the White Suit*, and other wonderful films. He did not speak to me for three days. He then told me that there were more brains round the table at a J W T– client planning meeting than at a meeting of the Cabinet. I did not ask him how he knew. H. A. L. Fisher would have probably disagreed, since in his *Unfinished Autobiography* he says 'To listen to Cabinet debates ... by the best political minds in the country is an experience which ripens the judgement as the autumn sun ripens the corn'. Maybe.

My job was to turn Pond's Cold Cream advertisements, which analysed Lady So-and-So's face and its most interesting spots, into different sizes. When it was later found that I could draw, I was put to inventing comic situations for Rowntree's Milk Chocolate in three frames, which ended with someone saying 'And Rowntree's has such an interesting flavour, don't you think, Mr Wagstaff?' But my drawings could never be published: all finished artwork was done by outside artists.

Bush House was a luxurious place for an office. It contained restaurants, bars, swimming pools, squash courts, a hairdresser and shops, all patronized by J W T 's staff. A memo came round while I was there saying 'All members of the copy and art departments are expected to have completed their toilets and their breakfasts *before* they come into the office'. However despite these temptations I soon realized that work in an advertising agency was not really my metier (despite the attractive money) and I looked elsewhere.

One evening, after a Galley Club meeting, Edward's Kay drank four double whiskies and kissed me for the first time – cause and effect, or supply and demand? I told her that I had just developed an insane desire to go and learn printing in Russia, and she told me that her friend Allen Hutt had done just that, so we went to his flat to meet him. That resulted in four of us, including Allen's Scots girl friend Sheila, a school teacher, going to eat at Durand's in Soho. We ate cervelle and Brie, with Medoc, followed by Armagnac with the coffee. Allen, then assistant editor of *Reynold's News*, the Sunday newspaper which was the first paper to print cartoons by Giles, had a face combining wildness with intellect. He said he would tell me the name of a man to get in touch with about Russia, but advised me to get a good typographer's job in England first, preferably in an advertising agency. Well, I said... We then argued about the introduction of tartan, the clan system, and why Glaswegians had bad teeth, on all of which subjects Allen was an expert; he also listed the number of railway strikes in England since 1914, told us about his work in Russia, not as a printer but in propaganda with a printing firm, and then related funny stories about communist campaigning in Fife. At one point Sheila introduced a bombshell by saying that there were three haggises beneath the table (it was quite true). We sat so long with our coffee and Armagnac that Ida, the waitress, pointedly removed our ash-tray. Allen then took us to a pub across the road and gave us Cointreau – and refused to let me pay even half of my share of the evening.

After another evening with him in 1940, the year when people were celebrating the invention of printing by Gutenberg in the Rhineland, I was thrilled by a suggestion of mine being followed by a telegram (remember telegrams?) from Allen saying 'Do thousand words on quote if printing had never been invented unquote copy by Wednesday next keep it popular = Hutt'. The article was printed in *Reynolds News* early in the year. On the same theme, I wrote a short story 'Death of Noted Inventor' (that was Gutenberg) which earned 'special commendation' in a *Time & Tide* competition and was printed in *Time & Tide* in May 1940. I also learn from an old scrapbook, that I went up to Heaven and interviewed Gutenberg: the interview was published in *Printing Review*, again in May. *Printing Review* also published an article I had written called 'Ingenious Typography', which dealt with a subject I had not seen in print before, 'stunt typography'.

I went on taking girls out whenever I could: cinemas and meals in Soho cost very little in those days, and some wonderful girls insisted on paying for themselves. I found one girl who had seen and remembered the life-size statue of Balzac by Rodin in Antwerp, and had been moved by it as much as I had been. She mentioned 'The Thinker', and as she spoke I placed my elbow on my knee and my chin on my hand. 'No – on the other knee' she said gently, and I was deeply impressed.

Saturdays and Sundays were days for taking out girls, or, since for a long time I didn't have a regular girl, for exploring London or going to the pictures or reading. One day, coming out from a film, I found a Punch and Judy show in quiet Leicester Street near Leicester Square. It was better than any film, deserving Hogarth, or Cruikshank, or Bentley, or Dubout, to illustrate it. There was a little girl so lovely in her Saturday clothes that I nearly wept when she gazed up at Punch. Her head was about the size of the rest of her body; her white cotton dress was, I suppose, the size of two men's handkerchiefs. It was exactly one millimetre longer than her torso in every direction. Her little arms and legs shot out of her body like spokes on a star-wheel. She had an ice-cream which she forgot to eat, and in her awe of the drama she backed slowly away and came up sharply against my legs. I think she was going to cling to them when her father put out an arm from nearby and collected her. There were two small boys with their arms round each other. One had knickers coming down at least twelve inches below his pants. Another small boy, trailing his macintosh like a small man taking home a drunk friend, had freckles and wire spectacles, and laughed louder, more explosively, than anyone in the crowd. The man taking round the bag got a shilling from me, but when I thought how much I had enjoyed the whole thing I had to add another half-crown. Walking home along the River Thames towpath, I was intrigued by a small boy with bare feet beating his socks on the ground. Why was he doing that? He explained, obviously pitying my dullness, that he was trying to dry his socks to prevent his mother knowing that he'd been paddling.

6. To Bradford in Yorkshire

IN 1939 I was lucky enough to be given a job with Percy Lund
Humphries, then perhaps the most forward-looking printing firm
in Great Britain. The works were in Bradford, and they had a publishing office in London presided over by a remarkable man called Eric
Gregory.

That meant having a farewell party. From 7.30pm to 10pm on a lovely
May evening, we sailed in a private launch on the Thames from Westminster Pier down to Greenwich and back again. We were about 20,
supplied with lots of ham rolls, cakes, apples, beer, claret cup, cheap
sherry, and two small bottles of gin (for a 'Dog's Nose'). All my best
friends, male and female, were there. Allen Hutt arrived slightly the
worse for wear, with his charming Scots girl friend, who sang 'Will ye no
come back again?' and other Gaelic songs, and I made a speech in Gaelic
which she gave me, which meant – it transpired – 'I love you'. Back up
the river, after sunset, there was a beautiful moon.

Bradford is in Yorkshire, a part of England I did not know. I found
that in Yorkshire they think of themselves as Yorkshiremen first and
Englishmen second. I also soon found that Bradford pubs were real family affairs. They were full of women and children as well as men. In one
pub there was a microphone to which women went and sang, to everyone's pleasure, whenever they felt like it. As a Scot, not an Englishman,
I felt very much at home.

In Lund Humphries, my title, invented for convenience since I was
still actually a learner, was 'Assistant Manager, Composing Room'. The
desk I took over had been vacated by a young man called Michael
Clapham, who had gone to the ICI-owned Kynoch Press in Birmingham. He warned me, in a letter, that Lund Humphries was a crazy mad-
house, and I gave him my views on that. When I next heard of him he
was Deputy Chairman of ICI.

My new desk contained a small collection of typographical specimens printed in German. They were set in two weights of sanserif,
positioned asymmetrically. They were so elegant that I had to find out
more about them. It appeared that they were the work of a Swiss typographer called Jan Tschichold, to whom Lund Humphries had just given
an exhibition in their London office at the suggestion of the designer

Edward McKnight Kauffer. I found myself suddenly aware of bits of printing which actually excited me. There was also a booklet in the drawer in yellow cartridge paper covers entitled *Typografische Entwurf-stechnik* ('How to draw layouts'). It said that compositors (for whom the booklet was written) should learn how to draw their layouts in pencil so accurately that costly corrections in proof would not be needed. The illustrations showed exactly how Tschichold did it, and it did not look too difficult. It seemed better than Francis Meynell's practice (of which I had just been reading) of having a printer set up twenty or more trial proofs for a Nonesuch Press title-page before he was satisfied.

When I discovered that this Tschichold was neither dead nor aged ninety, but alive and living in Basel, I wrote to him, and in July 1939 I used a vacation to go and visit him. He was then aged 37, a benign gold-spectacled little man who took me to a cafe–restaurant beside the swift-flowing Rhine. Here we sat for a summer's evening, among trellis roses and beautiful girls, drinking Rhine wine and attempting to exchange ideas on typography. My German and his English could hardly stretch to a whole evening, and my eyes wandered to the girls, who were clearly wondering why we did not ask them to dance. I wondered myself. However I did not dare to suggest this, and when words failed between Tschichold and myself, we beamed at one another.

The next morning I explored Basel, and bathed in the Rhine. I changed into a bathing costume and walked about one and a half miles upstream, jumped in, and floated back down. You had to shoot beneath a great bridge and then swim like hell to get in to the bank in time to catch hold of ropes hanging out from the enclosure in which you had left your clothes. If you didn't make it, you got ashore about a mile downstream and walked back. People were drowned there regularly.

In the afternoon I went to visit Tschichold in his flat in Leonhard-strasse. His wife was away. The living-room was square and entirely white except for a black lino floor. The tall windows had floor-length white silk curtains and there was a fine modern painting on each wall. The furniture was Bauhaus. It was, I thought, the most beautiful room I had ever been in.

We drank china tea and Tschichold showed me sheets of his new book on Chinese colour prints, and, later, the collection of books in his study. Among the things he said – in English, which I jotted down in my diary that evening – were:

'I am no more interested in my book *Typographische Gestaltung* – what others want to make of it, they can.'

'It doesn't matter what others think of my typography – I only know "Das muss sein". (It must be). If it satisfies me, it is good.'

'It is more difficult to design a book than draw a landscape.'

'Japanese colour printing, with thirty blocks, puts ours in the shade – so does Chinese civilization.'

'I am the only man in Switzerland who can make a book. No one in France. A few in England – De la Mare, Gill, Morison.'

'Koch says consciously, I will make German art. He was a Nazi.'

'Germany cannot be communist, they are too bourgeois. Germans are not balanced.'

'Greatness and ideas come from *one* man, not from movements. For example, Jesus, Confucius, etc.'

Tschichold, a German born in Leipzig, but not a Jew, had been put in prison by the Nazis for a short time, *persona non grata* because of what they called his 'Kultur-Bolschevismus' (advanced views on art and design). He was then allowed to emigrate to Switzerland with his wife and child, and continued his work to radically reform typography.

He gave me several examples of his printed work, and I found a few more in Basel bookshops. A month later, war broke out, and we did not meet again for over six years.

When I got back to Bradford from Basel, I found that the room I rented from Mrs Buchsieb contained too many ornaments. I began counting them, and found that the room itself contained one hundred and thirty-six separate *objets d'art* and eighty-nine pictures, prints, calendars, plates, mirrors, and texts on the walls. I decided I could stand it no longer. I placed all the vases in queue on the piano beside the door as a sign for their removal, and put a lot of other stuff out of sight, leaving the mantelshelf quite bare. I stood back to admire the effect, thought enviously of Tschichold's room in Basel, left a box of my own matches looking rather like a night-watchman's hut on a slum clearance site, and went out to post a letter and have a drink.

When I returned, the room was exactly as it had been before my ministrations, except that Mrs Buchsieb was standing in the middle of it looking like a dive-bomber about to strike.

The less said about that scene the better. A couple of days later I had to go down to London to join another war; but when in India and Ceylon a bit later, I did manage to find a few contributions for my old room, if that was how Mrs Buchsieb wanted it. For example, a boomerang paper-knife, whose handle was a kookaburra, and a photogravure print in three colours of Sydney Harbour Bridge, slightly out of register....

* * *

'War? There ain't goin' to be no war! W'y, I ain't been fitted wiv me effing gas mask yet!'

'Blimey, Bill, we all thought you 'ad it on!'

In 1938 it was difficult to believe that Europe was quite mad enough to start another war. I had had the 1914–18 war in the background of my entire life. My mother's brother had been badly wounded in Flanders. As I grew up, I read the *Times* War Annuals and many other books on our shelves, including Dick Sheppard, Beverly Nicols, Richard Aldington, Liddel Hart, R.H.Tawney, Robert Graves, and others, and had decided to refuse to fight. The theory was that if everybody refused to fight, the government could not declare war. I was even prepared to be shot for it, provided the Left Book Club and the *Daily Herald* handled the publicity and let people know for what I was being shot. To fight Fascism with Fascism's weapons, poison gas, thermite, bullets and shells, was to become Fascist oneself, wasn't it?

In 1938 Edward Young and the friends he sailed with all joined the London River Fire Brigade, which operated from the Prospect of Whitby, a favourite pub of ours on the river. I tried to join too, but it was sailing chums only, and I was refused. So I joined the London Police War Reserve. It was expected that when war broke out, London would immediately be heavily bombed, and the Police Force was trebled to meet the anticipated emergency. We attended lectures in Hammersmith Police Station given by elderly police sergeants, all raconteurs of high quality. They explained how to detach a suffragette from Buckingham Palace railings (which many of them had done) in front of a crowd, without appearing to use force, by placing a firm finger beneath her nose; how desirable it was to separate a middle-aged drunk from the two ladies holding his arms, because he probably had his Slate Club's funds in his pocket, which he was supposed to be investing; that it was useless to arrest a man beating his wife in the evening because she would never bring a charge against him in the morning; and that a policeman never drew his truncheon except to push a body off a live electric rail or hit a Chinaman carrying a knife. And finally, 'A policeman cannot be seen to be annoyed. It is not an offence to throw things at a policeman – it's a privilege.' When we were each issued with a truncheon, I was furious because they were not the real thing in dark *lignum vitae* but cheap substitutes in white deal.

Contrary to everyone's expectations, London was not bombed by the Germans immediately war broke out in September 1939. Around Christmas Eve the junior War Reserve policemen like me were being passed into the armed services. I announced that I was a pacifist. Telling the young Police Inspector who was my boss, and whom I much admired, that I intended to be a conscientious objector was one of the most difficult things I had ever done in my life, but he was sympathetic. He said that in due course I would be called before a Board, and if found to be sincere, I would be given a non-fighting job – which could include dangerous work like bomb disposal.

When I went home and told my parents, they were horrified. I had never thought how much it would mean to them. They were the last people in the world that I wanted to hurt. Many of my friends, male and female, had sympathized with my being a pacifist – they were pacifists too. But conscientious objector was different. I disapproved of war – we all did. But lives were already being lost bringing us our food. It was time to change one's mind. I cancelled my application to be a C.O. and tried to get into the navy.

The Naval Recruiting Officer in Oxford wouldn't have me. One good eye (6/6) and one bad eye (6/36) meant rejection. As I was going out of the door, I turned and said, 'I have a cousin who is a Lieutenant-Commander. Does that make a difference?' 'Why didn't you mention that before?' said the Recruiting Officer, and I learned that the Navy is, sensibly, a family business. 'Let's see, with that eyesight you can't keep watch at sea, but you can be a Writer or a Telegraphist'. 'Does a Telegraphist wear bell-bottomed trousers?' 'Yes' 'Well, I'll be that, please'. When, a bit later, the destroyer in which I had illicitly become an Ordinary Seaman docked close to my cousin's cruiser, on which he was Gunnery Officer, I tried to see him to say thank you – but he refused to see me.

There was some time to wait before I was called up. I worked on the *History of Printing* in the Bodleian Library in Oxford, and listened to the evacuation of Dunkirk on the wireless, not realizing that I could have gone and helped, as many others did.

I wrote a synopsis and several specimen chapters and sent them to Allen Lane. He sent them to Stanley Morison for his opinion. Before I was called up, I went to see 'Uncle Stan' (as Allen Hutt called him) in

Fetter Lane, E.C.4   M/M 309

Allen Lane, Esq., Penguin Books Ltd,
Harmondsworth, Middlesex.

Dear Allen Lane,
The author of your *Short History of Printing* has attempted a very difficult task, and
in the portion you have sent me, by no means without a measure of success.
Nevertheless, I doubt whether you would be justified in publishing it in its
present form.

  During the past 25 years a very great deal of work has been done by specialists of various nationalities upon various departments of the history and practice
of printing. In consequence the writer of an elementary manual needs to possess
a very wide range of reading. Without expecting acquaintance with the latest
monograph by an obscure professor in Germany or elsewhere, it is disappoint-
ing to find the authority for a statement regarding early Sumerian seals given as
H.G.Wells, who is in no sense a specialist but is himself depending on specialists.
In not a few other portions of the manuscript reference is made to secondhand
authorities. Moreover, there are not a few statements made in the course of the
work which need scrutiny. I do not think it is the case that scholars are agreed
that the Codex Sinaiticus is the earliest manuscript of the gospels. Nor, I believe
is it true that Adolf Hitler changed his name from Schicklgrueber. Inquiry I
think will show that it was his father who made the change. I have, however, not
made it my business to note small errors which, after all, are quite easily
corrected.

  The important thing, I think, is that it is not possible for you at this time to
put out a book on this subject, which is written in disregard of recently published and authoritative works such as Ruppel's *Johann Gutenberg*, Berlin 1938, and
Andre Blum's *Les Origines de l'imprimerie*, Paris, 1935 or 36. It will simply not do to
discuss the spread of printing, outside Germany on the basis of Winship's
Gutenberg to Plantin.

  Yours,
  [signed] Stanley Morison.

Letter from Stanley Morison to Allen Lane, 1939.

London. Morison always dressed in black, looked like a pope, and, I had been told (inaccurately), never relaxed until he had had two Napoleon brandies. He would not say anything about my chapters, but we argued a few points, and he told me books I ought to read, and said magisterially 'It is hopeless to think of writing a history of printing in a provincial library like the Bodleian'. He later wrote a not unkind letter to Allen Lane, which I was later shown (see p. 37) which was of crucial importance to me, since it enabled me to reach the vital stage when at last I knew what I didn't know. But the History was never finished.

Allen Lane generously forgot to ask back the advance he had given us.

Drawing for cover of *Penguin's Progress*, 1946.

7. Typographer's war

THE gates of Portsmouth dockyard opened onto a parade-ground on which crowds of sailors in white blouses were being drilled, waved flags, and swarmed around in squads. There was Nelson's own wooden-walled ship *Victory* in a dry dock, with beyond her, cranes and grey warship masts above the dockyard wall. It was September 1940: the Navy had already been at war for over a year.

Curiously, almost the first thing that happened to me was a kind of printing. We New Entries were given our new clothes, and to my astonishment I watched two elderly seamen solemnly cutting our names in reverse on small blocks of wood, which were then handed to us, with an ink pad, to print our names on the white vests and blouses we had just been given, and on anything else handy, such as our friends.

It was a new and very different kind of life I was entering. It may not have been as difficult for me as it was for some of the other younger New Entries, who had never been away from home in their lives. Those of us who had been boarders in an English Public School knew something about living a rough life among strangers.

I was already learning to be a typographer: I now had to learn how to be a seaman, which I also found fascinating, but it meant (or did it?) forgetting about typography. My career in the Navy was complicated by defective eyesight (in one eye only) which debarred me from an 'ordinary' career as a watchkeeper. I was admitted into the Navy as an Ordinary Telegraphist – about which of course I knew nothing; but in order to obtain a commission more quickly, I was allowed to change over, no questions asked, to Ordinary Seaman, which was more fun: the Telegraphists were quiet types, the Seamen were every kind of riff-raff.

Eventually I was posted to HMS *Windsor*, a destroyer operating in the Channel and the Atlantic. After a few months we ran over a German acoustic mine: no one was hurt, but the ship was badly damaged. We were sent home on survivors' leave.

When I was made an officer (entitled Sub-Lieutenant, Royal Naval Volunteer Reserve) I found that the only way I could continue to go to sea was as a British Naval Liaison Officer (BNLO) in allied submarines. I was very lucky to be sent to a splendid boat, the Free French mine-laying submarine *Rubis*, operating from Dundee in Scotland. As Liaison

Officer, I had to look after the British naval codes and ciphers, organise the coding and decoding of all signals to and from the Admiralty, and look after the allied morale, including making sure that our allies understood all the orders they received. I soon discovered that my French commanding officer, Lieutenant de Vaisseau Henri Rousselot – a young man only five years older than myself – understood his orders a great deal better than I ever could: he was outstandingly competent. I also had as my staff a British Leading Signalman and a Leading Telegraphist, to actually send the signals I had enciphered.

Apart from fighting the war, at which *Rubis'* officers and crew were very good, we had hilarious arguments round the wardroom table when we were travelling submerged. To reach our mine-laying areas off Norway or Jutland, we had to travel far north to go round the German declared minefields, so our periods beneath the surface were prolonged (usually all day-light) and we spent a lot of time talking. A favourite subject was denigrating everything English – such as English cooking, English eating habits, English fashions and English driving. But when the captain launched an attack on English printing, I had to intervene. 'Tell me' I said, 'Tell me *one* well printed series of French books *half* as well printed as our Penguins?' The captain thought hard, and then (very intelligently) replied 'Editions Nelson'. I happily pointed out that Editions Nelson were all printed in Edinburgh. As a matter of fact, the Captain, First Lieutenant, one other officer and several of the crew had all married Scottish girls. It helped that I myself was a Scotsman. They were prejudiced against the English, but occasionally we met an English man whom they much admired.

The first time I went to sea in *Rubis* was not on a wartime patrol, but to make a film for the Fleet Air Arm in the waters off Dundee, designed to show young airmen the difference, from the air, between a submarine, a whale, or another ship. We now had six officers on board, but there was room for only four when eating at the wardroom table, so very often, while they ate, I lay on the captain's bunk in his cabin just outside the wardroom. I was reading a book on his bed one day during the filming when I became aware of a certain amount of commotion. When it was over, I asked what had happened. We were travelling on the surface, on the diesels, which required air; the small hatch above the diesels was therefore open. The order was then given to dive. Owing to a careless misunderstanding, the hatch was left open. In the few seconds it remained open, after the dive, the submarine took in tons of sea water.

Author with commanding officer of Free French Submarine *Rubis* (Lieut. de Vaisseau Henri Rousselot), Dundee, September 1941.

The book I was reading at that moment described how an American submarine which made the same mistake was lost with all hands.

Life on board *Rubis* certainly had its moments, including excellent French cooking and a ration of red wine. But I gradually found that in general I had very little to do except eat, sleep, and read books. After supper, before surfacing when it became dark, we started playing bridge: a very different kind of bridge from the polite games I had watched my mother playing in North Oxford; our interesting bad language in both French and English was far from boring.

During my time on board *Rubis*, my friend Edward Young was in British submarines, a real submariner, climbing his way up to eventually become the first RNVR officer to command a submarine. I always hoped our submarines would one day coincide somewhere, but they never did. We just missed each other once in Lerwick, in the Shetlands.

After a year, I had taken part in seven patrols; the first was exceedingly exciting, and none were boring. I then wanted to do something more difficult. I was transferred to the Inter-Service Topographical Department (ISTD) in Naval Intelligence. It was my bad luck that the department was housed in an Oxford college, and Oxford, where my parents lived, was as far from the sea as it is possible to be in Great Britain. The work was of course very interesting, and there was a connection with my earlier life: the reports we were producing were printed at the Oxford University Press. Having been told that we had difficulty in getting these reports out of the Press, because they were so busy printing *War and Peace* and *Anna Karenina* for the Oxford World Classics series, I went one day to investigate, and met, for the first time, the illustrious John Johnson, Printer to the University. He had installed a bed in his office and told me that he had never been further out of his office, since the war began, than the letterbox on the pavement outside. They were printing a lot of secret work for the government, but Johnson was also at that time building up his priceless 'Sanctuary of Printing' – a collection, perhaps the first ever made, based on all kinds of neglected ephemera, e.g. bus tickets and printed paper bags, as well as books. Johnson, originally an archaeologist by profession, was I think a genius and, in his own views on most things, a fanatic. The 'Sanctuary of Printing' is now housed in the Bodleian Library in Oxford.*

To get to the college in which my Intelligence Department was housed, I had to walk every day past both Blackwell's and Thornton's bookshops: an enrichment of my reading if impoverishing my purse. One day I came out of Thornton's with Harris Nicolas' *Letters of Lord Nelson* in seven volumes, an event that unexpectedly affected my private life a year later.

Then, on a visit to London, I met a pre-war naval friend outside the Admiralty, who was building up an organisation of sailors and soldiers whose job was to survey enemy-held beaches prior to invasions. 'It's all done at night' he explained, 'and no one can see in the dark, so eyesight doesn't matter. Won't you join us?' So I did, and joined this new small force called Copp (Combined Operations Pilotage Parties, a name designed to obscure its real purpose), stationed in a yacht club on Hayling Island, in Chichester Harbour near Portsmouth. I was shown my bunk, 'but of course you won't see much of that.'

*See The John Johnson Collection (Catalogue of an exhibition). Bodleian Library, Oxford, (with a portrait photograph of Johnson). 1971.

Our landings on enemy beaches had to be by swimming in from a fol-
boat (folding canoe) or canoe outside the surf, taken there by a submarine or motor-boat. Our rigorous training, in cold waters, depended very
much on the effects of weather, currents and tides. We wore rubber suits
which were supposed to be water-tight and took one hour to put on and
one hour to take off. This was in the days before 'wet-suits'.

The last episode in our training meant visiting Glasgow to practise
launching canoes from a submarine on the river Clyde. Three days had
been allocated for this, but the weather was so good (and so, we said to
ourselves, were we) that the exercise was completed in a day, and we had
two days free. The only useful telephone number I had in my diary for
that area was that of a Wren whom I thought I had never met. My
mother had met her in Oxford, liked her, and sent me her phone number; she was in fact the cousin of an old friend of mine and we had met
when I was a child. I rang her, obtained a reluctant agreement to have
supper, and arrived at her Wrennery in Gourock in the only taxi, which
happened to be a Rolls-Royce. At supper I discovered that she too had
just bought the seven volumes of Nelson's letters, and since she was
beautiful and had trim ankles, I asked her to marry me. Her name was
Antonia (Tony) Maxwell Carlisle. There was just time to meet her parents, and ask my commanding officer Geoffrey Hall to be my Best Man,
before we sailed as we thought, wrongly, for the invasion of Sicily.
Geoffrey asked if I had a photo of my intended, was shown it and
admired the wrong girl (my fiancée's younger sister, also a Wren). After
ascertaining that she would probably be chief bridesmaid, he accepted,
and immediately wrote to her what I thought was a very forward letter.

So we sailed, and found we were being sent to India.

Our training having been all in cold water, we were now the first
Copp party to operate in the Far East. We started re-training, wearing
only thin overalls, in the warm water of the Indian Ocean.

We lived first on the east coast of India, and then in the north of
Ceylon. We made a successful reconnaissance-survey of a Japanese
beach in Burma, and then were given targets in Sumatra. I found that
Edward Young, now in command of HMS *Storm*, was based in Trinco-
malee, and I went to ask him if by any chance he could be our carrier
to Sumatra. As he had just taken part in a landing operation on another
Japanese beach, which had been betrayed, and they had been nearly
sunk by Japanese gunboats, he politely declined, unless he was ordered
to take us. I spent a happy couple of days with him and made a series of

drawings for *Good Evening*, a two-page daily 'newspaper' which Edward produced on every patrol for his ship's company. We went to Sumatra in another British submarine and did what we had to do without serious problems.

By then we had spent a year and a half in the Far East and it was judged that we had been out there long enough; other parties were now trained and longing to come out for their own operations. We were sent home. I was offered the command of a new party, but the war was now nearly over, and I wanted to get married and return to typography. Tony and I got married before the war actually ended, and Geoffrey, to everyone's surprise, married her sister Mary – whom he had never met until we got home – just after us. He later became a Rear-Admiral, Hydrographer of the Royal Navy.

Naval Party 735's badge, 1943: 'We've had it'.

8. Post-war beginnings, and Robert Harling

THE war was still on. I went back to ISTD (the Inter-Service Topo-
graphic Department) in Mansfield College in Oxford. Tony and I
found a flat in Iffley Road, and used to meet for a sandwich lunch
in the Botanical Gardens by Magdelen Bridge. One day Tony said that
she had passed a dashing naval officer in the High who had 'undressed'
her as he went past. I instantly knew that Robert Harling was back in
Oxford.

Harling had been a friend since before the war. He was now becoming rather important in my life – and in the lives of other young men
and women then coming out of the services.

Younger than Stanley Morison, Francis Meynell, and Oliver Simon,
Harling was a link between them and the new generation just beginning
to become designers. In January 1936 he wrote an article for *Printing*
magazine entitled 'What is this "Functional" Typography? The work of

Robert Harling, *c.* 1990.
(Photo by Phoebe Harling.)

Jan Tschichold. The man is different!' This was, I think, the first printed notice of Tschichold to appear in this country. In November 1936 appeared the first issue of *Typography*, an innovative periodical conceived, edited, and designed by Harling, and printed by James Shand at the Shenval Press. In the third number, Summer 1937, the first article was by Tschichold himself. The covers of *Typography* were enlivened by large Victorian wood letters in strong colours; Harling was one of the first to appreciate Victorian graphic virtues, and before 1939 had written two books, *Home – a Victorian Vignette*, and *The London Miscellany*, drawing largely on Victorian images. At the same time, he was advising the typefounders Stephenson Blake, designing their literature and also three popular display typefaces, *Playbill* (1938), *Tea Chest* and *Chisel* (1939); and among other things was art director of a leading London advertising agency. He was also a weekend sailor, and took part in the Dunkirk operation, about which he wrote in *Amateur Sailor*, a book that John Masefield said was the best eye-witness account of it ever written. He then joined the Navy, served in corvettes, and described that in *Steep Atlantic Stream*. He was then called into naval intelligence, under Admiral Godfrey, and worked with Ian Fleming, who became his close friend. I believe that my own call into naval intelligence was due to Robert Harling.

He was a pithy talker, apt to produce strings of bon mots. He neither smoked nor drank, but he liked women, and told me 'I don't know any happily married couples – I make it a rule not to'.

As the war ended, he was looking ahead on behalf of his younger friends, and telling us all to buy houses quickly. In 1946 he cross-examined me on what I liked doing best, and what I was best and worst at. He said that the most money would be in magazine-making in two years or so. The secret of production, he pronounced, was to get everything moving simultaneously. He insisted that the chief value of anything designed was the pleasure it gave to its designer. He added that his writing was the only thing that he was dead serious about. I had already noticed that his writing was very much part of his designings: when designing an advertisement, he nearly always also wrote the copy, with great effect. It makes designing a lot easier if you can alter the copy as you want.

Robert now suggested, in October 1945, that I write a story for boys, and also suggested a book on the nineteenth-century illustrator George Cruikshank. He may have thought I could do both simultaneously: he himself was always doing not less than four jobs at once, each one of which would have been a full-time task for anyone else. At that particular moment he was designing books, and also commissioning the illustrations, for a Mr Gottlieb, who operated under the names of John Westhouse (books for adults) and Peter Lunn (books for children). He was also producing a quarterly magazine called *Convoy*, which was nominally edited by Robin Maugham. However, everything in it, text and illustrations, seemed to have been commissioned by Harling, and of course he also designed it.

I opted for Cruikshank.

When I started I had a lot of fun. I knew nothing about Cruikshank as a person, but I was familiar with his illustrations for *Oliver Twist* and *Robinson Crusoe*; I had been given, as a child, an edition of *Crusoe* with the Cruikshank illustrations, curiously enough printed in Ayr in southern Scotland. I had to do the necessary research (and there was a lot of it) in the secondhand bookshops in Charing Cross Road in central London, in my lunch-hours, because I had to earn my living during the day – I had no time for research in the British Library. Charing Cross Road then enclosed probably the greatest concentration of first-rate antiquarian bookshops anywhere in the world. I had some good experiences. Early on, and very encouraging to a novice like myself, I found a book with three original letters in Cruikshank's own hand, tucked in the back. Then I discovered A.M.Cohn's *George Cruikshank: a Catalogue Raisonnée of the work executed during the years 1806–1877*, London, 1924, cheap and invaluable, and, as far as I could find out, the last useful work on Cruikshank that had been published. Then one day I went into a little bookshop off Charing Cross Road in which the proprietor was moving books around and had a pile in his hand. I asked if he had a copy of Southey's *Life of Nelson* with Cruikshank's illustrations. 'No', he said, I thought rather pityingly, 'Cruikshank never illustrated Southey, but I do have a copy of Southey here in my hand', and passed it to me. It was a small book in green leather tooled in gold and blind, seventh edition, 1844, with eight wood engravings signed by Cruikshank. These illustrations, I discovered, were in every edition of Southey from the first, 1830, certainly up to the thirteenth, 1853, which I found later.

A few days later I found a handsome leather-bound scrapbook, with an engraved bookplate of Frederick Collins Wilson (who he?), containing 80 original etched plates (some by Leech but most by Cruikshank), taken out of books and pasted down. They included complete sets of *The History of the Irish Rebellion*, 1845, and the *Fairy Library*, 1853–64.

The collection saved me looking for the books themselves; they are among the very best illustrations Cruikshank ever made.

George Cruikshank lived for eighty-six years, from 1792 to 1878, and spent nearly all his life drawing. He was immensely prolific, therefore books with his illustrations were common, and usually not expensive. I bought all I could afford, and a few I couldn't, secure in the belief that when I had finished my book I would sell them, hopefully at a profit. It didn't work out like that. I wanted to keep them. I had become a collector.

I wrote my text in all sorts of places, including H. A. L. Fisher's study in Rock Cottage when we were living there a year or so later. The text was quite short: the most important part of the book was over ninety reproductions in line, and a 'select list' of books with Cruikshank's illustrations, comprising about 153 titles. The book was designed by Harling and published as the first of the English Masters of Black-and-White series by Art and Technics (James Shand's new publishing firm) in February 1948. It was my second published work: my first, as I wrote in the copy I sent to my parents, was David Hector McLean (co-publisher Tony), who came out on 15 November 1945. The second family edition (addition) was Andrew, who appeared on 1 May 1948.

9. Something completely different

I had spent five years in the Navy, had sailed on or under the North Sea, the Atlantic, the Mediterranean, the Red Sea, and the Indian Ocean, had walked on three continents, and flown in two aeroplanes. I had worn seven different kinds of hat, carried six kinds of gun, and been issued with an instantaneous death tablet. I had been cursed by seven Gunners Mates, kissed by one admiral (French, of course), and earned Their Lordships' Displeasure for losing a key. My drawing in colour of Their Lordships' Displeasure, now hangs, or it did once, in the Submarine Officers' Mess in Fort Blockhouse.

My desire for an outdoor life, which I had felt so strongly when leaving school, was more or less satisfied.

During those five years in the Navy, nearly all decisions in my life had been taken for me. I had done (usually) what I was told. Now, with peace in the offing, I discovered that I had to think for myself about everything, including a wife, a child, and a house – except we didn't have a house. What we had was an invitation to share a cottage in the country with a friend of my wife's mother.

I went down to Rock Cottage in Thursley, Surrey, to meet Mrs Fisher, the widow of the historian H. A. L. Fisher, who had sadly been killed in Oxford in the blackout. I found her – a white-haired old lady – on her knees scrubbing out the kitchen floor. The deal was for her to do the house-cleaning, and my wife to do the cooking. 'Surely' I said, 'we can get a girl from the village to help?' 'Oh, no,' said Mrs Fisher, 'the cottage is too far out of the village for that.' This, I discovered later, was not true. Mrs Fisher did not want to have to talk to girls from the village.

So we moved in, Tony and I and our four-week old son David. Tony inspected what she had to cook on. It was an ancient four-burner paraffin stove. As she had practically no experience of cooking on anything, she hardly knew what she was in for. Mrs Fisher also kept 400 hens and Tony had to collect the eggs and pack them for the local authority. We were allowed three eggs a week each, as rationing was still in force. Mrs Fisher's views on rationing were rigid. One evening when I was grinding coffee beans, I remarked innocently 'Isn't it good that coffee isn't rationed!' 'It ought to be!' growled Mrs Fisher. She would have died for her friends, or her principles. She was not easy to live with.

Antonia McLean in H. A. L. Fisher's study, Rock Cottage, Thursley, Surrey. Drawn by the author in January 1946.

I was now again working in the J. Walter Thompson advertising agency in London. Not having a car, it took me two hours to get there in the morning, starting with a walk across three fields to catch a bus to Godalming. My wife and I both wanted to live in the country, but this was a no-win situation. There had to be an easier way to live with the hares and hunt for the pounds.

The J. Walter Thompson Agency, now in Berkeley Square near Piccadilly, had asked me to go back to them to start a new book design department they had in mind, but they were not yet actually ready to go ahead with it. Their first task was to find space for all their people coming back from the war. I was given an easel and a stool and put in the corner of a large room with an enormous desk and an acre of fitted carpet. It was the office of the managing director, who was ill and subsequently died. Here I sat, out of everybody's way, with very little to do. I was asked to re-design the firm's stationery, a job that a year or two later I could have done with my eyes shut, but now, as a born-again novice, it was beyond me. It nearly broke my heart. Eventually the kindly art director came to tell me that he saw no hope of getting the book department started just yet (in fact, I don't think it ever did start) and I had better look elsewhere. Sorry.

So in 1946 I went to see Allen Lane at the Penguin Books Office at Harmondsworth where I had visited Edward Young nearly ten years previously. Edward had left Penguins just before the war. Allen offered to take me on at the salary I had been earning as a naval Lieutenant, about £750 a year. I was to look after the production of Puffin Picture Books, a lively series of illustrated children's books, which suited me very well because they were printed by all the three main printing processes; letterpress, litho, and gravure. I could learn about these processes by visiting the printers concerned. Also enjoyable was meeting the artists, like Edward Ardizzone and Edward Bawden. They were commisioned by an outside editor, Noel Carrington, but the artists brought their finished work in to me. It was often in the wrong size or shape.

In 1947, a new series of children's books was started, called Porpoises, edited by Grace Hogarth. One of the first was *Paul, the Hero of the Fire*, written and illustrated by Edward Ardizzone. In September I had to take colour proofs to his studio in Maida Vale. Ardizzone was in shirt sleeves, in a rather grubby basement studio, littered with matchsticks and cigarette-ends. Ardizzone had a tummy, a large face, flabby cheeks, domed forehead, and longish loose grey hair. He was a very nice man indeed. He took me out to lunch at a nearby pub, where we found his wife and son Phil, aged fifteen. We discussed lithography and illustration in general. Ardizzone said that in order to live and keep his family, he had to draw four finished illustrations every day of his life. I mentioned the French illustrator Dubout, and the Villon illustrated by him that I had just bought, which was in my pocket. Ardizzone said that he didn't think that Dubout would reflect Villon's tenderness. I don't think Ardizzone ever illustrated Villon himself and I doubt if he knew Dubout's work. Looking again at the Villon, I thought that Dubout illustrated the book (tender? or savage? certainly coarse) quite superbly: it is a memorable book in every way. Ardizzone's work is tender, and charming, and gentlemanly, but I think not deep. He admitted the impossibility of illustrating *Oliver Twist* without being dominated by Cruikshank. I found that while sitting with Ardizzone, the people round us in the pub began to look like Ardizzone characters.

Another illustrator with whom I became very friendly was Victor Ross, who illustrated a Puffin Picture Book *English Fashions*. Victor was born in a German Jewish family so rich that it was never thought he would have to earn his own living, so he was never taught a profession. He came to London for a holiday, by himself, on what turned out to be the last train out of Berlin before the war. His family all perished in the ovens. He was eventually allowed to join the Pioneer Corps (a most un-military figure) and spent the war in a British uniform. After the war he realised that he must find a job. He had two possible qualifications: in food and wine, and art. He told me that he decided against the restaurant business (for which he was well qualified) because it meant getting up at four or five every morning to go to the markets. He became an illustrator, starting out by calling on restaurants and food firms. At Fortnum and Mason, he was asked to design a price ticket for goods in their windows, for which he was paid £5. Next time he passed the shop in Piccadilly he noticed that his ticket was now being used as Fortnum and Mason's symbol. He was too shy to go in and demand a large extra fee.

He married an extremely nice Englishwoman, Katharine, who was secretary and office-mother in the publishing firm of Heinemann. Victor always did the cooking if he and Katharine were having a party, which was often. He used to relate how one evening on his way home he remembered that he needed a bottle of sherry. Finding himself outside Berry Brothers (who he did not know) in St James's Street, he went in to buy a bottle. They insisted on him tasting seven or eight different sherries, and when he tried to pay for the bottle he wanted, there was a crisis because they could not change his pound note: cash was never seen in their lordly shop. Poor Victor. His illustrations for *English Fashions* were a remarkable achievement for someone who had not been brought up in England. Long after he died, I used to find menus still in use which he had designed for leading London restaurants.

Allen Lane also gave me other odd jobs. One was to design and produce *Penguins Progress*, an occasional booklet describing new Penguin publications; in it I was allowed to use my own drawings of penguins climbing library ladders or chatting up authors. The only actual book I got to design while at Penguins was David Pye's *Ships* in 'The Things We See' series, in a larger format than normal Penguins. I think I see in its pages the influence of Jan Tschichold, who entered the Penguin scene in March 1947.

The war and subsequent economy measures had caused Penguin standards to be gradually neglected; and now many new titles and series were being planned and introduced. Oliver Simon, at the Curwen Press, told Allen Lane that he should call in Jan Tschichold, whose recent meticulous design of the Birkhaüser Classics in Switzerland was

SILVERBECK, STANWELL MOOR, MIDDLESEX

The technical  to which we referred

last developed into a production

which has only now become 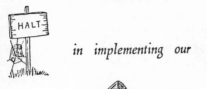. We are sorry

for the in implementing our

but hope that the enclosed will give you pleasure

this  and that good fortune will your

in the coming year.

Rebus letter for Allen Lane, 1946, sent with special edition of *The Ancient Mariner* given to his friends at Christmas. Printed in red and black. Reduced.

an obvious recommendation. Without doubt Tschichold was now the leading book designer in Europe, but he did not speak much English. Allen asked a lot of people, including myself, whether hiring J.T. would be a good idea. I think we all said no, there were plenty of good designers in England. Robert Harling said there were at least six good ones in London, and Allen should take them all on and 'make them knock spots off each other'. Allen heard all our opinions carefully, and went off to Switzerland with Oliver Simon to invite Tschichold to join Penguins as typographic supremo.

In February 1947 Tony and I decided to spend my war gratuity on a skiing holiday. We went to Zuoz in Switzerland because it was high. As a result we hardly ever saw the mountains, or anything much else, because we were nearly always in cloud. There were two coincidences on that holiday. The first was that the much-talked-about glamorous dancing instructress at the big hotel in Zuoz, when she came to give a demonstration in our smaller hotel, turned out to have been the chief bridesmaid at a wedding in London in the early days of the war, at which I had been Best Man. Her rapturous greeting of me on the hotel dance floor gave me a reputation I had hardly earned. The second was that on our train journey home, exhilarated and comatose, I saw a man pass down the corridor whom I recognized: it was Tschichold on his way to Penguin Books and looking rather lost. We clasped each other warmly.

His brief was to take charge of all Penguin typography, from the least item of stationery upwards. When he accepted this assignment, before arriving in England, he very wisely asked for two examples of every item of stationery to be sent to him. When he arrived at Penguin, he brought every one of these specimens with him, with annotations on each which were a lesson in lucid typographic criticism.

Tschichold's office was next door to mine, which made it easy for me to take him my problems from time to time. The worst of these were faults in the artwork for my Puffin Picture Books, commissioned not by me but by Noel Carrington. To reject wrong artwork would mean delay and possibly a refusal to redraw it ('that's how Carrington told me to do it!'). I found that Tschichold was a genius at adapting and adjusting so that no mistake was visible. In fact it often looked better than it would have done if it had been correct in the first place.

On Penguin books themselves, Tschichold did not make radical alterations, but small and telling improvements. He also tidied up the drawing of the Penguin itself, originally drawn by Edward Young but which in the course of time had suffered debasement. Tschichold did not simplify his job by introducing any standardisation of title-pages or text: every book he touched was a separate and individual work of literature, and received the typography he considered appropriate to it.

He composed a four-page leaflet headed 'Penguin Composition Rules', which was circulated to every firm of printers working for Penguin. It made a great impact on the whole British printing industry. Some English printers were stupid enough to resent having a 'German' typographer (Tschichold was in fact now a naturalized Swiss) teaching them how to set type in English. When they tried to argue with him, sometimes in my presence, I enjoyed watching his fairly weak command of English suddenly fail altogether, making argument impossible: Tschichold would smile inscrutably and get on with his work. He had a sly sense of humour, but on questions of typographic principle he was adamant. It was a great privilege to work in the next room to him. He was always even-tempered and approachable; I never saw him flustered.

By the time I was working in Penguins, Tony and I had moved from Mrs Fisher's Rock Cottage and found a tiny house of our own in Colnbrook, quite near Harmondsworth. When Tony's surgeon uncle, Sir Heneage Ogilvie, came to have supper with us, his Rolls-Royce was slightly longer than our house was wide. Living with Mrs Fisher had been an experience we did not regret. She was nearly a saint, and certainly a remarkable character.

We invited Allen Lane and his wife Lettice to dinner. I had bought a bottle of expensive sherry to mark the occasion. 'Allen, will you have sherry, or gin?' 'Oh, half and half, thank you' was the dismaying answer.

Allen was ebullient, enthusiastic, exciting to work for. He did not appear ever to have read a whole book, but he had a superb instinct for books; he was after all the pupil of his uncle, the great John Lane of the Bodley Head. Allen's facade was that of the club-man, most at home when telling stories in front of the smoking-room fire. He was charming to his juniors, like myself, but often difficult, to put it mildly, especially as he often said one thing but did another. Any meeting in his office which became irksome, as when printers asked to have their mounting bills paid, tended to be interrupted by telephone calls. Beaming smile, but the telephone rang immediately. A long conversation with his farm manager, followed by profuse apologies. 'I am so sorry. Now, what were we going to talk about?' The phone rang again, this time about his yacht. More apologies. 'Now...' Again the phone, and an

Detail, reduced, from pen-and ink portrait of Antonia McLean by Claude Harrison, Colnbrook, June 1949.

animated chat with his accountant. When the printer opened his mouth again, in walked Allen's wife. 'Ah! Lettice! You must meet... Now, let's all go across to the Peggy Bedford and have a drink!' Instead of a cheque, the printer got, and accepted, another large printing order.

I was by now getting back to the position, in thinking about printing and typography, that I had reached before being called up for war service – even, being by now five years older, slowly feeling my way further ahead.

It was, of course, enormously helpful to have Jan Tschichold in the next room, to see, watch, and talk to. His *Penguin Composition Rules*, printed in 1947 and reproduced in my *Jan Tschichold, Typographer*, 1975, was, in only four pages, an almost complete manual providing the basic rules for type composition for books. Most of it was now familiar to me, but it was wonderful to have it in such a short and accessible format.

What I wrote about the Rules in 1975 seems to be still valid today:

> 'Their importance to the British printing trade as a whole cannot be over-emphasized. Today, a quarter of a century later, they are still exactly valid, and still have to be insisted on: ignorance and carelessness of typographic detail are still regrettably common in British printing. Tschichold's Rules deserve to be read closely: word by word and to the end. It will be seen that their aim is not to promote a designer's aesthetic whims but to aid pleasing communication between author and reader – which is, after all, what typographic design is all about.'

I might have stayed in Penguins, but I was longing to be my own master, not an employee, and there was also one young man in the firm who regarded me as an enemy who wanted his job – in fact, the last thing I wanted. I was already doing some work outside Penguins: in 1947 I was invited by F. H. K. Henrion, then acting advisor to the Conservative party, to write and design a booklet on typography for their agents in the next election. They wanted to emulate the Labour party, which had just commissioned a perfectly splendid booklet on the same subject from Michael Middleton, called *Soldiers of Lead: an introduction to layout and typography for use in the Labour Party*, 1948. I wrote and designed a rival booklet, on Henrion's instructions, which we called *Words into Type. Notes on the Planning of Printing for the Conservative Party*. Henrion approved it and took it in to show the publicity officer who had asked for it. In the meantime he had left, and another chap took over who had different ideas. To cut a distressing story short, four consecutive publicity officers all had different ideas. Finally Henrion and I decided enough was enough, and resigned. What the Conservatives eventually produced was a pathetic four-page leaflet headed by an erratum notice.

Also in 1947, Harling printed in *Convoy* an article I had written and illustrated, called 'Moving Moments' – moving, usually out of kit-bags, with luck into a house, was what so many of us were doing in those days. A page is reproduced on p. 61.

Then my friend Vivian Ridler, who had been free-lancing in London for some time, was invited to Oxford to understudy Charles Batey and eventually become Printer to the University. He very kindly said that if I left Penguins, I could take over several of his freelance jobs. That meant that I could earn in a couple of days what I was getting from

Penguins in a week. When I told Allen Lane, he said this was a good idea for me, and if it didn't work out, I could come back to Penguins whenever I liked. I doubt if he really meant it, but it was comforting.

While I was beginning to practise as a freelance, the Royal College of Art in London was being re-organized under a new principal, Robin Darwin, who was an old Etonian, a descendant of Charles Darwin, and, before this new job, a painter and Professor of Fine Art in the University of Durham. Darwin revolutionized the Royal College, which it badly needed, creating six new schools of design, including the unheard-of one of Fashion, each with its own professor. He set out to make the place as civilized and civilizing an institution as the Cambridge college where he had been an undergraduate. He knew that the country needed designers and that they had to be educated to the highest level.

The first Professor of Graphic Design was Richard Guyatt, and I was asked to become the first tutor in typography under him, on a three-day-a-week basis. This meant that I had to invent a three-year course in typographic design, possibly the first ever to exist in this country and perhaps in the world. I had to prepare a syllabus, write and deliver regular lectures to the students, collect printed specimens to hand round, organize exhibitions either from my own collections or by borrowing from others, bring in outside designers and experts in related fields to meet and talk to students, and supervise the school's own printing equipment and collection of types and see that it was properly used. And defend it from being thrown out, as was recommended by Robert Harling, who said correctly that designers nowadays did not need to handle type. Dick Guyatt was a skilled artist who had designed posters for Shell, and had now to run a department whose tutors were mostly older than him and already eminent in their professions, people like Edward Bawden, Abram Games, John Nash, and Roger Powell, Britain's leading bookbinder. They were soon joined by Edward Ardizzone, Reynolds Stone, Barnett Freedman, and Berthold Wolpe. We were all part-time.

Neither Dick nor I had any professional qualifications: they did not then exist, just as typography as a recognized profession did not exist.

At that time, in 1948, Switzerland was regarded as *the* centre of typographic excellence in Europe. It was from Switzerland that Tschichold had been selected to come and overhaul Penguins. Swiss posters, which we saw reproduced in the Swiss magazine *Graphis,* were the best in the world. Dick Guyatt and I decided that we ought to visit Switzerland and see how it was done.

Revise proof urgently, please.

THE RED HOUSE
BEAUMONT · THORPE-LE-SOKEN · ESSEX
Thorpe-le-Soken 245

entirely

revelations, etc?

30·XII·'49

Dear Edward: in my little booklet for the British Council on modern design I am saying that I think Penguins' success (when other cheap series had failed) was largely due to their design. Can you give me anything interesting about the genesis of the design? I can say it was by you can't I? Was it first, second, tenth, twentieth shot? Did A·L· exert much influence on it? Did a committee sit & unanimously agree on that design? Were you at that time production manager of Bodley Head, & incidentally how old were you? Had you had your first woman? I shall put that in, of course.

Thank you for your Christmas card, which I expect is still in the post. Love to Diana and the family

Ruari

None other

Some.

That's what they called me.

Let's see I must have been about 22

Naturally. I remember her very well. She was ... Oh well never mind - but can I tell you about my Lantern? - much more interesting.

Heavy reciprocations

Diana swears we sent you one - & come to think of it if I remember asking our your address specially. I thought yours well up to standard - thank you.

For typical results of committee work see Pan Books covers.

Letter to Edward Young and his reply, 1949. Reduced.

59

This was sanctioned by the Principal, and we set out. We visited the leading Swiss art schools, we met the distinguished designer and illustrator Imre Reiner, we collected examples of Swiss printing, and we looked, as we walked along the pavements, for pretty girls. As we never saw any, we assumed that they must all be locked up on the tops of Swiss mountains. Certainly the snow in the Alps had something to do with Swiss typography, which relied heavily on white paper. The secret of the best Swiss posters, we decided, was that they left out all words: when words were included, they looked ordinary.

We finished our trip by going to Paris. The Swiss all got up very early. As our train drove into the Gard du Nord in the early morning, not a soul was working in the French fields. When we emerged from the station, there were lots of pretty girls – and they were getting the taxis, irrespective of taxi queues. We went to a café on the Boule Miche to have a drink before parting for the week-end. As we sat enjoying the spring sunshine, a pretty girl came into the café in a sleeveless blouse. The waiter went up to her, lifted the shoulder of her blouse with a finger, looked down inside, gave a beaming smile and made a sign of approval with index finger and thumb and pursed lips. The strain of Swiss seriousness slipped away.

One of my jobs at the Royal College of Art was to invite people distinguished in the design world to come and talk to the students. Beatrice Warde was an obvious person to ask: she was glamorous in appearance, a brilliant extempore talker, and editor of *The Monotype Recorder*, at that time the most influential design periodical in Britain. It always contained specimens of new Monotype type faces and an article of great importance either by Stanley Morison or herself. When she came to the College, I had to introduce her to Dick Guyatt, the Professor of Typography, who had never met her. She beamed at him and immediately asked 'What do you think of art?' Dick blenched, but came back calmly with a grin and a phrase which I, also unnerved, have sadly forgotten. However, Dick made a good impression, and Beatrice of course entranced my students.

She was kind to me: in Summer 1952 she published a special number of the *Recorder* entitled 'Typographic Transformations', in which I found a whole page illustrating my redesigns for *The Colnbrook Chronicle*, printed in colour (see next chapter), and also some redesigning of small booklets I had done for the National Union of Teachers. Facing those reproductions there is a photograph of an audience of typographers listening to a lecture by Joseph Thorp, author of *Printing for Business*, 1918, the first text book of typography ever addressed to laymen print-buyers.

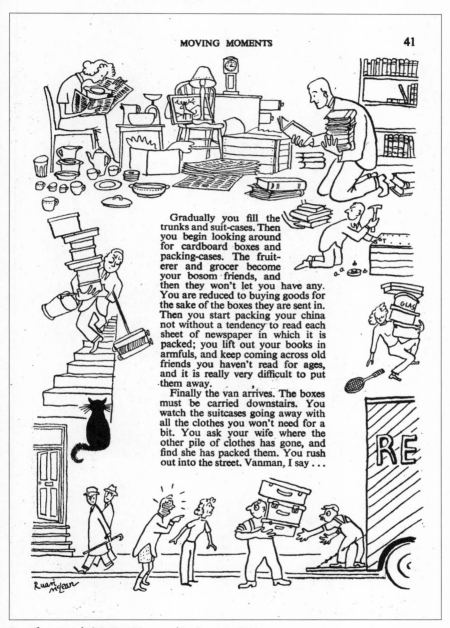

Page from article 'Moving Moments' in *Convoy* magazine, 1947.

Family Christmas card, Colnbrook, 1948. Reduced.

The photograph is remarkable for showing Sir Francis Meynell sitting next to Stanley Morison, and other recognizable faces include Harry Carter, Herbert Spencer, and Allen Hutt.

In 1955 Beatrice published *The Crystal Goblet*, a book of her own essays, and gave me a copy inscribed in her own elegant calligraphy, with 'her profound compliments to a writer she trusts and admires'.

Beatrice Warde, with Stanley Morison, 1960s. (Photo courtesy of St Bride Printing Library.)

I did not have many chances to meet Beatrice again. She did not come to Double Crown Club dinners, we thought because there was a club rule that ladies could not be members. But that was not the case. Stanley Morison had divorced his wife for her, (and Beatrice had left her husband Frederic for him) but finally Morison decided that as he was a Catholic he could not marry her. If ladies could be members of the Double Crown Club, the first had to be Beatrice: but while Morison was a member it was agreed this could not happen. When Morison died, on 11 October 1967, Beatrice and his secretary Miss Gaskin were with him*. Beatrice must then become the first lady to be elected a member; when she came to see us in Blackheath around then, I remember her discussing with my wife what she should wear at her first meeting: something in 'black silk' had high priority.

* N.Barker, *Stanley Morison*, Macmillan, 1972.

10. Typography and parsons

THE vicar of Colnbrook (a village between Heathrow Airport and Windsor Castle) had inherited from his predecessor a sad-looking little monthly news-sheet, in out-of-date types, posing as the parish magazine. Its appearance said exactly the opposite of what the vicar, Guy Daniel, was himself trying to say to his parishioners. He did not want something 'arty'; he wanted something simple and straightforward. He invited one of his parishioners who happened then to be teaching typography at the Royal College of Art to help make it look at least of its own time. The parishioner (me) invited selected students to come out to Colnbrook for a meal and make drawings of some aspect of the village that appealed to them. As a result we were able to put a new drawing on the cover every month. The circulation doubled, and the vicar, putting the price up to fourpence, even saw a modest profit. That was in 1949, and the redesign was later illustrated in the *Monotype Recorder*.

It was my first attempt to help a parson design a parish magazine. Parsons need typographers: but typographers don't always need parsons. I found that parsons who consulted me about their magazines either had no intention of following my advice, or accepted it without acknowledgement, let alone payment. So when I received a letter from an unknown parson in Birkdale, near Liverpool, saying that he wanted to turn his parish magazine into a religious *Lilliput*, and had been given my name by a friend, I sent him my standard off-putting reply. Apparently this annoyed the parson so much that he asked me to meet him at Euston Station. I met a young man who changed my life. He did not look like a parson. He was about my age. He wore a sporty dog-tooth grey suit, without a dog-collar. I learned that when at Oxford (Brasenose College) he had won prizes for ballroom dancing, and later married Jessica Dunning, an elegant actress. After training at Wycliffe Hall and being ordained, he had joined the R.A.F. during the war as a chaplain. Stationed at a large bomber station, he discovered that his orders were to think of himself as an officer, which meant playing strip poker or shove-ha'penny with the other officers and having virtually nothing to do with the 7,000 'erks'. He therefore resigned. He was then sent to a tiny parish in Essex where he had hardly any parishioners. He started a

Marcus Morris, editor of *Eagle*, *c.* 1950.

commercial market garden. He then moved to Birkdale, reputed to be one of the wealthiest parishes in Britain, where his main activity was expected to be attending cocktail parties.

He actually meant business. *Lilliput*, that famous and delightful pocket magazine conceived by Stefan Lorant in 1937, which pioneered in this country unlikely juxtapositions of photographs, was a good model for an innovative parish magazine. My parson's name was Marcus Morris, and his parish magazine was called *Anvil*.

He wanted, as well as help on *Anvil*, a range of letterheadings and other stationery for himself and his publishing activities – and was prepared to pay for it. I had just bought a copy of the Kynoch Press Type

THE

COLNBROOK
CHRONICLE

No. 25   Fourpence   Jan. 1949

The re-designed Colnbrook parish magazine, 1949, actual size. Drawing by Monica Goddard. Type in black, background terracotta.

Marcus Morris's parish magazine *Anvil* for Birkdale, Merseyside, July 1950, actual size.
Drawing by Sheila Robinson, printed in four colours.

Book designed by Harry Carter in 1934, which showed wood engravings by Eric Ravilious as stock blocks which could be used in any Kynoch Press printing. Marcus soon had his new stationery, printed in green, with Ravilious blocks in black as decorations – and paid for it all, not because he was rich (he was in fact heavily in debt) but because he thought he needed it. And with his encouragement I commissioned a series of cover drawings from Sheila Robinson, while he commissioned articles from C. S. Lewis, C. E. M. Joad, Harold Macmillan, and other top figures. One of Marcus's friends was the Rev. Chad Varah, and one evening I was invited to dine with them at Pruniers in St James's Street, then the very best French restaurant in London. I was intrigued to find, over the coffee and brandy, how much more than I these two young parsons knew about wine and women.

By this time I was working three afternoons a week in an advertising agency above the Mac Fisheries shop in Mount Street, Mayfair. I was also still teaching at the Royal College, and had one or two part-time jobs with publishers. Marcus, always trying to make *Anvil* profitable, now had a new idea. With three children of his own, he had found that children's comics were being imported from America in large quantities; none was admirable and some were actively vicious. Parents and educationalists were trying to ban the American comics, but Marcus said it would be wiser to drive them off the market by producing something much better. He had found an artist, Frank Hampson, who was now drawing for *Anvil*. He thought Hampson was the man he wanted for the new comic he had in mind, and paid him a retainer out of his own stipend to prevent him going elsewhere.

In the new comic, the first 'hero' was to be called Lex Christian, 'a tough, fighting parson from the slums of the East End of London'. He then became airborne, a flying padre, and a strip was drawn by Hampson which was nearly sold to the *Sunday Empire News*, but the editor who liked it, Terence Horsley, was tragically killed in a gliding accident. Marcus decided to go ahead and produce an entirely new children's weekly of his own, to be called *Eagle*. He and Hampson made a dummy and every Sunday night, after a full weekend as parish priest, Marcus climbed aboard the sleeper to London and hawked the dummy round Fleet Street. Everyone turned it down. As he told me later, he became very close to both bankruptcy and a nervous breakdown. He was paying out to Hampson and others more than he was earning, and the debts of *Anvil* were mounting into thousands.

Marcus called on me one day at Holden's, the agency where I was now working (see Chapter II, p. 87), to show me the dummy, which I had not previously seen or had anything to do with. He was wondering if he could borrow enough money to finance publishing it himself. One look at the dummy told me that it was far too big a project for Holden's to touch, and we were not publishers. At least I didn't give Marcus any false hopes. Then, in November 1949, he phoned to say that the dummy had been bought by the Hulton Press, whose main publications were *Lilliput, Picture Post, Housewife*, and *Farmers Weekly*. I knew that Hulton used the Curwen Press for their design work. I was pleased for Marcus's sake, but there would be nothing in it for me. The great Oliver Simon at Curwen would do the typography.

What happened was different. Apparently Oliver Simon gave the job of designing the heading for *Eagle* to a girl in his office, a competent girl whom in fact I knew, and I can only suppose that she did not take the job seriously. Marcus, still almost penniless but installed in a West End flat in which a bottle of Gordon's Gin was prominent on the sideboard, called me in to look at what Curwen Press had sent. It was so uninspired that he asked me to have a go. Hampson had already drawn the Eagle symbol, using as a model the top of a brass inkwell Marcus had bought at the white elephant stall at the vicarage garden party. I recalled a typeface called 'Tempest' which I had seen in Robert Harling's magazine *Typography* in 1937, which had the right visual connotations. It was strong, had movement, and the curves which ended the crossbars in E and L seemed to suggest eagle's feathers. I sketched my idea on the back of an envelope, sitting on an arm of Marcus's sofa, and Marcus liked it. The 'Tempest' type had been designed by Berthold Wolpe, then working in Frankfurt with Rudolf Koch, but now in London. We asked him to draw the word EAGLE in these letters, which he did. It was accepted by the management at Hulton, and from then on I was hired as typographic adviser to *Eagle* at £5 a week. Marcus asked me to find a flat we could share during the week – his family were in Lancashire, mine in Essex – and I found one in South Audley Street, just round the corner from Holden's office in Mount Street. Marcus was not perturbed when we found that the other floors in our building, and indeed nearly all the other houses in the street, were occupied by prostitutes. Doors slammed at intervals above and below us all through the night until breakfast time.

Being fully occupied all day, I could never meet Marcus until the evenings. He had usually spent the day meeting and interviewing contributors, or discussing plans with the Hulton Press management. Marcus did all the editorial planning and commissioning of strips, articles and illustrations. When I arrived at the flat each evening, I usually found Marcus briefing an artist. To begin with, on recommendations from Hultons, he went to the leading strip artists working in London. Time and again he explained carefully what he wanted: the artists went away and came back not with what they had been asked to do, but with what they thought was needed. They could not believe that a young parson who had never edited anything except a parish magazine knew better than they did what was right for this completely new children's paper. They found themselves dropped, and Marcus had to find other people who would listen to him. It slowly dawned on me that for the first time in my life I had the privilege of working for a man who knew exactly what he wanted and who would accept nothing less.

My responsibility was to lay out the text and mark it up for setting, and to design the titles for the strips and stories. The type I chose for the strips, which I thought had the right informal-looking character, was appropriately called 'Cartoon'. It had been designed in America by Howard Trafton in 1936, and was available in only two weights. I used it on nearly every page. The story headings were usually better in hand-drawn lettering, to give movement and variety. While I was counting words, calculating column widths and pondering type sizes, Marcus was sub-editing typescripts. We were often still at it at two, three, or even four in the morning. By then I was ready to agree to anything, but Marcus never let anything go until he was satisfied and I had agreed. He would argue about a comma or a hyphen endlessly, and curse me for being lazy if I said it didn't matter. Every word and every syllable in the early numbers of *Eagle* was chewed over until Marcus was sure it was right. I cared about English too, but I didn't have Marcus's stamina.

Gradually the thing took shape. Early on, our hero Lex Christian became Dan Dare, and ceased to be a padre, merely chief pilot of the fleet, with the cheerful Digby as his Sancho Panza. And Frank Hampson found himself drawing not one but four pages in full colour and one in black and white for each issue. He soon had a staff of assistant artists.

On the editorial side, Marcus had two chief consultants, the Rev. Chad Varah and James Hemming.

Chad, chief scriptwriter and general adviser on literature, was dark, lean, and amusing. After the days of *Eagle*, Chad turned his considerable energies into founding the Telephone Samaritans, and organizing them world-wide. His name 'Chad' had originally convinced me that he couldn't be English, probably because I remembered from stamp-collecting days that Chad was a small state in Central Africa. Much later, I realized that he was named after a much-revered Northumberland saint who died in 672.

James Hemming was a psychologist, educationalist, broadcaster and author, and one of those very rare people who make you feel, after talking to them, that the world is a better place. It was Hemming who, with Marcus, established certain principles for *Eagle*: the hero in difficulties had to get himself out of trouble by skill and courage: 'with one bound he was free' was not allowed. And Germans, Japs, and other foreigners, must not automatically be villains; and in any gang of children, one or two must be coloured. Religion in the paper must not be obvious: preaching was forbidden. But the moral values for which *Eagle* stood underlay every page.

Publication was due in April. Hultons was already aiming to sell a million copies a week, but no printing machine in the country which could do this was available. At that time, *Picture Post, Everybodys, Illustrated*, and *John Bull* all printed a million weekly. Eric Bemrose, an energetic printer-engineer in Liverpool, undertook to build the photogravure press required and have it ready in time. It was said that when *Eagle* finally went to press at one end of the new machine, Bemrose was still tinkering at the other. There were 20 pages, 8 in full colour, in each issue.

Easter came. We were both going home to our families on Thursday evening. I said unthinkingly to Marcus, 'Well, cheerio, Marcus, have a good holiday!' Marcus looked bleakly at me. 'I suppose you don't realize that Easter is the time when most parsons think they are so overworked that they deserve a nervous breakdown.'

At the last moment, publication of the first issue was advanced by a week: we had been told that a rival paper might appear before ours. 900,000 copies of the first *Eagle* were printed without anyone in London seeing a colour proof. Publication day was Friday 14 April 1950 and all newsagents were, as usual, given strict instructions not to show a copy anywhere in advance. Nevertheless on Tuesday morning I saw *Eagle* on sale (3d) at our local shop in Mount Street, and bought a copy. I rang Marcus at Hultons in Shoe Lane. He had not seen it. Some un-parsonical language flowed.

Front page of *Eagle*, March 1951. The lettering for EAGLE drawn by Berthold Wolpe.
Reduced from 305 × 275mm.

So *Eagle* had started. It was an instant success. Children loved it, and so did their teachers.

For some weeks, all the editorial work was done by Marcus, with help from Chad Varah. I did the production work myself, sitting with Marcus every evening in our flat.

As soon as articles were approved and I had marked them up for typesetting by Bemrose in Liverpool, and illustrations were marked for size, they were sent north by train. The bits and pieces came back at intervals to Hulton Press, where Marcus collected them; and once a week he and I made a final paste-up of the complete issue, parcelled it up, and took it to Euston to send back to the printers by rail. Having finished the issue and parcelled it up, we often went out for a meal before going to the station. At that time I was driving the first car my wife and I ever owned, a little blue Austin 7. One week, when I had the car in London, Marcus and I drove into Soho, parked, and left the *Eagle* dummy in my briefcase in the locked car. When we returned to the car, the briefcase was gone. It was never seen again. If that had happened on any previous occasion, there would have been no *Eagle* that week; but the dummy stolen (it was the seventh issue) was the first one for which every page had been duplicated. It was therefore possible for us to reconstruct the dummy next day, in panic but with complete accuracy.

It was about this time that Marcus was in the General Manager's office being congratulated on the latest issue, which had just come in from the printer. 'How far ahead are you?' asked the General Manager. Marcus looked puzzled. 'Well, we're just about to start on the next issue. Is that what you mean?' The General Manager nearly had a fit. 'Spend any money you like' he said, 'but for God's sake get as far ahead as you can – you should be six or seven issues ahead!'

Even after *Eagle* had been appearing for some time, Marcus and a secretary were the only people working full time on the paper. Full time? He was also running his parish in Birkdale. Eventually he had to go to his Bishop and ask whether he should not give up his parish and move his family down to London. The Bishop, to his eternal credit, said 'You now have a parish of over a million children – of course that is more important'. So *Eagle* really became a parish magazine – but of a special kind.

Marcus was soon planning a companion paper for girls. *Girl* was first published on 2 November 1951, and its title masthead was also drawn for us by Berthold Wolpe. It was followed by *Robin* (for the youngest age group) and then *Swift*, for those between *Robin* and *Eagle*. As well as the four weekly papers, I had to design the books that accompanied them. Each paper had to have its own Annual, and *Eagle* soon had a yearly *Sports Annual*, a *Book of Trains*, a *Book of Aircraft*, and *Dan Dare's Spacebook*. There were also ephemera which needed careful designing. In 1951 the Dean of St Paul's Cathedral allowed us to advertise a Christmas Carol Service for all our readers, to be conducted in the cathedral by Marcus Morris. We had no idea whether anyone would come: in the end, we were told that more people were inside the cathedral than it had ever held before. My small son David read one of the lessons, and I carried more chairs than I could count. It became a yearly function; by 1959 Marcus and Chad Varah were conducting Christmas services for children in eleven cathedrals all over Britain.

As soon as each of the new papers acquired its final editorial pattern, Marcus handed it over to an attractive girl editor (whom he had selected and appointed; Ellen Vincent at *Eagle* was the first) and let her get on with it. There was no interference. Marcus was available for consultation only if wanted. I often found him asleep on a sofa in his office in the afternoon while his four papers came out successfully every week. Eventually the Hulton Press management realized this and gave Marcus other assignments, such as trying to save *Housewife*, a once good and now ailing monthly.

Marcus liked living well, and was soon able to do so. He reckoned that his talents had earned him some of the douceurs of life. He told me that at Oxford he had watched his friends drinking in order to get drunk; he did not wish to appear a pussyfoot, so he trained himself to drink level with them and stay sober. Whether this was really due to a mental decision, or a cast-iron stomach, I never knew. I was lucky in having what I preferred to call a hard head, and we had a certain amount of hilarity in our evening dinners. I never saw Marcus drunk and only once do I remember seeing him slightly flushed. What I do remember is a series of meetings in night clubs: there was a convention among the senior Hulton executives that you could never conduct serious business in the office during the day, and the best time and place was the Gargoyle at two in the morning. I often watched tough advertising types plying Marcus with champagne or brandy, or both, thinking that this inexperienced young parson would be an easy victim. After the eighth brandy it was Marcus who was still cool and collected and it was they who were on their knees.

Girl magazine art competition lunch, 1950. From l. to r., Marcus Morris, Robin Darwin (Principal, Royal College of Art), author, Vanora McIndoe (Editor of *Girl*).

Lunches and dinners were the most convenient times for Marcus and me to meet. As Dan Dare, on the front page of *Eagle*, went from strength to strength, it was clear that the whole world – well, a large part of it – was hanging on Dan's adventures. Chad Varah, who was scripting the story at that time, got Dan Dare onto Venus, but did not know what he was to do next. Marcus wanted Venus to be the sort of place Earth might be if we weren't all such fools.

One time I had lunch with Marcus when he had just come back from a holiday in the South of France; he had not enjoyed it, had spent too much, and caught a cold. While we were sipping our gin-and-tonics, he wrote down a list of the seven deadly sins, and marked both of us. He reckoned that he himself was guilty of six out of the seven. The one of which he acquitted himself was accidie, sloth. He said he knew what was wrong with himself, but not how to cure it. He was no longer interested in just editing children's papers; he had no ambition to improve the world, but he did want to exercise his own power and talents. Should he resign from the Church? It would have been the Church's loss if he had left it, but he decided to stay.

I was now dividing my time between my own office in Wyndham Place (close to Baker Street and a very good bookshop in Marylebone High Street) and Hultons in Shoe Lane – which was no longer a lane but a wide street leading down to Fleet Street, Ludgate Circus, and the River Thames. The Hulton offices were in a dismal block with a lift run by a dismal liftman who had once said that he would like to kill Edward Hulton, not noticing that Edward Hulton was at that moment standing beside him in the lift. From that day Mr Hulton nearly always took the stairs.

In late 1952 I was invited to go and talk to John Pearce, the Managing Director of Hulton Press. Would I take over the typography of *Picture Post*? This was odd, because the Assistant Editor of *Picture Post* was Michael Middleton, an extremely able typographer, and also a friend of mine. In any case, there was nothing wrong with *Picture Post's* typography: what mattered there was how the pictures were laid out. When I went to see Michael, I explained the position to him, and he generously agreed to my joining the paper as typographical adviser, provided I did not touch the typography. So I said to John Pearce 'Thank you, yes'. I found that Michael was in fact rather a busy man, because the editor, (the third since the paper's great days under Tom Hopkinson) became regularly *hors de combat* after lunch, and Michael had to run the paper by himself.

As I was still fairly heavily engaged on the children's papers for Marcus Morris, George Rainbird (with whom I was now in partnership, see p. 89) negotiated a salary for me with Hultons which was paid to Rainbird, McLean Ltd and was rather more than I was actually drawing from my own firm. He also arranged for them to provide an office for me in Shoe Lane, where I had a secretary, paid by us, who worked full-time at Hultons.

At that time, Rainbird, Mclean had got the job of making a single book out of the nine booklets written or edited by André Simon on all aspects of gastronomy (including wine); this had been planned in 1939 but held up by the war. In fact a new section had been published every year of the war, and each had been beautifully designed and printed by Oliver Simon at the Curwen Press, and were now collectors' pieces.

JAMES LAVER

VICTORIAN VISTA

London
HULTON PRESS
MCMLIV

Titlepage opening of *Victorian Vista*, 1954. Reduced.

All we had to do now was to put the nine sections together and make them into a book for the publisher William Collins. It turned out to be not as simple as it looked. Straightforward reprinting was ruled out because our required page size was smaller than the original Curwen Press page size. Also when we looked at the texts editorially, we found that there was no sort of consistency in measurements, definitions, use of capitals or italics, use of Latin or other languages for derivations; each section had been compiled and written without reference to any of the others. It had become an editorial job of far greater complexity and labour than could possibly be done in the office by any of our staff. There was also a lot of revision now required by André Simon. It so happened that my mother, no longer occupied with domestic duties with young people in Oxford, and now living in Tunbridge Wells with my retired father, was enjoying her new career in editing for London publishers. We gave her the job. It was the perfect assignment for her, and it was easier for her to see me occasionally in Shoe Lane, because we had a lift.

The book was finally published in 1952, with decorations by John Leigh-Pemberton. It is not nearly so distinguished in appearance as the Curwen Press originals, but it is a great deal more scholarly and contains no fewer than 840 pages. I doubt if any work on gastronomy ever published contains more facts.

So I found myself fully occupied with both Rainbird, McLean and Hulton Press work when in Shoe Lane.

My secretary in Shoe Lane was a girl called Ann, with delightful auburn hair, blue eyes and a jutting chin. One day she bawled me out in front of a client. I wish I could now remember what she said, and who the client was, but I remember saying to myself that she would have to go. However, before I could give her this news, she gave me hers: she was going out to Singapore to marry a Professor of History. I see, lucky old him, I said to myself, and thought no more about it. In 1960 I went, on my first visit to the United States, to a design conference in Aspen, Colorado. At the first day reception, we were queuing to be introduced to the keynote speaker, Professor C. Northcote Parkinson, when a voice behind him shrieked 'Ruari!' It was Ann. The keynote speaker was her husband. As I heard later, it was Ann who had ensured the success of *Parkinson's Law* by getting it first published as articles in *The Economist*.

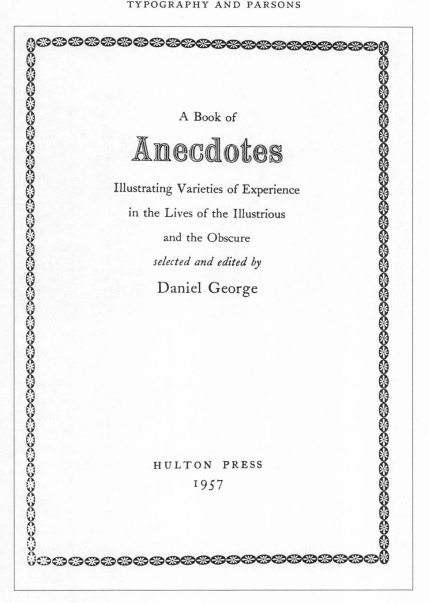

A Book of

Anecdotes

Illustrating Varieties of Experience

in the Lives of the Illustrious

and the Obscure

selected and edited by

Daniel George

HULTON PRESS

1957

Title-page opening of *Anecdotes*, 1957. Reduced.

Frank Dowling, editor of *Picture Post*, and the author photographed by chance playing darts in a London pub, by Bert Hardy, 1953.

On *Picture Post*, in 1952, I was obviously in the way. At last, the editor thought up a job for me. 'You can take charge of two Coronation issues planned for 1953', he said. This was ideal (at least for me) as they had nothing to do with ordinary issues and involved special illustrations to be commissioned and completed well in advance of the actual ceremony. The Coronation itself would of course be reported in regular issues.

I was glad not to have Michael Middleton's job. Whatever the time of day, or night, including Sundays, he had to be on alert. If an international crisis occurred, someone – probably Michael – had to organize immediately a team of writers and photographers to go and cover it, wherever it might be. The current editor had once achieved the distinction of sending three teams of reporters and photographers to within a few miles of each other in Central Africa, and was no longer considered reliable for this kind of thing.

Picture Post's correspondent for the reporting of religious ceremony at that time was Tom Driberg, MP. It was laid down that office boys should never be sent to Driberg's flat, so I had to go myself with proofs, and was intrigued to see a young Guardsman waiting in attendance. Around this time, H. M. Queen Mary died, and Driberg was asked to write a piece on her for the next issue. He ordered everything we had on the spike (matter written but not yet used is put 'on the spike' until needed) to be laid out for him, and dashed over from the House of Commons to write his piece. He never looked at any of the material we had collected, but wrote some 500 brilliant words in fifteen minutes, which had to be transmitted by teleprinter to the printers in Watford. Driberg, like Alexander Woollcott of the *New Yorker*, cared passionately about punctuation and other niceties of writing, and if anyone altered anything he had written without permission, there was an explosion. Unfortunately, the teleprinter at Watford delivered everything not only without punctuation but entirely in capital letters. It happened that I was in Watford when it came through, and I had to sub-edit it back to what I could only guess was what Driberg intended. If there was an explosion, I never heard it.

An explosion came, but for another reason. We had commissioned covers for both *Picture Post* Coronation issues from John Brinkley, a friend who was a superb calligraphic craftsman. He produced beautiful floriated Victorian designs which were sentimental and therefore popular, without being banal. The first cover, the royal coat of arms surrounded by a wreath of summer flowers, surpassed our expectations. When the second cover came in, featuring 'God Save The Queen' in elaborately decorated floral lettering, I was so enchanted that I wanted to show it off before it went to the printer. Since it was after lunch, the Editor was not with us, so I took it proudly to show the General Manager, a large genial man who I thought was a friend. 'Ah, yes', he said, 'very nice. Just leave it with me, will you?' Next morning, the Editor was informed, on the telephone, that Brinkley's cover was not suitable. No reason was given. We were told to have a colour photograph of the Queen instead – the only cover the management considered possible on a Coronation issue. That bloody fool McLean had cocked things up. I never forgot the lesson: NEVER show anything to the management. I now learned why Harold Ross, Editor of the *New Yorker*, always kept the door between his editorial offices and the management firmly locked.

Brinkley's rejected cover can be seen – only in monochrome – on a full page of The Studio's *Lettering and Calligraphy*, 1954.

About this time, someone in Hulton Press commissioned a series of articles from a famous journalist Claud Cockburn, who lived in Ireland. Cockburn was known to enjoy his liquor, so a young man – an engaging character, born a White Russian Prince, whose main job was to look after Edward Hulton and pay his bills in restaurants, was deputed to meet Cockburn at Heathrow and have him in the office next day at the right time and sober. They met and became instant friends, went on a drinking spree, and ended up, both unconscious, on the floor of a room that had been booked for Cockburn in the Pastoria Hotel off Leicester Square. The hotel management made the wrong assumption and for a long time afterwards if either of them appeared there he would be told, 'Your friend hasn't arrived yet, Sir'.

Claud was the best story-teller I had ever heard. We met in the Shoe Lane pub regularly, and one Friday evening, at the end of a tiring week, I invited him home to dinner with us in Blackheath. Driving along the Lower Road to Greenwich, we decided that we would each like a whisky; the pub we stopped at did not sell whisky, which must make it unique. In the same street I also found a post-office which did not sell stamps.

Claud was tall, with a domed forehead, beaky nose, round black-rimmed spectacles, and very alert – but kindly – eyes. He reminisced brilliantly all through dinner. I ought to add that he had not yet written *In Time of Trouble*, the autobiography in which so many of his stories were finally printed.

It was only when he tried to light his cigarette half-way along its shank that I realized how far the drink had taken him. It was clear that we had Claud for the night. I got him up to the spare room, provided pyjamas and a toothbrush, and wished him good-night. When I went up a little later to see if he was alright, he was asleep on the bed with his boots on. I got them off and covered him with an eiderdown.

The next morning, Saturday, Tony and I had arranged to visit my parents in Tunbridge Wells. Claud asked if he could sit at the dining-room table and finish an article for *Punch*. It wouldn't take more than a few minutes. No, he didn't want lunch, he'd be away long before that. Our very competent (and pretty) Dutch au pair, Mieke, promised to provide lunch if needed.

We returned to Blackheath on a lovely summer evening. Mieke was sitting with her feet out of the drawing-room window overlooking the drive. Her agitated gestures indicated that Claud was still in the house. She had noticed that every time she entered the dining-room, the level

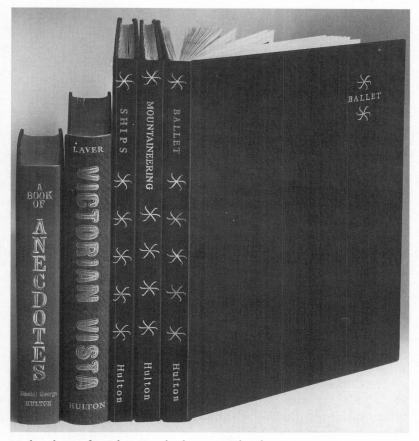

Binding designs for Hulton Press books, 1950s, reduced.

of whisky in the bottle on the sideboard had fallen. By late afternoon the bottle was empty and she was ready to jump out of the window if he should start on her. (Claud, with all his faults, would never have done that without encouragement.)

So we had Claud for another night. The next morning, Sunday, I took him firmly to the station and put him on a train. When I returned and looked inside the cupboard for the gin, as we felt we needed a celebratory drink, I found that bottle was empty too.

With the children's papers thriving, and *Housewife* also being looked after, Marcus needed something else to do. A new Sunday newspaper was an obvious good idea, and was given a programme. It was to be called *Seven Days* (later changed to *Sunday Star*). It was to be edited, under Marcus, by a formidable partnership: Claud Cockburn and Maurice Richardson. One was entitled to wonder. As journalists these two were brilliant. As characters, both were wild, enjoyed wild friends, and were apt to be what was euphemistically called 'unreliable'. Life was never dull in their company.

Seven Days got as far as a dummy run, which went to press at the Sun Printers in Watford. The party included Claud, Maurice Richardson, a secretary, a young and talented journalist called Lady Caroline Blackwood who was devoted to Maurice, and myself. Maurice at that time reviewed crime fiction for the Sunday *Observer*, and it was Friday. He brought with him that week's pile of books for review, and sat in the middle of the back seat with the secretary on one side, Lady Caroline on the other, the books round his feet, and me on the pull-down seat opposite. Claud must have been sitting with the chauffeur in front. When the car moved off, Maurice picked up each book in turn and handed it to Lady Caroline. She opened it and told him what it was about and who the characters were. Maurice, with hardly a pause, dictated his review to the secretary, who took it down in shorthand. Maurice was, of course, showing off, and interlarded his dictation with witty and sarcastic comments about the authors, most of whom he knew. He had an appreciative audience. When we arrived at Watford, I heard the secretary dictating it all back (in Hulton's time) to the *Observer*, where I was fascinated to read it two days later.

Our own new newspaper was then put together in an atmosphere of hilarity, sandwiches, and flowing wine, with periodic calls back to Marcus, mostly by me, asking for advice: I remember getting a maelstrom of conflicting advice from everybody, while Lady Caroline tried to pull me away from the phone.

There was one projected feature in the paper which had been discussed and agreed between Maurice Richardson and the artist Lucian Freud in a night club a few hours earlier, and whose non-appearance I much regretted. This was a political cartoon, which Lucian had gone home to draw, promising that it would be ready when we called. So we made a diversion to his house and I was sent to collect it while the limousine waited, its inmates watching agog. I had never met Lucian, and was not prepared for what eventually opened the door, obviously straight out of bed: a figure with a haggard face, terrifying staring eyes, hair standing on end, and wearing a woman's summer frock. Of course the drawing was not ready; had not been begun. If it had appeared, it might have scared the public as much as the artist scared me – which would have greatly pleased Claud and Maurice.

If Hulton Press had been managed on a basis of sanity, Marcus would have had all the opportunities he wanted. But it wasn't. Edward Hulton eventually sold Hulton Press, without informing his editors or even his company secretary. Odhams, the new owners, allowed Marcus to break his unexpired Hulton contract (*Eagle* was an inconvenient competitor for their own children's papers) and through George Rainbird he was invited to join the American-owned National Magazine Company, whose Managing Director Ben McPeake was one of George's close friends. Here Marcus really could exercise his talents. He soon became its Managing Director, and converted the modest profits it had been making to such large ones that the American Directors held the firm's Annual General Meeting in London for the first time, and gave Marcus lunch. At lunch, they said to Marcus 'We think you ought to have a Rolls-Royce'. 'Oh,' said Marcus, 'that's very kind of you. I believe you can get a very good secondhand one for seven or eight thousand pounds.' 'We don't mean a secondhand one' was the reply, and they took him across the road to Barclay's showrooms and bought him a brand-new and very large Rolls-Royce saloon.

Lettering drawn by Berthold Wolpe for the *Eagle* and *Girl* children's paper titles.

11. 1951 and all that

IN 1950 Tony was diagnosed as suffering from rheumatoid arthritis. 'You are very young,' the doctor said, 'it will burn itself out very quickly.' It never did. She was put into St Bartholomew's Hospital in London, and kept there for a year. We had just moved to a house in Essex, with two children by now and two Swedish au pair girls. The idea had been for me, now free-lancing, to work as much as possible at home, and go up to London only two or three days a week. With Tony in hospital and the pressure of work, that was now impossible. I continued sleeping all week in London, seeing Tony each evening, and going home at weekends to see the children.

I was in the meantime finishing a booklet *Modern Book Design* for the British Council, yet another job I owed to Robert Harling, who had recommended my name. In the very first sentence I made a point that runs through the book, I hope not too didactically: 'Printing in this country, and particularly book-printing, has had a chequered history, but its beginning was a good one. William Caxton, our first printer, came to printing through literature: it is still the best approach.' And a few pages later, I insisted 'An absolute principle of good typography, as of calligraphy, is that the words should be close together (not further apart than the width of the letter "I"), since the virtue of a page of type is in its closely woven texture, which it will lose completely if the words are too far apart.' I later brought in Bernard Shaw and wrote 'Shaw's incursion into typography illustrates a fundamental truth about book design – or at least the design of printed literature – which is that it is the writer's and not the artist's or the technician's mental equipment that must come first. The real art of the book is achieved by working from the inside out; it is literary and internal, and in no way analogous to a coat of paint or a streamlined cowl.'

The booklet was published in London by the British Council in 1951. It was translated into Swedish and published in Stockholm in 1956. It was then expanded into a full-sized book published by Faber & Faber in 1958, where I expressed the same thought more drastically: 'Designing for print is a continuation of the work of writing. Ideally, the author, having done the writing, should then do the designing.'

While I was finishing the booklet, Robert Harling invited me to follow my work on Cruikshank with another book for Art & Technics, this time on a living artist, the wood-engraver Joan Hassall. When I went to meet her for the first time I found her living in the house in Notting Hill (in London) in which she had been born. Her father was the famous poster artist John Hassall (1868–1948) and it was an experience to be given tea by her in the large room which had once been her father's studio. From that meeting came an invitation to stay in her house for a short time to work on the book. So I moved in. Joan Hassall was very kind, but I felt that she did not entirely approve of me, partly because I usually went out in the evenings to visit Tony when she thought I ought to be working, and more than partly when I broke her downstairs lavatory seat. I think that I was standing on it in order to investigate some curiosity in the cistern, and I forgot to pay the plumber when I received his bill. I finished my introductory essay on Joan in 1952, but then Art & Technics was closed down and my text came back to me unused. *The Wood Engravings of Joan Hassall* was taken and published in 1960 by Oxford University Press and reprinted several times.

Eagle burst on the world in 1950. At the same time I had begun to work in Holden's advertising agency, in Mount Street, close to Piccadilly. Holden's was a Birmingham firm who had been so impressed by a young man called George Rainbird, with whom they had worked during part of the war, that they had invited him to start a branch office for them in London. He set this up in the late 1940s, and in three years was making a profit, with South-Eastern Gas Board, Vickers Armstrong, and Whitbread's Brewery among important clients.

Before joining Holden's, Rainbird had worked for a large Midlands engineering firm, and when he left them they gave him, remarkably, as a leaving present, a small collection of finely printed limited editions – which opened his eyes to book design. He soon began to use books for advertising: he commissioned Compton Mackenzie to write a book for Vickers, and then started the Whitbread Library and wrote one of its small books, *Inns of Kent*, himself. For design and production he used the newly-founded firm of Adprint, headed by Walter Neurath, later the founder of the great publishing firm Thames and Hudson. Neurath and his then partner Wolfgang Foges were, like Stephan Lorant and Jan Tschichold, brilliant men who had managed to escape the Nazis and greatly enriched Britain and other countries. Neurath and Foges originated the highly successful Britain in Pictures series of well-illustrated introductions to aspects of life in Britain after the war, now regarded as classics.

Someone recommended me to Rainbird as a book designer, and I joined his studio in Holden's on a part-time basis, chiefly to design publications for new clients. One of my first jobs was the About Britain Guides, a Rainbird idea for 1951, the Festival of Britain year. The idea was offered to the Festival of Britain's Publishing Committee, and they called a meeting in our office to decide whether they could give it their approval.. The committee was headed by Gerald Barry, Director of the Festival, high-powered and high-minded. He was ready, I believe, to accept the idea but not to leave it in the hands of a little-known advertising agency with an office above a firm of fishmongers called Mac Fisheries. The meeting was my first sight of George Rainbird's genius as a salesman. Gerald Barry and his committee were soon listening respectfully to everything George said.

There were to be twelve titles in the series, and later Northern Ireland became no.13. The poet Geoffrey Grigson, a friend of ours, was appointed as overall editor and myself as production editor. Each book had its own editor, e.g. W. G. Hoskins for *Chilterns to Black Country*. Appropriate experts were chosen to supply maps, detailed tour guides, and area portraits. Michael Huxley, Editor of the *Geographical Magazine*, was appointed to be pictures editor, which turned out to be bad news for me. The selling price of each book, with illustrations in colour, was settled at 3s.6d. To make this viable, the printing quantity had to be 50,000 per title.

I had to collect the illustrations and show them to Michael Huxley. Once a week, on Friday evenings, Huxley and I sat down together, each having done a week's work in our own offices, to choose what was to go into the books. Everything I chose was immediately turned down by Huxley. Not content with that, he tried to insist that I always agreed with him. At the end of each evening we found ourselves sitting glaring at each other, speechless with hatred. Eventually that misguided man wrote a paper headed 'Reasons why McLean and I do not agree' and presented it to George Rainbird. George rushed to my defence and unhappily chose exactly the wrong argument for Huxley: 'Our job is to be popular, not aesthetic.' Of course, Huxley thought of himself as being the best chooser of popular pictures in the country.

But one member of the committee became a good friend. Colonel Penrose Angwin, at that time Director-General of the Ordnance Survey, was concerned with all maps in our Festival Guides, and I saw a lot of him. On one occasion he suggested something of which I knew George would not approve, and still as George's employee and not yet his partner, and still, I suspect, a little afraid of him, I said 'George will go up in the air if we do that.' 'He'll come down again' said Angwin cheerfully. It was a good lesson, which I took to heart.

We worked hard, and in a little under a year found that we had edited, designed and produced some 650,000 books containing no major mistakes, under the eyes of an exacting committee, and on time. The profits went to A. N. Holden & Co., who did not offer George a directorship. In February 1951, we had dinner together, and George said to me 'Ruari, if you live to be a hundred, you will never make a good art director of an advertising agency. Would you consider going into partnership with me to set up a book design and production firm?' It seemed like a good idea.

George was my senior by twelve years. A large man physically, he was also the opposite of everything that was small, narrow or mean. When excited by a new project or idea – which happened often – his imagination expanded and soared. He saw the widest implications and possibilities, in a series of flashes. Time and again, when we went into book publishing, he made a success of something that had been lying in front of the leading professional publishers for years, which they had missed. And he was a brilliant salesman.

George Rainbird liked many things: books, pictures, food, wine, men, and women (provided he wasn't married to them): but what motivated him most was a determination not to be poor. As a small boy he had been given a puppy by his parents, who had not realised that it needed a license which had to be paid for. They could not afford the license and the puppy had to go. George never forgot that tragedy.

Rainbird, McLean Ltd was founded in February 1951, less than a year after the first issue of *Eagle*. George was determined that we were going to be big. Our capital was only £600 – £400 of his and £200 of mine – but he insisted that we should employ the best lawyers and the best accountants he knew of in London. He made me move my bank account into the same bank as his, so that we shared the same bank manager, who would know us both and from whom nothing would be hidden. He introduced me to his tailor and his doctor, who had been Bernard Shaw's physician. He also, and most importantly, introduced me seriously to wine. Wine became a passion for both of us, and a useful ploy in business. André Simon became a good friend and ally of George's, and in their company I was given a grounding in wine that I could never have acquired for myself. Unless you have tasted a great claret and a great burgundy, how can you know what wine is all about?

And I could never have afforded such wines, or known how to order them, without the help of these friends.

Our first client was the publishing firm of William Collins.

Collins had been chosen to market the About Britain Guides, and George had to attend meetings in the offices of the Chairman, W. A. R. 'Billy' Collins, later Sir William. George noticed a framed print on Billy's wall taken from Thornton's *Temple of Flora*, 1802, one of the most superb colour-plate flower books ever produced, which George knew (but of which at that time I had never heard). As George left the office he murmured to Billy 'I see that we worship at the same temple'. Billy replied that he had three copies of the *Temple* and had asked his people to produce a book about it, but they didn't know how to start. George came away pondering; within a week or two we had produced an editorial plan, costs, and an extremely handsome dummy with a calligraphic title-page, in the early nineteenth-century mode, drawn by my friend John Brinkley.

Billy Collins was delighted, and George received an order for what was to become the first Rainbird, McLean book. As George wrote later 'We came to the conclusion that if the great House of Collins did not know how to produce a beautiful book on such a beautiful subject, there must be other publishers in the same situation, and that we could fill the gap...'

Our second book was also for Collins. Sydney Goldsack, Collins' advertising manager, was keen on cricket, and out of his and George's enthusiasm came *The Book of Cricket*, photographically illustrated and with an erudite and amusing text by the exuberant journalist Denzil Batchelor.

Meanwhile, Tony was at last allowed out of hospital.

Early in 1951, we moved into London, and bought a house in Blackheath with a long walled garden, a lawn, fruit trees, and a small pond in which we soon had four, and eventually seven, goldfish. Blackheath is on high ground above the River Thames at Greenwich. In May 1954, the Queen and Prince Philip returned to London in the royal yacht HMS *Britannia*, after a tour of the Commonwealth. We hired a room overlooking the river in the 'Cutty Sark' (late 'Union') tavern, right on the river, and gave a party to watch the royal return. We had about 50 people, and the proprietor was afraid it might make the ceiling of the room below fall down, but it didn't. The moment that *Britannia* came in sight at the end of Greenwich Reach was very impressive, with an enormous Admiralty flag at the fore, Royal Standard at the main, and Union Jack at the mizzen, and a great new White Ensign at the jack staff. She was painted blue and there was a Marine band playing away on the deck aft like a lot of toys: of course no one could hear them. It was magic to see the royal party go past, almost within touching distance from the windows of the pub.

Later in 1951 we had the Festival of Britain. It had been planned, since 1947, ostensibly to celebrate the centenary of the Great Exhibition of 1851, but with the real aim of saying 'Cheer up, Britain, the war's over, let's enjoy ourselves'. It was important for the Royal College of Art: one of the Festival's leading features, the Lion and Unicorn Pavilion, was being designed by three of our professors, Robert Gooden, Dick Russell, and Dick Guyatt. Contributions by other members of the College ran throughout the Festival. I had a tiny job: the Guide for the Pleasure Gardens in Battersea Park. What I enjoyed most was meeting Hans Tisdall, who designed the Piazza, the Gardens' centrepiece; he also drew my guide's cover. At the very last moment someone realized that the Gardens would need a poster. I had to design it. Fireworks were a key part of the Gardens' entertainment, being let off for twenty minutes every night. I wanted the poster lettering to say 'fireworks' and got a girl student, Sheila Stratton, to draw beautiful firework lettering under my instructions. I never kept a copy. Our poster was reproduced in colour in vol. 46 of *Penrose Annual*, and was credited to Publicity Arts Ltd, even though all they did was to print it.

A year later, Marghanita Laski wrote in *The Observer* 'Do you remember those first wonderful evenings, strolling along the Embankment and looking across the river, no hurry to cross it, to crowd through the turnstiles, but first to savour from a distance the thrilling magical change? Do you remember the first sight of the Skylon – "yes, that's it, look, that must be it!" – a needle of spider-web delicacy? ...Do you remember the colours that glared across the river, olive and scarlet and yellow and blue, balls and windmills and walls and doors, dabs of pure colour such as we didn't know we had always hungered for until at last they were there? ... And then we crossed the river, pressed through the gates, saw, for the first time in our lives, design as beautiful as possible all around us. We saw, for the first time in England, gaiety that wasn't corrupted, elegance that wasn't pompous... one remembers with such pleasure, the beauty – the yellow flock wallpaper in the Lion and Unicorn, the shining loaves of bread, the fruits of agriculture, the pearls-against-velvet mystery of the planetarium, the fantastic power of the fountain in the Ships Pavilions'.

That was all true. When I stood on the Embankment at the bottom of Northumberland Avenue, and saw the lights and colours of the Festival across the river on that first morning, it was so utterly beautiful and exciting that I wept.

Marghanita's article ended: 'It was nice, wasn't it, last year, Festival Year? It was the nicest thing that happened in England in the whole of my life.' How I agreed with her.

All in all, 1951 was quite a year for a young typographer. Well, I was now 34. It included the publication of my booklet *Modern Book Design*, the continuing success of *Eagle* and the first issue, in November, of *Girl*, the publication of five *Eagle* and *Girl* annuals, all designed by me, the About Britain Guides, a Prospectus and other items designed for the Royal College of Art, the Guide and Fireworks poster for the Festival gardens, *Lincoln Choir Stalls* and other booklets for the Friends of Lincoln Cathedral, and, for Rainbird, McLean Ltd, various publicity leaflets and books.

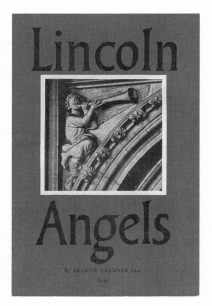
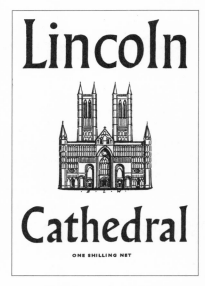

Two covers for Lincoln Cathedral booklets, *c.* 1950–51. Lettering on both covers, and drawing of the cathedral, by Berthold Wolpe. *Left:* printed in black on red; *right:* black on yellow.

12. Typography and Partners

WORK continued to flow into the new business, most of it from George Rainbird's fertile fieldwork but some of it introduced by me. Our first big book, after *Redouté* and *The Book of Cricket* for Collins, was *Fine Bird Books 1700–1900*, with a page size of 19 × 14 inches, the biggest book I had ever designed. It included sixteen plates printed in Amsterdam in 8-colour photolitho offset, and twenty-three black-and-white plates printed in collotype. It involved hilarious trips to Holland with Sacheverell Sitwell, one of the book's authors. Sachie, the younger brother of Sir Osbert and Dame Edith, was very tall, with a mischievous grin, and was a good listener as well as a good talker. He was a superb guide when we visited the Rijksmuseum, and when we were in a library which he had last visited twenty years before, he remembered exactly in which drawer or shelf could be found the prints for which we were looking.

Fine Bird Books, 1953, was followed in 1956 by *Great Flower Books 1700–1900* in the same size and with the same number of really beautiful plates, and again a characteristic text by Sachie Sitwell. The lettering on the jacket was drawn by Berthold Wolpe in what later became his typeface 'Decorata'.

By 1953 we had begun a connection with the National Magazine Company (owned by Hearst in USA) through George's friendship with Ben McPeake, their Managing Director. The National Magazine Company owned *The Connoisseur* magazine; the first book we designed and produced with the *Connoisseur* imprint was *The Queen's Silver*, by A. G. Grimwade, and it was also one of the first books ever printed by the Westerham Press. Rowley Atterbury had just founded the Westerham Press on a small loan from an aunt, and he soon became one of my closest friends. He had been working since the war in Faber & Faber's production department and had become so dissatisfied with the service given by Faber's normal printers that he decided to set up his own press and do better. He became the outstanding printer-designer in Britain of the post-war period. We were happy to give him all the work we could, but the time came when he let us down so badly on a crucial Christmas delivery date that the board of Rainbird, McLean solemnly sat down and passed a resolution never to employ him again. That did not last

Rowley and Mary Atterbury, Westerham Press, 1950.

long: Rowley had to be forgiven. We had many further and important collaborations, but Rowley was never easy to work with, although always amusing. Many years later, George Rainbird accepted Rowley's invitation to become Chairman of Westerham Press, and found that Rowley continued to go his own sweet way without consulting him – up with which, as George said, there was no putting. Rowley was aware of, and devoted to, quality in everything. In printing, he was certainly the most critical expert of his generation; but he was not, and could never become, a 'group man'. Max Rayne, the millionaire owner of the Hamlyn Publishing Group, found this out when in order to help Rowley, and with Rowley's permission, he bought the Westerham Press. He gradually realized that Rowley could not be 'disciplined' into a big business, and generously gave him back his Press at no cost – which Rowley accepted with alacrity.

It was not only books that we produced. George proposed to Shell a

Michelin-type Guide for Britain, which they eventually turned down, for political reasons. However a little later Vernon Nye, the Shell-Mex and British Petroleum Publicity Manager, asked if we would like to design a Christmas card for them – it seemed that all the suggestions he had made to the directors had been turned down. As George said, at that time we would willingly have taken an order for printing lavatory paper. He got his friend John Leigh-Pemberton to design something in the Shell tradition, which was accepted, and came away with an order for more than 300,000 cards in four colours, very useful for the firm in those early days.

This was followed by a book for Shell for the Coronation in 1953, called *Royal Progress*, with text by James Laver and colour-plates by Leigh-Pemberton. Then came the Shell Wild Flower series, perhaps our first major break. They started as wall sheets for schools, showing arrangements of wild flowers for each month of the year, collected and drawn by Rowland and Edith Hilder. They then appeared as advertisements in colour in nearly every colour-printed magazine in Britain. The series

Berthold Wolpe, 1976. (Photo by Sue Fowler.)

95

continued for several years, covering many aspects of natural history and wild life, illustrated by several other distinguished artists (and with my typography). They then became books.

George found that the Managing Director of Shell-Mex, C. M. Vignoles, loved wine. A series of gastronomic lunches ensued, alternately at Shell-Mex House in London and in the country house George had recently bought at Whichford in the Cotswolds. At our lunches, the wines were planned by André Simon, and at one of theirs, Shell invited Cyril Connolly to provide conversation. He brought his wife Barbara Skelton, certainly the most attractive woman I had ever met. It was well known that during the war, in Egypt, Connolly had found her in bed with King Farouk, which resulted – since she was a British cipher clerk – in her being promptly moved to another job. She subsequently married Connolly, but not long after our Shell lunches she left him for his publisher, George Weidenfeld. George Rainbird thought about the appearance of Farouk, Connolly, and Weidenfeld, not really good-lookers and all biggish in shape, and murmured 'There's hope for me yet'. Later, however, she returned to Connolly, perhaps because of his beautiful voice. She was also the author of an extremely good short novel, *Born Losers*, 1965, and a collection of short stories, *A Love Match*, 1969.

So the firm flourished. We had ideas, took them to publishers with dummies and detailed costings, and usually came back with orders. The publishing risk was taken by the publisher; the books we designed and produced had to make a double profit, for us and the publisher, and they usually did. If they did not, we could not lose on that project, but obviously were unlikely to get further orders.

George had the ideas, and the ability to find clients and sell them. And when a project became a job, he drove everyone in the office to get on with the production. I had first to design and make the dummies on which the ideas were sold, and then to design and oversee the production of the books themselves. In George I had found another colleague who knew what he wanted, and trusted me to get on with producing it without too much interference. It was a hectic but enjoyable life: our tastes and senses of humour seemed to tally.

Douglas Edy, who had been our accountant at Holden's, joined us as soon as we could afford his salary, and became the ideal Company Secretary, gloomy and pessimistic but obedient, at least to George. One day while George, Douglas and I were having a directors' meeting, the telephone went on George's desk. Douglas answered it, listened, muttered

'Thursday', and put the phone down. George said 'What was that?' Douglas replied, 'Your secretary asking what day it is'. Immediately after the meeting was finished, George went downstairs and sacked her. According to George, she then burst into tears and asked him to lend her his handkerchief.

On another occasion, Douglas watched one of our secretaries answering the phone with hand-fluttering and the words 'Rainbird – Rainbird – you know, rain, the thing that comes down – bird, the thing that goes up'.

Ideas began to come in from our friends. The most fertile with ideas, in the early days, was Geoffrey Grigson, the poet and freelance writer, who had become a good friend of both of us. One day we invited Geoffrey, James Fisher, the naturalist, and Charles Gibbs-Smith from the Victoria & Albert Museum, to come and discuss the idea of a new children's encyclopaedia. Gibbs-Smith's speciality was not to know everything but to know where it could be found. Oxford University Press were then publishing such a work in twelve large volumes, which we thought was behind the times and very boring: we wanted to produce an encyclopaedia using the strip techniques of *Eagle*. Something quite different came out of the meeting. 'All knowledge', said James Fisher, 'can be summed up under three heads – people, places, and things'. 'And ideas' added Geoffrey. Within seconds George Rainbird had conceived the jackets for three of the four books: David's Napoleon for *People*; Canaletto's Venice for *Places*; and Michaelangelo's Creation for *Ideas*. Later, I found a colour photograph for *Things* in the Swiss magazine *Du*.

The plan – four volumes for adults, not for children – was quickly sold to a publisher, and Geoffrey Grigson was appointed as full-time editor. We had to find him an office and hire staff for him. The choice of editorial secretary must have been felicitous, for Geoffrey married her. As Jane Grigson, the cookery writer, she kept him well fed for the rest of his life, and a large public also enjoyed her books. Before this happy settling down, Geoffrey had had a tempestuous short affair with the wife of a Swedish professor he'd met in the British Museum Library, and when she went home, he wrote a series of poems which we printed for him (because we loved him) in a small book entitled *Legenda Suecana*. I took a lot of trouble designing it, and invented a typographical patterned paper for the covers, paper on boards. There was a curious result. Perhaps a year later, I saw in a shop a tea towel and kitchen roller towel with patterns which I thought attractive and bought them. When I took them home and looked again at them, I found that they were enlarged versions of the patterns I had made for *Legenda Suecana*. They had been produced by the new firm of Laura Ashley. 'Oh boy,' I thought, 'I am going to sue them for breach of copyright and win a large sum in royalties.' It took a long time to remember that the covers had been printed not by the printers of the book but by Rowley Atterbury at Westerham; and when I talked to him, I discovered that Laura Ashley's husband, then a neighbour of Rowley's, had gone to the press and asked for some type borders, and had been given a loose sheet of what I had designed. I received two free roller towels.

Although the individual entries in each volume of *People*, *Places*, *Things*, and *Ideas* were commissioned from experts, Geoffrey found that when put together they did not form a coherent whole. He had to rewrite nearly every one, a surprise for him and a shock for us, as it greatly increased the time the books took to produce.

George had sold this series of books three ways: to an English publisher, to an American publisher, and to a publisher who sold books from door to door. He had begun to find the formula which led the firm to real money.

We were soon making enough profits to believe that we could produce books for ourselves – a thumping fallacy, as we soon found out.

In 1954 we formed a second company, George Rainbird Ltd, whose directors were Sacheverell Sitwell, Sir Alfred Beit, the financier, George and myself. Sir Alfred provided some capital but played no editorial part; Sachie provided contacts and editorial advice. Since he had no pied-a-terre in London, he was glad to accept George's invitation to share a flat in Montagu Square. It was the first flat that George had ever been able to furnish for himself with some degree of luxury. Having bought the furniture, he purchased a large Medici Society print of a Canaletto to hang in the living room. Sachie protested; he was used to real Canalettos. I was glad to see that George remained firm. He loved Canaletto, he couldn't afford a real one and was not going to be pressurized into snobbism.

George came back into the office one day bubbling with enthusiasm over some paintings of flowers which he had seen in the office of Billy Collins. They were, he said, equal to, or better than, anything done by

Opposite: Cover design printed on paper on boards for Geoffrey Grigson's *Legenda Suecana*, 1953. The design was 'borrowed' by Laura Ashley Ltd, enlarged, and printed on roller towels and tea-cloths.

Redouté. They had been painted by a young artist called Charles Raymond, who, as George had taken the trouble to find out, was poor, even starving. Billy Collins, with all the resources of William Collins & Co. Ltd that we didn't have, was not prepared to do anything. George was.

Sachie Sitwell's advice was sought. The subject of old garden roses (of which I regret I had never heard) was chosen as a theme for the artist to draw and us to publish. The project was planned as a series of six volumes, each with eight colour plates of Raymond's paintings. Sachie would write the text for the first, and author–poet Wilfrid Blunt for the second volume, with botanical notes throughout the series by the distinguished horticulturalist James Russell.

Raymond would be paid an income on which he could live, while producing the paintings. At a meeting in January to celebrate the start of the project, he turned up in a new car, wearing a suit made of silk which was so thin that he was shivering – but ecstatic. He was to paint the flowers in the Hampshire garden of Trelawney Dayrell Reed, a friend of Sachie's and the painter Augustus John who lived nearby. Dayrell Reed resembled Don Quixote in more than just his appearance. He had recently been prosecuted for discharging a shotgun at aeroplanes flying overhead in the King's Cup Air Race, which he alleged were using his garden as a turning point. He endeared himself to me by presenting me with an autograph poem written and given to him by his friend James Elroy Flecker – which is now in the National Library of Scotland.

The old roses came into flower, but progress was slow because Charles used a brush with about two hairs, which he frequently wore out, painting meticulously and laboriously with tiny strokes. We had to admit that the results were miraculously beautiful. What we did not know, as publishers, was how to market such an unusual work. Subscriptions were invited, to begin with from our friends. But the long list of subscribers, printed in the books, actually headed by Her Majesty the Queen Mother, was not enough. Collins' salesmen, responsible to us for selling to the trade, were, it seemed in this case, out of their depth in unfamiliar waters. A pity, because the books were beautiful and the texts were entertaining and authoritative.

Charles painted twenty-four roses before we had to stop him. Two volumes were published by George Rainbird Ltd in 'special' and regular limited editions of 160 and 2,000 copies respectively, before George decided that we had a publishing flop on our hands. The eight unpublished paintings were framed and hung on George's walls for the rest of his life; and our friends who bought copies of the books, if they kept them, found that over the years they increased considerably in value.

Gardens and flowers were one of George Rainbird's passions. It was an area in which I failed him. I enthused to George about a rose in Dayrell Reed's garden and it turned out to be a peony; it may have been the moment when he first wondered whether I was a suitable partner.

While we were working on *Old Garden Roses*, Sachie took us to meet Augustus John at his house in Fordingbridge. John was then a very old man with paper-thin ears and piercing pale blue eyes. We discovered that no well-produced book of John's drawings had ever been published, and soon saw why. He was almost impossible to deal with, and any serious dealing had to be completed early in the day, before the wine was brought out.

Persuading Augustus to co-operate in the production of a book of his drawings, and bringing it to a successful conclusion, was perhaps one of the most difficult things George ever achieved. Augustus changed his mind, broke all his promises, attempted to seduce my secretary who took him proofs, repeatedly insulted George, and tried to back out from the whole project; but George patiently poured oil (and wine) to soothe every crisis, and won through. We even got Augustus to draw a self-portrait on a litho plate (which he said, untruthfully I think, that he had never done before), and it made a magnificent frontispiece. The most moving thing about all those visits to Fordingbridge was, for me, to see the beauty of his wife Dorelia in her old age, and to recognize in her the young girl of his early drawings.

The next book we brought out for ourselves was an edition of Joyce Cary's *The Horse's Mouth* with illustrations by the author. Joyce Cary's eldest son Michael had been one of my closest friends at the Dragon School, and my wife Tony was Joyce's niece.

Joyce was enthusiastic about the project, but he was already suffering from disseminated sclerosis (multiple nerve damage), brought on, it was believed, by having been a passenger in an airliner which crashed after aborting take-off at Heathrow. As I had done with Augustus John, I took him a prepared lithographic plate, and, like John, he made a superb self-portrait, which became the frontispiece. He was already losing all strength in his wrists and hands, and could make no more lithographs; but with his arm supported in a sling, suspended from above his head as he lay in bed, he gallantly made eight pencil illustrations for the book. The edition itself was interesting. An American professor, Andrew Wright, was in England writing a book about Cary, and he agreed to edit our volume for us and to include, in an appendix, 'The Old Strife at Plant's', a chapter Cary had written and then discarded. Michael Joseph, Cary's British publisher, had just begun to reissue the Cary novels in a standard format, the 'Carfax' editions, in which *The Horse's Mouth* had already appeared. Professor Wright found several *hundred* misprints in it. Cary's handwriting was atrocious, and he left proof-correcting to his wife Gertie, who, like her niece my wife, had many talents but not that one. *The Horse's Mouth*, first published in 1944, had already been translated into French, German, Italian, Spanish, Danish, Finnish, Norwegian, and Swedish, and many of the misprints came to light when translators queried a puzzling word and found that it was not at all what Cary had written.

Joyce Cary saw and approved the format and design for type-setting and binding, but he died on 29 March 1957 without seeing the completed book. We had given it to Curwen Press to print. It was published for Christmas 1957 in an edition of 1500 copies, too many for a limited edition and too few for an ordinary one. We had got it wrong again; but what was wrong was our marketing, not the book itself. George's comment on it in *The Rainbird Archive*, 1985, was 'in my opinion the most beautiful book (in its class) ever printed by Rainbird's, but a financial disaster. The publisher (Michael Joseph) did not like it!'

In 1958 George decided that he and I should part. He needed more capital for the business, and wanted my shares to sell to someone else. He could also, now that the firm was established, buy what I was doing for him from somebody cheaper. He was right, from his point of view. It was a worry for me, since I was now paying school fees for two sons, with a daughter still to be educated.

When he told me that I had been earning far more while working with him, I held my peace. For some time I had, in fact, been paying more into the firm, from my Hulton Press retainer, than I had been drawing out in salary.

I could see now that it was time I went. The firm was becoming big, and big firms were not my forte. I had, after all, progressed through the war by avoiding big ships, and after five years ended up (as I had to confess to my sons) second-in-command of a two-man canoe. But working with George had been fun. George had given me the chance to design books which would never have existed if he had not conceived them.

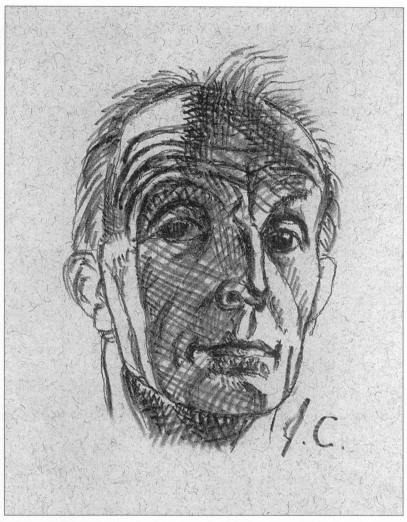

Self-portrait drawn on stone by Joyce Cary shortly before he died, March 1957; used as frontispiece for the Rainbird, McLean edition of *The Horse's Mouth*, with illustrations by Cary, 1957. Reduced.

They included some very big books, such as *Fine Bird Books*, *Great Flower Books*, and the *Album de Redouté*, of a kind that few designers ever get a chance to handle.

And there was the *Wyndham Bible*. George succeeded in circumventing the special copyrights vested in Oxford and Cambridge and Eyre & Spottiswood by doing a deal with Collins, who had a licence to print the Bible in Scotland. The *Wyndham Bible*, in the authorized King James version, contained every trimming that George could think of, including Roger van der Weyden's *Descent from the Cross* in eight colour plates, forty-eight plates of Old Master paintings in colour, selected and introduced by Geoffrey Grigson, a Concordance, eight pages of family Register on imitation vellum, decorated by John Brinkley, the Epistle Dedicatory, and of course the Apocrypha. The printing quantity ordered by the publishers to whom the idea had been sold was 100,000. We had a hundred extra copies printed on India paper and bound in white vellum for presentation to ourselves and friends. How many other typographers of my generation had the chance to make typographical layouts for a new Bible?

It was entirely set in Monotype Plantin by Benhams of Colchester, then perhaps the best Monotype composing firm in the country. It had to be printed by Collins, because they had the licence. Collins 'Clear-Type Press' was not famous for good printing. However, Collins at that time could not cope with such a large printing order, and it was farmed out to R. & R. Clark in Edinburgh, who of all the printers in the United Kingdom were the ones I would have chosen if I had had the choice. Things are not always what they seem: an inverse situation had occurred when Penguin Books produced the 'million Shaws' – ten books of Shaw's plays in a run of 100,000 copies each. R. & R. Clark were the only printers allowed by Shaw to print his plays, but in this case Clark's couldn't cope and the books were printed by Collins. I don't think anyone noticed the difference.

The Connoisseur Period Guides were another series I was glad to have been allowed to design and produce. They consisted of six well-illustrated volumes containing essays by experts in fifteen or so fields, such as furniture, painting, architecture, silver, and glass. Each volume ended, at George's insistence, with an article by H. M. Nixon on bookbinding and by myself on printing. The overall editors were Gwynne Ramsey, Editor of *The Connoisseur*, and Ralph Edwards, lately Keeper of the Department of Woodwork in the Victoria & Albert Museum.

Title-page opening for *Southill*, one of the earliest Rainbird, McLean books, 1951. Reduced from 190 × 250mm.

As every article came in, I had to sub-edit it, organize the illustrations, and send it to the printers. An article on 'Costume' seemed to me to contain some pretentious nonsense, and I communicated my doubts to Ralph Edwards, the working editor, whom I did not then know, and who did not know me. He was furious at my interference, and I was put (by telephone) very firmly in my place. Unfortunately I had pencilled some comments in the margins of the author's typescript and had forgotten to rub them out. They went back to the author with his galleys, and he sent them to Ralph Edwards. The subsequent explosion was heard in Wyndham Place and I was summoned to attend Edwards at his house on the banks of the Thames at Chiswick Mall.

I was shown into his drawing-room and was admiring his collection of English watercolours on the walls when Edwards came in. He stood at the door and shouted abuse at me without stopping for several minutes – ten, I think. My temperature rose, I nearly walked out, and then the absurdity of the situation struck me and I remained calm, staring at him with some amazement: I had not been cursed for so long a time even by a Gunner's Mate in the Navy.

Then his wife came in with a silver tea-tray and said 'Are you ready for tea?' Ralph Edwards replied, 'Mr McLean hasn't been paying a blind bit of attention to me. Yes, please.' If I had quailed, or stormed out, as I nearly did, I would never have gained his respect, but now all was sweetness and light. It was, I heard later, his normal technique to bully his subordinates.

During the seven years I worked with George Rainbird, I designed and produced some seventy books for Rainbird, McLean; at the same time I was also designing *Eagle*, *Girl*, *Swift*, and *Robin*, and a not inconsiderable series of children's annuals, books and ephemera, such as service sheets for the cathedral carol services, and I also designed some general books for the Hulton Press Book Department under Frank Waters. For a time I was also editing and designing the *Journal* of the Society of Industrial Artists.

A conflict of interest lurked beneath the surface between George and me, as it must always do between the business man and the designer. George's determination, first to survive, and then to make a fortune, meant that for him delivery dates came first. For me, getting a difficult, complicated and loved job right (i.e. as I wanted it), even if a little late, was more important. George was senior partner. I was used to working on deadlines, and as far as I know I always met them; but there was never a time when I could afford to be leisurely. George hounded me, and everyone else, and I sympathized with him; the mails must go through. I don't remember ever having a serious disagreement, let alone a quarrel, but the pressure never let up. He may have resented that I had a few other jobs beside Rainbird, McLean, but so had he. We had both promised to put every and any outside penny we earned professionally into the common kitty.

George was not abstemious in any way, nor ever self-indulgent. Wining and dining our clients, and occasionally ourselves, was part of the business and an important part of both our lives, once we could afford it. After a year or so, we shared, during the week, a flat on three floors in Wyndham Place, near Baker Street, with offices, kitchen, and a bedroom each. We had an excellent charlady/cook called Mrs Uzzle, who prepared office lunches, some of which were memorable. After one particularly successful lunch, when we went in to congratulate her, we found her, surrounded by piles of dirty plates, asleep, with a contented smile on her face and her feet in the oven. She lost favour when, while dusting the mantelshelf in George's room, she swept to smithereens a beautiful glass goblet engraved by Laurence Whistler, brother of Rex the painter, which George had just bought.

When we could afford another important addition to our office staff, we took on Joy Law, who became mother–manager of our increasing secretarial staff, manager of the editorial side, manager of office lunches, helpmeet and soother-down of everyone in every crisis (of which there were many) and a loved friend. She stayed with the firm for long after I left, saw it through some of its greatest triumphs, to which she contributed greatly, and finally, for a rest cure, went to the Royal College of Art to take over their publications.

To celebrate my departure and to show his independence of such troublesome creatures as typographers, George then produced a book which he designed himself and had no typography in it at all: *Heads, Figures and Ideas*, a large folio made from the famous sculptor Henry Moore's sketch-books, which George had been shown when taken to meet Moore by Geoffrey Grigson. All the wording was written by George in his own brand of calligraphy. Some 27 copies each contained an original water-colour drawing by Moore. They are now priceless.

George Rainbird went on to achieve success after success. The firm's greatest breakthrough was *Tutankhamen*, published in 1963. George tells the extraordinary story of how it came about, in his autobiographical bibliography *The Rainbird Archive*, 1985. It started, at a party, with an argument between George and the American journalist Fleur Cowles about what was 'the most beautiful and rare collection of art treasures in the world'. Fleur Cowles immediately said 'the Tutankhamen Treasure.'

The Treasure, in Cairo Museum, had never been photographed under studio conditions: how George and his sculpture photographer F. L. Kenett eventually achieved this is an adventure story in itself. It was stipulated that each time the seal was broken on a glass case, it had to be in the presence of the Director of the Museum, the Chief Conservator, the Keeper of the Collection, an army officer of not less than the rank of major, and an armed soldier. The book was given an authoritative text by Christiane Desroches-Noblecourt, the leading Egyptologist of her day, and the 75 colour photographs by F. L. Kenett were stunning. No wonder it was an immediate success and in George's word 'established us, once and for all, as being serious publishers'. It has continued to sell in millions and in several languages.

George was a visionary, not just an able organizer and business man. Time and again he saw publishing projects which the professional publishing world had missed: for example, in 1968, *Madame de Pompadour*, by Nancy Mitford, and *A History of Warfare*, by Field Marshal Montgomery, were Rainbird books.

The Keble Martin *Concise British Flora in Colour* is another great story. The book, illustrating the whole of the British flora with 100 plates in colour, had taken the Rev. Keble Martin over sixty years to complete. It was turned down by at least seven leading publishers, who could not envisage printing more than a few hundred copies. George printed a first edition of 50,000 copies and made another fortune – as well as one for Keble Martin.

In 1965 George sold a majority interest in his firm to Lord Thomson of Fleet, who later bought the whole of the capital. George retired from running his own business, and became chairman of all Thomson Book Publishing interests, a position from which he finally retired in 1982.

I am happy to say that he and I remained friends; his autobiographical bibliography *The Rainbird Archive* was the last book on which we worked together. He died, aged 81, in 1986.

A file containing all the correspondence between him and me on the Archive – and George's letters, all in his own hand, are personal and amusing – is now in the National Library of Scotland.

My partnership with George ended in 1958, and another partnership, although I did not know it at the time, was just beginning.

13. *Motif*

BEFORE I left George Rainbird we had moved the Rainbird, McLean office to Charlotte Street, on the northern edge of Soho – with Bertorelli's homely but famous restaurant just two doors away. I had my own office papered in four-inch wide black and white vertical stripes, which so impressed Peter Kneebone, a young designer friend, that the next time he came to see me he was wearing a shirt with identical black and white stripes.

One day after lunch I came back from Charing Cross Road with a strange little book containing a religious text printed in lurid Victorian chromolithography, c.1845, and bound in what was clearly meant to look like carved ebony, but was then called black papier-maché. It cost me £4. 10s and must be extremely rare, I thought; I had never seen anything like it. My new secretary admired the book and came back from her lunch with another book exactly like it, which she had picked up in Foyles, for 7s. 6d. I naturally thought she had bought it for me. No, that was not the plan: she was now collecting Victorian books herself.

This secretary, tall and ash-blond, was Fianach, the eldest daughter of Douglas Jardine, erstwhile captain of England's cricket team, and one of my boyhood heroes. He had nearly brought England to war with Australia by defeating Don Bradman. I found that I could work with Fianach: she was a girl of strong character, who did not take no for an answer. She was friendly to those who deserved it, and unfriendly to printers and others who broke promises.

When after a few weeks with her in my office, I came back from that interview with George Rainbird, and announced (no doubt with rather a pale face) that I was leaving the firm, and had no idea what I was going to do next, she immediately offered to take another job and work for me in the evenings without pay, until things improved.

This could not, of course, have been accepted, but luckily something else turned up. A friend who had heard that I was now out of a job and needed cheering up (as he hoped) began taking me out to lunch. At each lunch he insisted that we drank a bottle of claret together, which he soon increased to two bottles. I was amazed to find how enjoyable this was. His motive, I gradually discovered, was really to inveigle me into a new business he planned to start, with me as one of the partners.

Fianach Jardine, later Lawry, and the author, *c.* 1961.

His other partner in this enterprise was a charming fellow who during the war had been aide-de-camp to General (later Field-Marshal) Sir William Joseph Slim. I heard that he got this job because when all the hard planning before a battle had been done (by General Slim) he was an amusing person with whom to go fishing. My friend was also amusing, but I did not see myself as his partner in a business of which, the more I heard about it, the more I was doubtful; so I declined with thanks – especially for the claret. I believe that he then mentioned my situation to the printer and publisher James Shand, which was good of him. Shand had previously published (and printed) three periodicals: first *Typography*, before the war; then *Alphabet and Image*, and then *Image*, all edited by Robert Harling. They had each lasted for eight issues, and had been, in the world of printing, of outstanding editorial and visual merit. Harling, James Shand explained to me, had always refused payment, enabling him to provide the copy when it suited him, not Shand. James now invited me to start a new periodical for him, and proposed to give me a modest salary, a room in his Frith Street office, and to pay Fianach's salary. In return, I had to provide him with my copy when

Shand required it. We would also get a commission on any work we could put in the way of the Shenval Press at Hertford, which James owned with his father and brothers. This allowed me to return to free-lance work on very acceptable terms.

The furniture in my Charlotte Street office, mainly a large desk and two Windsor chairs and some book cases, belonged to me. Fianach and I hired a costermonger's barrow and wheeled it down the road to Frith Street on a Saturday, in July 1958, nearly winning a prize in the annual Soho waiter's race for which it was thought we had entered. Life began again.

The new magazine was given the name of *Motif*. The word came from the artist Charles Mozley, on the pavement outside 58 Frith Street after a Soho dinner, and was immediately accepted. James Shand's wife, when she heard the new name, said she always liked words with an 'f' in them. James asked Mozley to do a cover design for the first issue. That was at midnight: by ten next morning, Charles appeared in my office and plonked ten finished cover designs on my desk. We happily chose one. Apart from a small drawing on page 84 of the first issue, Charles never made another contribution to *Motif*; I cannot think why.

James Shand had two main reasons for starting another periodical. The first, which he could use to persuade his brothers and fellow direc-tors, was that it would be a good advertisement of the Press's capacity in the world of art publishing, in which field they wished to be leaders. The second, and perhaps the most important for James, was that it would be an enjoyable relief from boring commercial work.

I presume that when he costed it, he planned that it would never lose too much money, but he never considered it as potentially profitable in itself. I could not see why it should not make a small profit if properly managed, and wanted it to do so in order that it would live longer. It was therefore frustrating to find that once we got it going, James paid not the slightest attention to even minimal efficiency in the way his Frith Street office handled our subscriptions and sales. Once, on a sudden whim and without informing Fianach or myself, he cut the printing quantity of one issue to below the number of copies for which we had actually received orders, so that neighbouring and friendly bookshops like Zwemmers on whom we depended for support could not supply their customers. Crazy; it happened only once, and the printing order went back to 2000 for all subsequent issues. It showed how little James cared for that side of the operation.

What he did care about was the contents, and the link it gave him with the world of art and artists. He gave me a complete free hand as editor. He never told me what to put in the magazine and never rejected anything I had chosen. All he demanded was that I should have my copy ready when his machines needed it. Of course I showed him the intended contents for each issue when I could get hold of him, and there were often technical or tactical problems for which I needed his support.

In *Motif* 2 (Feb 1959) James Shand wrote 'MOTIF is not edited, designed and produced only for the specialist, be he painter, sculptor, typographer or architect. MOTIF is for the receptive whole man (whether, by profession, artist or laundryman) who can get visual pleasure from Pollock's abstractions, Mies van der Rohe's skyscrapers, Paolozzi's sculptures, or Stewart's sun, moon and stars.

'The point is, perhaps, worth emphasizing. While he is doing an actual job, a man must be a specialist – whether he is mending a fuse, carving a wood-block, or cleaning a fish. But for life as a whole, men and women must be whole, and must not be specialists. Today, more than ever before, scientists must understand the imprecision of art: and artists must know where the scientists have got to, because that is where man has got to. The artist who knows nothing about science is as dangerous as the scientist who knows nothing about art.'

I was empowered to pay contributors – not much, but something – but far more important was the fact that we could offer artists pages of white paper on which we could print, in colour or black-and-white and in the finest quality, anything they chose to draw. That was something they could not get anywhere else at that time (or, as far as I know, since).

Early in 1960, Willy de Majo asked me if I was going to the annual Design Conference in Aspen, Colorado, for which he was the London correspondent. I said of course not, I couldn't afford to. 'Nonsense!' he replied, 'You can't afford not to!' That was clever. He had me hooked.

What made it possible was a contribution to my expenses by James Shand, on the strength of my promising to do my best in promoting *Motif*: we wanted American sales and contributors.

So I went to New York, where I met Charles Wrong, my oldest friend, who was on his way to teach English at a co-ed school in California. We had breakfast together in a drug store where I was fascinated by a new experience: to be offered fried eggs sunny side up by a red-haired negress. She has haunted my memory ever since.

I hadn't seen Charles for a long time. 'Charles', I said, 'can you tell me

The author and James Shand discussing *Motif*, with pages from *Motif* 5 and 6 on the wall behind, 1961. (Photo by John Hedgecoe.)

who said, and of whom, "you can always forgive a man for having an ace up his sleeve, but not for saying that Almighty God put it there"?' Charles immediately replied correctly that it was said of Gladstone by Disraeli. 'All right' I said, nettled by such a quick reply, 'when and where did he say it?' Without hesitation Charles replied, 'At eight-thirty pm on the evening of October twenty-ninth, eighteen-sixty-four, at Ashton-under-Lyme' and added 'in the Oddfellow's Hall.'

While in New York I wanted to meet Milton Glaser, the designer whose work I had seen in the *Push Pin Graphic*, an entertaining broadsheet sent out free to anyone who asked for it. We could not possibly pay him for a contribution: he was already one of the most successful artist–designers in the States; but I could offer him up to twelve pages in colour in which he could do anything he liked, and he accepted this with pleasure. In due course we received in London a 'bestiary', twelve pullout pages of animals, birds and insects, six in colour and six in black-and white, which we published in *Motif* 7 in 1961. The American Institute of Graphic Art awarded its Gold Medal to both Glaser and me for this (mine should have gone to James Shand for paying and printing it). Glaser must have been awarded more gold medals than I have drunk martinis in America, but it was my only gold medal ever. It was embedded in the centre of a large cube of transparent plastic. Perhaps it was one of those gold-covered chocolate coins. I couldn't even prove that.

I met and made friends in New York with warm-hearted Paul and Stella Standard, the booksellers Herman and Viv Cohen, and Fritz and Annie Kredel, and was much moved by my first experience of New York hospitality. To be invited to have dinner with the Standards was an experience: Paul and I were put in chairs with a glass each and a book, while Stella disappeared into a tiny kitchen, from which emerged a flow of swear-words and then a delicious meal.

To get to Aspen from New York, you have to fly to Denver, with a touch-down at Milwaukee. Coming into Denver was amazing: it is on the edge of a vast country where all the farmers fly, and there were more private planes parked at Denver than there are cars at Heathrow. Aspen had once been a silver-mining village, had fallen into decay, and was now being turned into a beautiful location for holidays and conferences. I wrote in *Motif* 'The ad-weary traveller is battered by ugly all the way across America and then gets at Aspen the same sort of shock as we got when we had our first sight of the Festival of Britain on the South Bank: a glimpse of a world created by design...a sparkling landscape of brilliant sunshine, lawns, contemporary architecture, and items which have no familiar names, since they are part of the future, not the present: such as a group of white stone blocks arranged by the Bauhaus artist Herbert Bayer; Buckminster Fuller's geodetic dome, placed over a swimming pool; and the Aspen Health Center's doorway painted by Bayer with man-sized letters in red, yellow, blue and white'.

The main speeches were given in an orange and blue Big Tent designed by Eero Saarinen, and since nearly all the 450 conferees wore tropical shirts and shorts, the scene was pretty colourful. Relaxations included swimming, sunbathing, dry martinis, 'stingers' (a carefully measured mixture of Crème de Menthe and brandy with cracked ice), ascending the longest skilift in the world, and a vintage car rally. I waved copies of *Motif* about to justify my existence.

The keynote speaker at the conference (theme: The Corporation and the Designer) was Professor Northcote Parkinson, now, as already mentioned, husband of my ex-secretary and author of *Parkinson's Law* recently published. The British contingent included Leslie Julius of Hille Furniture, and Paul Reilly, head of the Council of Industrial Design, who incidentally made a brilliant short speech about English design to a group of young Americans who didn't know it existed. The other speakers included Eliot Noyes, architect and designer of the IBM typewriter and the IBM Pavilion at Brussels International Fair, and Traugott Malzan, designer of new and stunningly designed Braun electrical appliances in Frankfurt. After each speech the audience broke up into small discussion groups and thrashed out, with no inhibitions, the problems of designers and corporations. The whole atmosphere was serious but relaxed.

From Aspen it was back to Denver, from where I flew to Chicago to visit the Newberry Library, the Art Institute and its Picassos, the great printing firm of Donnelly's (printers of *Life* and the Sears Roebuck catalogues among other things), Bob Hunter Middleton, and Art Paul, the Art Editor of *Playboy* magazine. At that time *Playboy* had a circulation of nearly two and a half million copies a month and was one of the best designed and best illustrated magazines in the world. Art Paul kindly accepted my invitation to contribute some pages of his drawings to *Motif*, which appeared in *Motif* 12 with a witty commentary by London journalist Reyner Banham. He also put my office on *Playboy's* free list, where it remained happily for years.

I then had a few more appointments in New York, but no one had told me that it was useless to be in New York for the days on each side of 4 July, when everybody, but everybody, goes on vacation. An invitation came from Harold Hugo to join him, his friend and colleague Jim Barnett, and his son Tuck, on a fishing trip to Lake Richardson in Maine. Harold and Jim are both now dead, but if the Elysian Fields exist, they will be there, making friends as they did all their lives, and I hope I may be allowed to join them. I had met Harold through a friend's introduction, in London. His achievement had been to turn a small printing firm, the Meriden Gravure Company in Meriden, Connecticut, into a world leader in one kind of printing. He had specialized in reproducing monochrome subjects like drawings, manuscripts, etchings and engravings, and pages of print, to a standard previously thought unobtainable, except perhaps by collotype.

The one process the Meriden Gravure Company did not use was gravure. They had originally been specialists in collotype, a difficult and slow process with a serious restriction that not more than about 500 good impressions could be taken from a collotype glass plate. During the Second World War, the U. S. Army Map Service had demanded

Rocky Stinehour,
1970s. (Photo by
Tony King.)

higher standards of definition in map printing, for long printing runs,
than were normal; in response to this demand Eastman Kodak produced 300-line screens for photo-litho offset printing. Up to that time,
150-line screens were considered to be the finest that could be worked,
and, in letterpress printing, they could only be printed on the
smoothest paper, i.e. clay-coated 'art' paper – which was unsuitable for
war conditions since it could be ruined by a drop of water. Meriden was
one of the few firms entrusted with these new 300-line screens. After
the war, Harold Hugo decided that the future of Meriden (of which he
had now become Managing Director) lay in developing the use of these
new screens rather than in collotype. The screens were difficult to use

and he encountered opposition from his workmen – 'it can't be done!' – but he bullied them until they found themselves producing work of a quality that both they and everyone else had thought was not possible.

In an antiquarian bookshop in Amsterdam, I had found a book, *Baroque Book Illustration*, by Philip Hofer, Harvard University Press, 1951, whose subject was seventeenth-century engravings from copper. Some of its plates were printed in line (*not* half-tone) with a degree of fineness that I knew could never have been achieved by line blocks, which were, in the 1950s, the normal way a book designer would reproduce such subjects in a book. I would have been delighted if I could have had such quality in the six volumes of *The Connoisseur Period Guides* which I had to produce in 1956–8. *Baroque Book Illustration* surprisingly contained no mention of its printer. It took me some time to discover that the printer was Meriden, a name then unfamiliar to me.

By 1960, Meriden Gravure had closed down not only its collotype operation, but also all typesetting; they concentrated on photo-litho-offset, using only 300-line screens. Their clients were art galleries, libraries, and scholarly bodies requiring reproductive work, usually in monochrome, of the highest quality. Meriden could be competitive in price because they did not need to employ an expensive sales force, like other printers: their reputation was enough. Calling on clients was done by Jim Barnett and Harold. Harold always insisted on working directly from originals, not from photos of originals, and was so trusted that priceless books and manuscripts and drawings regularly travelled to and from their owners in Harold's car or pockets. The Metropolitan Museum of Art in New York was not permitted to part with its treasures in this way, so when they saw what he could do, they got Harold to set up a reproduction camera in the museum basement, and craftsmen from Meriden came to operate it. On a later visit to New York I was allowed into this room to watch the photographing of a collection of Inigo Jones drawings. The drawings were in different tones of pencil or chalk, on different kinds of paper; each one was studied minutely by the experienced craftsman operator, and many were photographed several times with different filters or exposures.

It was possible for a firm like Meriden to have no typesetting facility because that could always be bought in, and many clients preferred to procure their typesetting themselves. Meriden had also formed a close liaison with the Stinehour Press in Vermont, which was, in its own way, as distinguished and remarkable a firm as Meriden. It had been founded after the war by Roderick (Rocky) Stinehour, who after flying in the Navy wanted a peaceful life away from cities, and bought a small forest in Vermont which included a house, and, incidentally, some printing equipment in a barn. He became interested in printing and set up the Stinehour Press to produce books by letterpress, a few years earlier than Rowley Atterbury set up Westerham, with very much the same ideals and the same intuitive skills. After Harold's death, Meriden and Stinehour amalgamated, and became one firm in Vermont.

Printing is something that we all need and use, like clothes and shoes, and we get our letterheadings and our invoices and our wedding announcements and parish magazines and even our books, pretty much like everyone else's; but occasionally someone like Baskerville or Stinehour or Atterbury comes along and turns it into something quite different, a true source of visual pleasure for those with eyes to see.

Stinehour's name became known in Europe through his periodical *PaGa* (*Printing and Graphic Arts*), of which the first number came from Lunenburg, Vermont, in February 1953. It was edited in Boston by Rollo Silver, with an editorial board of Ray Nash and Stinehour himself. It got better and better until it petered out, as these things do – their proprietors tend to have too many irons in the fire – in 1965. *PaGa* is still a useful component in any typographical library.

We called in at Lunenburg on our way to the lake. Rocky's family had just come down from entertaining 200 people at a book-launching party on top of nearby Mount Washington, and despite our intention to stay in a motel, we were most hospitably fed and pressed to stay the night. Next day we reached Lake Richardson. To reach the 'camp' (a series of log cabins with a luxurious central restaurant) we had to park the car and cross the lake in a motor boat. Since I had to be back in New York three days later, but the others were staying for a week, Harold generously arranged for me to be flown out of the camp by a seaplane. Seeing that the lake was full of floating logs, I assumed that somewhere a flight path had been cleared.

We had a lot of fun fishing (I caught nothing) and finished each day in front of our own log fire, whisky in hand. I grew to love Harold – always even-tempered and humorous – and Jim Barnett equally so. They had been through the Great Depression together, which I learned was a bond perhaps comparable in our country to having been in the trenches of the First World War.

On the morning of my departure, a tiny speck over the tree-tops turned out to be my seaplane. The pilot refused to get out for a cup of

Edward Bawden, 1903–89, a dear friend from days at Penguin after the war to the end of his life.

coffee, uttering the ominous words 'weather's closing in, I want to take off right away'. I was wedged into the open back seat by my suitcase. The door was fastened by string. The pilot said, 'Gee, I can't see anywhere that's clear of logs.' Then he started the actual take-off. The nose of the aeroplane went up, and from then on we certainly couldn't see what was in front of us. I resigned myself to a premature but spectacular death. However, we soared away safely and my friends, probably even more apprehensive than I was, dwindled into specks on the lakeside and then disappeared out of sight. The pilot flew me to his headquarters, where I was supposed to get into one of his land planes and be flown to Portland Airport; but by then the weather really was bad, and I was taken by car.

When I got home I continued my search for artists, preferably not too well known, to whom I could say: Please draw for *Motif*, no payment, but you can have twelve pages to do what you like in. The first person I thought of was Robert Stewart, a Glasgow artist who was head of textile design in Glasgow School of Art. He was more than that: he was a brilliant graphic artist and one of those few who, like Edward Bawden, combined being both fine artist and designer. He had designed superb silk squares for Liberty in London, but when the ones I had given to my wife and other girl-friends wore out, I found I couldn't get new ones: he had gone on to ceramic jugs and mugs, and then started on three-dimensional plaques which combined painting and sculpture. Then it was murals: there is a great example of his work in the chapel below Glasgow Cathedral. Robert made the cover and inside illustrations for *Motif* 2.

In *Motif* 6 we had Hans Unger, who was then making memorable posters for *The Observer*, the *Radio Times*, the BBC, and London Passenger Transport. Hans, born and educated in Germany, and a Jew, had left his country before the war and gone to South Africa. When war broke out he joined the South African army. He was captured by the Italians, and knowing that if he was handed over to the Germans he would be tortured or shot, he escaped by hurling himself over a cliff from a moving truck. He survived, badly injured, and now lived alone in North London. As I got to know him, he became one of the friends I most loved. He lived on a main traffic route, and told a story of how he was woken, early on a summer night, by a crash beneath his windows. He went out to help and found a car piled up against a tree, in which a girl was trapped by the leg. She and her husband were in fact returning from their honeymoon. The car's boot had sprung open. Hans saw a cricket bat and seized it to try and prize up the metal frame pinning the girl's leg. 'Oh, no, you can't use that!' cried the young man 'That's my new bat!'

Hans hated the world of advertising, although highly successful in it, and decided to learn how to make mosaics. After designing a mosaic mural for the new office of Penguin Books, he took on an assistant and obtained several important commissions; but was then nearly killed when a huge and heavy frame fell across him: he survived with two broken legs. Hans used to come and spend Christmas Day with us, but after we moved to Scotland he never came. I then heard that he had died and was appalled when I discovered later that he had taken his own life. I missed him terribly.

Motif's predecessors *Typography*, *Alphabet and Image*, and *Image*, had never included painting or sculpture as subjects. We had included sculpture from the start: Elizabeth Frink had been in the first issue. We wanted to include painting, but were deterred by the cost of colour, really a necessity. James Shand solved this problem by a system of co-operation in the making and use of colour blocks with certain private London galleries. But who was to write the texts of our articles? I chose Robert Melville (whom I had never met) because of all the writing on art that I read in London at that time, his articles in the *New Statesman* and *Architectural Review* made for me the most sense. James and I invited him to lunch, and I nearly fell off my chair when I heard James offering Melville £50 for a thousand words, since our going rate for other contributors was £5 a thousand if they were lucky.

We started with Alan Davie, who generously made a painting for our cover reproduced (in *Motif* 7) in brilliant flat colours by silk screen. In later issues we did William Scott, Reg Butler, Peter Blake, Michael Fussell, Ceri Richards, and Francis Bacon, as well as other articles on painting not illustrated in colour.

Motif ran for thirteen issues. It achieved the first of its purposes, asserting Shenval Press's reputation as a leading printer for the art world. But in 1967 James Shand used to disappear for days or even weeks at a time, and nobody knew where he was. We did not know that he was ill, and in fact dying.

The thirteenth issue, all of which James had discussed and agreed with me long previously, lay in proof for over a year, since James, if he ever appeared, could not be talked to. He died in November 1967, and *Motif* 13 was published posthumously as his memorial. I wrote of James in that issue: 'Whatever his prejudices, they were fiercely and entertainingly expressed. He was gifted both as writer and designer. Many witty but unsigned shorter pieces (in addition to several important articles which he did sign) appeared in *Typography*, *Alphabet and Image*, and *Image*, and *Motif*. He also contributed occasional book reviews to the *New Statesman*, and was once a member of the BBC Critics. Although he could not draw a straight line or a circle, he was in fact solely responsible for many brilliant typographic and other covers. For example, he produced covers for *Process*, a process-engraving monthly periodical which he had rescued and published at his own expense for several years, sometimes using blocks we had made for *Motif* before we could use them ourselves. He was also, to his friends, the most generous of men; the number of people to whom he "lent" money and did not ask for it back, will never be known. His values were not of suburbia or the establishment: he remained a bohemian although running a large and successful business.'

It seems that at heart, or at least in some moods, he was ashamed of this success and the money it brought him. He envied all artists. One painter, later a Royal Academician, told me that James, with drink taken and in the small hours at the Gargoyle, had poured all the money out of his pockets (a considerable sum) and forced it on this painter 'as a token of my admiration'.

He was a strange and difficult man to whom we were devoted.

ABCDEFGHJ
KLMNOPQR
STUVWXYZ
abcdefghijklmn
opqrstuvwxyz

A NEW ALPHABET ENGRAVED ON WOOD BY JOHN WOODCOCK

Elephants

*Doctor
Zhivago*

In our last Editorial we asked 'where are the young British de-signers of lettering to maintain the Anglo-European tradition of men like Eric Gill, Reynolds Stone, Zapf, and the late Jan van Krimpen?' Pondering this, we decided to commission alphabets from three young British designers, and the results are on this and the following two pages.

First is a Roman alphabet engraved on wood by John Wood-cock. He has never designed a type face, but would be glad to do so if set a definite problem. By temperament he works most easily on making subtle variations on the Roman theme and considers this the letterer's most difficult task.

A style of lettering which could become a display face is shown in the word 'Elephants', used on the jacket of the recent book of that name by Richard Carrington, published by Chatto & Windus. Woodcock's recent work has included the jacket for *Doctor Zhivago*, published by Collins, part of which is shown here, and a series of calligraphic press advertisements for Penguin Books.

John Woodcock, aged 35, was born in Yorkshire. He was edu-cated at Barnsley Holgate Grammar School, Barnsley School of Art and the Royal College of Art. He now works as a freelance designer and teaches at St Martin's and Brighton Schools of Art.

94

122

ABCDEFGHIJ
KLMNOPQRS
TU abcdefghijkl XY
mnopqrstuv
VW wxyz *Michael Harvey 1959* &Z

Robert McLaughlin

SIN

The alphabet above was drawn by Michael Harvey with street lettering in mind, although the method of manufacture would considerably affect the design. As it stands, it would make a powerful display face for title pages and book jackets.

Below are shown some words from a book jacket Harvey designed for *The Notion of Sin* by R. McLaughlin, published by Michael Joseph.

Harvey, aged 28, trained as an engineering draughtsman, but at the age of 21 read Eric Gill's *Autobiography* and was fired with enthusiasm to become a letter cutter. He took evening classes, started cutting in wood and then spent his summer holidays learning to cut letters in stone under Mr Joseph Cribb, who was Eric Gill's first apprentice and still continues this work at Ditchling Common in Sussex. In October 1955 he was taken on for a trial period by Reynolds Stone to assist in letter cutting on monuments, and giving up his draughtsman's job he moved to the Dorset village of Litton Cheney where Stone lives. He is still working as Stone's assistant, and as a sideline produces a considerable number of lettered book jackets for Heinemann, Chatto & Windus, Michael Joseph, the Cambridge University Press and other publishers. He has never designed a type face, but would like to try; he would also like to design lettering for buildings and packaging.

95

An opening from *Motif* 4, (March 1960), showing new alphabets and lettering designed by John Woodcock, *left*, and Michael Harvey, *right*. Printed in black and red on cream paper. Page reduced from 305 × 240mm.

14. Victorian books

ONE of the best antiquarian bookshops in London during the 1960s was Bernard Quaritch, then at the head of Grafton Street, just off Bond Street. Amazingly, they kept a shelf marked 'Free books' from which customers could help themselves, a generosity I think they later regretted when they found themselves buying those books back again.

One lunch hour, I found, on the lowest shelf in one of the Quaritch ground floor rooms, two books, which I had never seen before, with handsome typography and coloured plates, at a pound or two each, and bought them. They were published in the 1840s by William Pickering, printed by Whittingham, and the author was Henry Shaw. None of those names meant anything to me.

These Henry Shaws, and the 'illuminated' Owen Jones books which I found a few days later, must have been lying around in bookshops all over the country all my life, and I had never noticed them. Having found them, I began to find many other nineteenth-century books with printed colour plates, mostly dusty and at very low prices. I began to take notice of the names, and styles, of printers like Edmund Evans, J. M. Kronheim, John Leighton, and George Baxter. When I looked them up in the printing reference books I had on my shelves, I could find nothing. It was only considerably later that I found some of them mentioned in Basil Gray's perceptive *The English Print* (1937). Later still, I found three books about Victorian colour printing written early in the twentieth century, while some of the printers were still alive, by Courtney Lewis, R. M. Burch, and Martin Hardie; but they answered only a few of the questions I wanted to ask. Coloured illustrations in a printed book must be either original paintings, or prints, either hand-coloured or printed in colours. From the time that printing in Europe was invented (c. AD 1440), right up to the early years of the nineteenth century, nearly all coloured illustrations were hand-coloured, simply because to print illustrations in colour, whether from wood or metal blocks, or, from about 1800, lithographic stones, was laborious and therefore expensive. Hand-colouring was usually done either by the artist himself, who might do it for love, or by women and children, who were cheap to employ.

Plates coloured by hand were often fantastically beautiful, but there were limits to what was feasible in an edition of even so few as one hundred copies, let alone one thousand. Also, with hand-colouring, the colours in every copy could never be exactly the same: often they varied a great deal.

By the 1830s, most of all in Great Britain, there was a population explosion, and the number of people who could read and needed books was increasing so fast that a few far-sighted publishers and printers saw that to print in colours would soon become economical.

The plates in nineteenth-century colour-printed books had qualities which made them extremely attractive to me. The colours were bright, and of every shade; they were genuine colours, not simulations of colours by the ingenious three- and four-colour process of commercial colour printing normal in the twentieth century. The best printers in the Victorian period ground and mixed their own inks, which gave their work an individual quality which could be recognised. You could tell, usually at a glance, whether a plate was printed by Leighton, Evans, Kronheim, or whoever. Because they were not using standard inks, or the trichromatic process, prints made in only three or four colours could have exciting visual qualities rarely seen in modern printing; and when the printer used eight or more colours in a single print, as they often did, it had a richness indeed. The quality of the drawing in these plates varied, but that did not matter: the prints were intrinsically exciting, almost as if they were abstract art.

In the second half of the century, the contribution of the artist often became significant: Edmund Evans, for example, employed artists like Birkett Foster, Dicky Doyle, Walter Crane, Randolph Caldecott, and Kate Greenaway. But since none of them engraved their own drawings, the wood-engraver's and printer's contribution remained paramount.

In lithography, it was different. The artist could draw directly on the stone. Chromolithography (printing in multiple colours from lithographic stones or plates) was pioneered in Britain by Owen Jones, a Welsh architect who learned lithography and set up his own lithographic press in London in order to produce an accurate illustrated account of the Alhambra Palace in Spain, which he did in two handsome folios published in 1842–6. Since the plates were printed and the colours in every copy of the book were consistent (impossible with hand-colouring and in any case of a complexity with which hand-colouring could not have coped) he thus laid the foundation for scholarly art publishing in this country.

What I was discovering for myself all came, as I gradually learned, from quite a short period of about fifty years, roughly from 1830 to 1880. It was ended by the introduction of photographic process blocks, pioneered in the United States. The first number of the *Strand* magazine of London, which appeared in January 1891, contained line blocks, halftone blocks, and wood engravings. In the same year William Morris published the first book of his Kelmscott Press.

Some of the books I bought in my London lunch-hours were very large. Lewis Gruner's *Specimens of Oriental Art*, for example, published by T. McLean in 1850, consisted of two volumes over two feet in length, which got me into great difficulties getting on and off a bus in the Charing Cross Road. Some, on the other hand, were very small, down to Pickering's match-box-sized 'Diamond Classics': diamond type is equivalent to 4-point and could not be read without a magnifying glass. They did not contain any colour, but I had to have them because not only were they Pickering's first venture into publishing, but they were also the first books ever to be bound in cloth by a publisher.

At weekends, Tony and I hunted for books in country bookshops, particularly in the direction of Tunbridge Wells, where we drove regularly to see my parents.

In any one bookshop we might find only one or two of the books we were looking for, but in one small shop in Sevenoaks we found an entire room of Victorian colour printing, presumably a collection bought en masse when the owner died. I ought of course to have made an offer for the whole lot, but we did not have the money or the nerve.

Mr Pratley's shop in Tunbridge Wells became a regular haunt. Dear Mr Pratley, like Mr Pickwick, with twinkling eyes behind small round gold spectacles, when he knew our interests put aside piles of books for us, and even gave us items considered by the trade at that time to be valueless, such as books in incomplete original parts. Many books, in nearly every category, started life in the nineteenth century in monthly parts, at a shilling, with some text and three or four plates: Dickens, Thackeray and other novelists were all published in this way. The printed paper covers were usually undistinguished and unillustrated: the day of the dust-jacket had not yet arrived. These covers are now excessively rare and bibliographically interesting.

Another ally was Ben Weinreb, a great bookseller specialising in architecture, then near the British Museum in Great Russell Street. Admittedly I was a customer of his, but it was surely extreme generosity or foolishness to give me nine original parts of Owen Jones' *Alhambra*, in grey paper wrappers, each part inscribed to the Architectural Society (later the Institute of British Architects) by Owen Jones himself. It was always a privilege to browse anywhere along Ben's shelves.

Occasionally there was sheer luck, but not often. One day in a small bookshop in South Kensington I found a folio half-bound in red leather, entitled *The Art Exemplar*, intended to illustrate every known printing process or method of illustration. It contained 86 pages each with different original illustrations pasted down to illustrate the printed text. The bookshop proprietor had not looked at the book closely enough, and sold it to me as being of almost negligible value or interest. Each copy of the book had to be unique, as the illustrations, being originals, were always different. I found later that four copies had appeared in 'elephant folio' (one of which I now possessed), and six in oblong quarto. The copy belonging to the author, W. J. Stannard, is now in the Print Department of the British Museum; another is in the Royal Library at Windsor; the third, once belonging to the Earl of Ellesmere, and later mine, is now in Massey College, Toronto; the whereabouts of the fourth copy is not known to me.

Further afield, we sometimes visited Thorp in Guildford. This was a very large shop, like a cathedral, in which the shelves were packed with books three or even four deep; the staff had little idea where any individual book was. Our visits on Saturday mornings were punctuated by appalling crashes, as frustrated customers, trying to extract a tome, toppled over an entire stack. Clouds of dust rose up and the customer, often an elderly clergyman, had to be dug out and dusted down; but a new lode had been exposed.

The proprietors of the smaller bookshops tended to be highly eccentric and, occasionally, less than lovable. One was afraid of floods, and whenever it rained he shut up shop and retired to have coffee and could not be found. Another kept his best books under his bed, where he seemed to spend most of the day; his bedroom was the only room in the house that could be entered by the door, for in every other room books had fallen down and blocked the entrance, and the windows were fastened. In another shop, in Edinburgh, the books were in three basement rooms, but there was only one electric light bulb, which the grim-faced proprietor's wife, or sister, moved from socket to socket behind the customer, keeping a suspicious eye on him all the while.

In London, the shop of shops was Heywood Hill in Curzon Street.

It was next to Trumpers, where occasionally I persuaded myself that I could afford to have my hair cut. Handasyde Buchanan at Heywood Hill was an expert in fine flower books and showed me Redouté, Thornton, and other treasures I could not afford; he was also mad on cricket. The unfortunate thing about Heywood Hill was that it was stacked with books, new as well as old, which I wanted very badly indeed. Things got worse when John Saumarez Smith took over. The main bookshop seemed to specialize in everything in which I was most interested: Henry Shaw and Noel Humphreys jostled with C. E. Montague, Peter Fleming, Alice Meynell, and Mary Coleridge. The children's book department downstairs, run by the daughter of a friend of mine, was much worse. After a bit, I certainly couldn't afford Trumpers.

We found another bookseller in the depths of a wood in Kent. His name appeared in a printed list of antiquarian booksellers and because he was not too far from Blackheath, we made a Saturday morning appointment. We found, hidden away in a wood which seemed to imply that the occupants did not wish to be found, a tall, handsome man with white hair, who told me his life story. As a young man he had gone out to the Argentine – as I had once thought of doing – to work on a ranch. One of the amusements of his contemporaries was bare-fist fighting, which they did until one of them dropped. When he asked me how old I thought he was – always a difficult question – I underestimated by twenty years. In fact he was over 80.

His father had owned an antiquarian business, including books, in Chelsea, and when the old man died, the son had to come home and take over the business. He had disposed of it all except the books, which he brought down to Kent, and now conducted business only by post. The trouble was, I couldn't see any books.

He did have a small glass-fronted bookcase in the room in which we were sitting, and invited me to look through it. I extracted a beautiful blue leather binding, which turned out to be the work of James Hayday, the leading Victorian fine binder; and better still, it had a colour-printed armorial bookplate. Bookplates printed in colour are unusual. I was allowed to buy the book, and when home ascertained that the book-plate, belonging to Sir Joseph Walter King Eyton, had been printed in four colours by Charles Whittingham from wood blocks engraved by Mary Byfield. King Eyton himself was a book collector who specialised in commissioning exotic bindings and in having copies of books he fancied specially printed, in a few copies, on something unusual like green vellum. One binding in leather commissioned by King Eyton from Hayday had more than 57,000 impressions of tools (item 259 in *Catalogue of the Library of Joseph Walter King Eyton*, privately printed, London, 1848). The present location of this book is, I believe, not known.

The name of my new bookseller friend was Peacock, and it was clear that somewhere he had a lot of books about which he was keeping quiet. However, he invited us to visit him again. As he was elderly and his wife was frail, we invited them both to have lunch in our Volkswagen Microbus – in which four people can sit round a table – parked outside his front door. He then led me down a path through birch trees until we came to a brick building with a tin roof, the size of an aircraft hangar – it might have been a wartime bomb store – which was stacked with books on simple wooden shelves so tightly spaced that you could hardly walk between. There were many large unopened packing-cases, and at the far end there was a great pile of books lying higgledy-piggledy beneath a layer of guano, which also lay along the tops of all the shelves: birds were nesting inside the roof. The first I picked up there was volume 2 of an aquatint-illustrated account of India, in poor condition: I never found volume 1.

I was allowed free range through this potential Ali Baba's treasure house, and came out, after an hour or so, with a few not exceptionally interesting books which I bought at reasonable prices. I made one or two other visits on Saturday mornings, each time coming away with something, but never actually finding the shelf of Cundall's gift books, or a complete set of the Home Treasury series of children's books, in mint condition, which I was convinced must be lying just round the next corner. Many of the books had his father's bookplate, a wood-engraving of a peacock combined with the initials CJP, and I have often seen this bookplate in bookshops all over the country. My Mr Peacock died; I never heard when. His wife knew nothing about the books or his business. She found the name of a bookseller on a letter lying on his desk and invited him down to value and dispose of the stock. I was told that he took one brief look and offered her £500, which she accepted. That was about what it would cost to remove the books to London. To be fair to this bookseller (which I find very difficult) it was a gamble on which he might have made a loss, but I believe it paid off handsomely. For many years I continued to have dreams about finding a treasure on the guano-topped shelves in that isolated wood.

In order to find the answers to all the questions I was asking myself about the books we were bringing back home by the box-load, and which were not answered in any existing literature I could find, I had to write a book on the subject myself.

This meant, since I did not have the time to research in libraries (having my living to earn during the day), that I had to buy systematically, and try to find, and possess, every important book of the period printed in colour.

Victorian Book Design and Colour Printing was printed by James Shand at the Shenval Press and published by Faber & Faber in 1963. It was fortunate in its reviews: John Betjeman and Evelyn Waugh liked it, and there were kind notices from the anonymous scribes of the *Times Literary Supplement*, the *Economist*, and my then favourite periodical, *The Bookseller*. It appeared in conventional octavo format, but when it went out of print, my friend David Bland, the production manager at Fabers, persuaded Fabers to make a second edition in a larger size which was published in 1972. The new edition, which again all too soon went out of print, contained sixteen new colour plates, beautifully printed by the Shenval Press, and a superb collection of monochrome reproductions, in line and half-tone, appearing on every one of the 246 text pages: a fitting tribute to the hitherto largely unrecognized richness of nineteenth-century illustration.

While we were collecting Victorian books, especially those with printing in colour, it was a great pleasure to discover that our friend the engraver Reynolds Stone was also a collector of Victorian illustrated books. Reynolds became a dear friend over the years; we did not often see him in London, because he disliked travelling, but we had happy visits to Reynolds and Janet in their house in Dorset, in the south of England not far from the Isle of Wight and the sea. When he died in 1979, I was privileged to write an introduction for the booklet accompanying the exhibition of his work organised by the Victoria & Albert Museum; since it is relevant to the present book, I reprint it here with the V&A's kind permission.

Reynolds and Janet Stone moved to the Old Rectory, Litton Cheney, in Dorset, early in 1953. There, in Iris Murdoch's words spoken at Reynolds' memorial service in 1979, 'he lived the happy good loving life of a true man, creating with his wife and children a serene and beautiful home which was a refuge and a joy to his many generously welcomed friends, a place of pleasure and spiritual refreshment.' This with strange closeness echoes the words written by Eric Gill at the end of his *Autobiography* in 1940: 'And if I might

Jacket of *Victorian Book Design and Colour Printing*, 2nd edition, Faber, 1972, printed in colour. Reduced from 293 × 227mm.

attempt to state in one paragraph the work which I have chiefly tried to do in my life it is this: to make a cell of good living in the chaos of our world.' No such statement was ever made, or ever would have been made, by Reynolds. He never made any statement of belief.

The Old Rectory was indeed an extraordinary and magical-feeling place. The house itself, late Georgian, was as beautiful and elegant as houses of that period usually are, but it was not especially grand: it was its position that made it special. On one side tall beeches and elms, with an old church tower, made a picture that brought back echoes of a hundred Birket Foster wood-engravings; according to Lord Clark, Reynolds loved the splendid trees in his garden 'more than anything in the world except his family'. From the hills above the house, there were unspoiled views of Dorset countryside for twenty miles in every direction. From the side of the house, a stream ran down through woods, making rills, cascades and pools which Reynolds recaptured in many of his own engravings. He said once he would be content to paint for the rest of his life within his own garden. He and Janet had found the perfect environment for themselves and their life together. It was right for Reynolds, the perfect setting, but the extraordinary thing was that it gave the impression to visitors, immediately, that Reynolds had himself designed it; that they had stepped into a series of Reynolds Stone illustrations.

Another attraction, important to Reynolds, was that it was near the coast: one could hear in the calm after a storm, the rumble of the surf on the Chesil Bank from his front door. Fishermen regularly brought fish to sell to the house in the morning, lifted from the sea the night before. This happened on one of my own visits: we were having breakfast together and when Reynolds came back to the table, after negotiating with the fisherman, leaving the front door open, his eight-year-old daughter entered the room to say good-morning, and while she was standing there, a dove or wood-pigeon (a wild bird, not a tame one) flew into the room and perched gently on her shoulder making a moving symbolic picture. After that visit, Reynolds explained in a letter (dated 21 June 1960) that he was trying to accept fewer stone-cutting commissions, because they took up so much time: 'I expect you think I don't get on with work here, distracted by stray pigeons and other birds of passage. But this is not so, and I want very much to concentrate on drawing and engraving and I am uncomfortably aware of the passage of time.'

Reynolds Stone, probably *c.* 1946.

Reynolds had his work table for drawing and engraving not in a closeted sanctum or private studio, but in a corner of a large drawing room,* surrounded not only by his family and friends but by his much-loved collection of nineteenth-century illustrated books, all, apparently, in almost mint condition and picked up in Weymouth and Dorchester bookshops for pennies and shillings. These he treasured and studied, and was an expert in recognizing the styles of different artists and engravers. Dicky Doyle, Birket Foster, Edmund Evans, Linton, Swain, and the man with the hunting horn described on p. 161 of Gill's *Autobiography,* were nearly as dear to him as his living friends. When a book that I had edited, *The Reminiscences of Edmund Evans,* was published, he wrote to me (5 December 1967):

I am absolutely delighted with Edmund Evans. You have made one more of our Victorians, I mean the Victorians we are interested in, come to life. I know there is too much about spiritualism and too much piousness, both of which were very characteristic of the time.

*Described and drawn by Richard Guyatt in *Motif* 5, Autumn 1960, and painted by William Henderson.

It certainly is tantalising that you have not been able to put your hands on any original drawings by the dear old boy. I wonder who gave some of his blocks to the V & A and whether there is a line of enquiry there that might produce results.

Other names like Birket Foster and Thomas Miller come to life a little more. I particularly like the story of Birket Foster cribbing E. W. Cooke's etching of Shipping and Craft (a book I have had for a very long time), and the stuff about Caldecott, which is also worth having.

I have always loved The Three Jovial Huntsmen since the nursery. My copy, belonging to my mother as a child, is alas very battered, and of course the wonderful Dicky Doyle drawings from the Princess Nobody, issued as you have listed first in 1870, with a second edition in 1875, as Fairyland by the artist with a poem by William Allingham. Here the format is twice the size of the Princess Nobody, so it had not been necessary to fold the large designs or to chop some of the smaller ones. To my mind it is a glorious piece of colour printing and the designs if encountered in childhood remain in the memory for life.

He also over the years built up a collection of hand-presses,* which he regarded as objects of great beauty. They were used for proofing blocks, and occasionally for printing a small edition; for example, in 1968, he printed 125 copies of *The Other Side of the Alde,* by Kenneth Clark, a 16-page booklet which was also the first showing of his second typeface, 'Janet', retained for private use and cut only in 18 point in roman caps and lower-case and italic lower-case. It makes a splendid page and a fine black accompaniment to four wood-engravings. 18 point was the size for which it was designed, requiring a large page (in this case 10¾ × 7¼ in.) and some leading. If reduced to, say, 12 point or smaller, for use in normal books, it would be handsome but it is doubtful if it would have had sufficient obvious advantages over such comparable faces as Perpetua, Joanna, Juliana, or even Monotype Bembo, to justify the expense of such an operation.

Reynolds' only other typeface was Minerva, commissioned by Linotype to provide display sizes (i.e. above 14 point) to accompany the Bunyan typeface, designed by Eric Gill for his private press, which Linotype issued in 1953 under the name Pilgrim, in sizes from 8 to 14 pt, but which was unsuitable for cutting in larger sizes. Minerva was introduced to the public in *Linotype Matrix* No. 21, January

*See 'The Albion Press', by R. Stone, *Journal of the Printing Historical Society*, no. 2, 1966.

1955. The bold version of Minerva (perhaps the most successful part) was adopted for some years for article headings in the *New Statesman* (but not for the paper's masthead). Minerva had many other uses, but was discontinued in the early 1970s.

It was in his engraving of letter forms on wood that, I think, Reynolds' greatest achievement lay. His mastery of 'roman' – or what might better be called 'English' – letterforms was absolute. He engraved several whole-page displays of the roman alphabet in white out of black – some with numerals and some without – which seem to me the most beautiful things he ever did. They are well reproduced in the John Murray book. They are more satisfying, for some reason I search for but cannot find, than all the exquisite engravings of words and sentences for bookplates, title-pages and inscriptions. Could they give as much pleasure to someone who has not been brought up with our alphabet – for example an Arab, a Russian or a Japanese? Are they intrinsically beautiful, or is it a beauty of association and familiarity? The engravings of words have usually only one meaning, while the alphabets have all meanings inherent in them.

The alphabet, like Viola Meynell's dust,

> *Is flowers and kings*
> *Is Solomon's temple, poets, Nineveh.*

Reynolds Stone achieved the ultimate in purity of form for these shapes, his letters seem to make nearly every other artist's version of them just a little – or more than a little – fussy, quirky, less good. But I do not understand why.

When I once remarked to Reynolds that I had never seen him draw roman letters with any decoration on them,* he replied in a letter (12 March 1963):

Footnote on decorated letters. I love decoration, but the enclosed [see illustration] is not a decorated letter in your sense, I suppose. There is a valid distinction here. I don't, I admit, often feel the need to decorate the letter itself which would more or less degrade its form. Of course there are occasions when degradation is required and I expect it is a mistake to be too puritanical. But the forms have acquired a kind of absolutism akin, in a much simpler way, to the

---

*There are several in his *A Book of Lettering*, 1935 and often reprinted, which I had forgotten.

human form in our eyes. It is not usually necessary for the limbs of nymphs to start sprouting leaves however richly decorated their background may be.

In another sense I don't feel as bounded by or bound to the 26 letters of the alphabet as perhaps you think, but of course I agree about my limitations, which are obvious. But in general I don't feel limited as to what one may or may not do in 1963 because I don't feel that anything that has flourished in the past has come to a full stop forever. I admire enormously those who successfully experiment but I don't think that either geometry or loosened up geometry or amorphous blots are the only things we are allowed to play with today. One of the many good things about Motif is its generous inclusiveness.

Some other views were expressed in a letter (31 October 1970) replying to one of mine asking if he were coming to a Double Crown Club dinner:

Oh dear! I wanted to come to the Dwiggins dinner but have lost the list of talks. There is something awfully sick-making about Art Nouveau but I ought to try and understand Van de Velde I suppose. Modern minimal 'art' leaves me speechless (all those boxes at the Whitechapel followed by lengths of wood nailed together) and the trickling bits of metal in Cork Street and the Tate. There is probably a correlation somewhere with pollution and over-population. But cheer up you might say, David Jones and Ben Britten and dear John Nash are still with us ... One of the troubles of coming up to London from here is the continual increase in BR fares, and motoring is tiring, dangerous, and slow. I get more like Mr Woodhouse every day.

Reynolds Stone taught at the Royal College of Art for one day a week in the early sixties. His transparent honesty and sincerity, apart from his skills, made him a much sought-after tutor of individuals, but he was not happy as a lecturer. I heard him give a slide lecture on wood-engraving at the St Bride Printing Library, when he murmured diffidently, head down, into his notes, and whenever a slide of his own work appeared, about which his audience really wanted to hear him talk, he hurried on apologetically to the next slide.

Although by nature he was reserved, never pushing himself

forward, and, in public, sometimes seeming shy or diffident, he was in private a most outward-going and enjoyable companion. There was always a glint of humour in his eyes and a chuckle in his voice (which had a most characteristic baritone timbre): he loved poking fun, but gently. I saw him mostly in London, which in an important sense he hated (away from his home and his work), but I think that also he enjoyed London as a sort of half-holiday escapade, an opportunity to notice things, and meet people, who both fascinated and appalled him. There was nothing indecisive or diffident in his basic faiths.

His 'oeuvre' as an engraver is really astonishing, and, surprisingly, it gains rather than loses when it is displayed, as in the present great exhibition, in its near entirety. Among the highlights of his career were the clock device to head the leader page of *The Times* in 1949, the Royal Arms and lettering on *The Times* masthead, 1951*, and the Royal Arms to head the Court Circular since 1951; stamps for the Post Office in 1946, 1958, 1960, and 1963; the Royal Arms commissioned by HMSO and used in Hansard since 1956, and other versions of the Royal Arms for HMSO at various dates; the five pound note for the Bank of England in 1963, and the ten pound note in 1964; bookplates for various members of the Royal Family; and, in stone-carving, Winston Churchill's memorial stone in Westminster Abbey in 1965, and the memorials for Sir Max Beerbohm (in St Paul's Cathedral crypt) and for Duff Cooper (at Belvoir). Among his most widely-used designs were logotypes for Dolcis and Bally shoes, the London Library label, and devices for the firms of Grosvenor Chater, Rupert Hart-Davis, Hamish Hamilton, J. M. Dent, Blackwell's, the None-such Press, and the University Presses of Oxford and Cambridge – all of them certainly familiar to many who had never heard of Reynolds' name. Besides these, he engraved hundreds of labels and bookplates for private and public people, beautiful in themselves, but acquiring a new and unforgettable dimension when mounted and framed in multi-coloured groups.

Long before he began engraving, his craftsmanship was developed in the making of model sailing-ships, which he saw on holidays in Bridport harbour. He thought the trader sailing-ships of the nineteenth century among the most beautiful things man has ever

---

*The Royal Arms was later abandoned until brought back in 1981 and again dropped early in 1982.

made: like the Albion and Columbian presses which he collected, functionally perfect. No one who sees these models, happily included in the exhibition, can easily believe that they were made by a school-boy, and not by an elderly sailor who had spent a lifetime offwatch, making such models. Reynolds was also – as Myfanwy Piper tells us in her perceptive Art and Technics monograph of 1951 – accustomed to sketch in watercolours with his mother (who died suddenly when he was seventeen). In later life he returned more and more to water-colours, choosing nearly always as his subject trees in woodlands, reminding one of the sculptor Jacob Epstein's watercolours of Epping forest.

Reynolds did not write much for publication – how could he have had time to write at all – but when he did, he wrote extremely well, making one wish he could have written, for example, a much, much longer autobiography than the essay in this catalogue. He wrote reviews in the TLS, *Motif* and elsewhere, and selected, with a full and scholarly introduction, *Wood Engravings of Thomas Bewick* (Rupert Hart-Davis, 1953). In *The Wood Engravings of Gwen Raverat* (Faber & Faber, 1959), his eight-page introduction is as well and sharply written as her best-seller *Period Piece*. He rarely, if ever, involved himself in the commercial-artistic problems of actually designing books, maga-zines, or industrial literature; although he did design, not always with complete success, a few book jackets. He confined himself to a very few, comparatively narrow activities, mostly centred round the twenty-six roman letters of which he was, in his life, the greatest living master.

But the work of Reynolds Stone that will be loved most deeply for the longest time is surely the wood-engravings of the Dorset coun-tryside: the oaks and elms, often with a child curled in the branches, or playing underneath; the wind blowing across a cornfield, or over the Downs; a bird, an animal or a flower, in tiny but consummate detail, seen with a naturalist's vision that was strong, original and loving. RUARI MCLEAN

Our collection of Victorian colour-printed books was eventually sold to the University of Toronto as the Ruari McLean Collection, and is now in Massey College in Toronto. Tony and I packed eleven tons of books into boxes. They had to go, because my next book was on magazine design, and our house was rapidly becoming knee-deep in magazines.

But the wealth of Victorian craftmanship made me return to the period for two more illustrated books: *Victorian Publishers' Bookbindings in cloth and leather*, and *Victorian Publishers' Bookbindings in paper*. They were both published by Gordon Fraser, and beautifully printed: the first, in 1973, by Lund Humphries in Bradford, the second, in 1983, by the Roundwood Press in Warwick. In the paper volume, more than half the plates are in colour, and in both books nearly all the bindings are reproduced for the first time since their original publication. Even now, I am astounded by the richness and variety of their invention. Most of the cloth and leather covers are elaborately patterned, including decorative lettering, in which illustration plays a lesser part, and only a few have much colour, although rich in gold. The paper-covered books are nearly always rich in both illustration and lettering, but of a different kind. They are now difficult to find in good condition: paper can soon get worn and torn. I was often lucky in finding undamaged copies to photograph, borrowed from the collections of friends.

Victorian Book Design was in fact followed by two other books dealing with individuals of the period: *Joseph Cundall. A Victorian Publisher*, Private Libraries Association, 1976, and *Benjamin Fawcett, 1808–1893, finest of the colour printers*, Scolar Press, 1988. Both books were essentially essays with illustrated bibliographies rather than biographies.

Cundall fascinated me because as well as being author and publisher, he was also, for a time, a freelance book designer and also a pioneer photographer, who organised the first serious photographic record of the Bayeux Tapestry.

Fawcett was a superb colour printer who like Thomas Bewick chose to spend his entire working life in the countryside in which he was born, in his case the wolds of East Yorkshire.

Both books were fun to write, and the necessary research led to friendships with still-living descendants. In *Benjamin Fawcett*, my wife became co-author, and wrote an important chapter on popular science publishing in the nineteenth century.

15. Magazines

MY friend Allen Hutt wrote a book for Oxford University Press on *Newspaper Design*. He then proposed to follow it up with a book on magazine design. Oxford sent me his proposals and asked for my comments. I did not think very much of them, but the only way I could answer was to outline how I would tackle such a book myself. To my dismay, my synopsis was accepted, and I was told to get on and write it.

I had never thought in general terms about magazine design, but I had been concerned with designing, re-designing, or advising on, a lot of magazines of different kinds. I would never think of trying to teach anyone how to design an important national magazine, but I would know what questions needed to be asked before tackling such a job. However, I was also aware that many minor periodical publications were being produced, all over the place, by people who had no training in typographic design or even editing; a book on the subject could certainly give some helpful guidance to such people.

As a small boy, my parents wanted me to read books, and said that reading magazines was a waste of time, if not actually sinful. In spite of that, and partly because for eight years I was more in bed with tonsillitis than up, I managed to read a lot of magazines. My early education, and certainly my general knowledge, owed more tő magazines than to books.

There was first *Chick's Own*, in which words with more than one syl-la-ble were hy-phen-at-ed. Then came *The Rainbow* and *Tiger Tim*. We also already possessed old volumes of *The Boy's Own Paper*, on which my father had been brought up. What that magazine meant to its readers will probably never be appreciated by modern children who have so many more distractions in their lives.

Modern Boy started when I was about eleven, with a dazzling series of free gifts in its early numbers. Then I enjoyed *The Champion*, which gave me a deep (and largely unsatisfied) interest in dirt-track racing. Following came *Meccano Magazine*, now sadly defunct, and then *The Children's Newspaper*, approved by many parents because it was theoretically educational, but the only thing I can remember enjoying in it was the comic strip about monkeys called Pip, Squeak, and Wilfred. And then there was *Punch*. I think I learned more English, history, and general knowledge from old numbers of *Punch* than anything else except Arthur Mee's *My Magazine*, of which we had inherited a set of bound volumes. They all enriched my childhood. Then, growing up, I found *The Wide World, The Strand* (with contributions by Conan Doyle, Sapper, and P.G.Wodehouse), and *Windsor*, which introduced me to Ethel M. Dell and High Romance. I wept more over Dell's *The Altar of Honour* than over *David Copperfield*.

Then came *The Aeroplane* and *Flight*, which gave me a passion for cutting out and pasting down aeroplane photographs. My friends were flying them only too soon. Then, still growing older, I read the *London Mercury, New Statesman, Time & Tide*, and *The Spectator*; less seriously, *Vogue* and *Le Rire*. I was soon to be astonished to find that I shocked the mother of a French friend by buying the latter, and a Naval Officers' wardroom by proposing it should subscribe to the former.

After the War, I had to buy the *Radio Times* and *Vogue* for Tony.

I could not also afford subscriptions to the *New Statesman* and the *Architectural Review*, so I bought them regularly from bookstalls. Then I began to get involved in actual magazine design through two intelligent parsons, Guy Daniel and Marcus Morris. Magazine design became a regular activity in my working life, as described in Chapter 10. When I was asked to write a book on the subject, it gave me a welcome excuse to buy more magazines than ever before. This was not difficult, since my office was in Soho, the most international part of London. Bookstalls were packed with all the most glamorous periodicals from the Continent and USA as well as Britain. How truly glamorous they were, and I began to realise that there was an increasing number of magazines that were a joy to look at. Note: 'to look at'. The magazines I was now buying were predominantly *visual*. In fact, one well-known magazine art editor at that time was heard to call the journalists who wrote text 'The Wordies' – jokingly, but with disparagement. His layouts were made with a slot here and there to drop in a few words. It clearly didn't matter to him what words.

What was now happening was that the new teaching of 'graphic design' (no longer 'typography') in art schools everywhere, and in this country in particular at the Royal College of Art in London, was suddenly bringing results. A new breed of designers was now active, and everywhere finding imaginative publishers and editors anxious to use them. In England, a trade magazine for men's clothes, *Man about Town*, was bought by Clive Labovitch and Michael Heseltine and was turned into a sophisticated monthly, first, in 1961, as *About Town*, and then *Town*. It was very good while it lasted, until January 1968. *The Queen*, an old-fashioned woman's magazine, relying heavily on insipid photographs of the Royal Family and 'Society', was bought in 1957 by Jocelyn Stevens, then aged 25, and with Mark Boxer as art editor, became one of Europe's most lively magazines, full of serious articles and brilliant illustrations. In USA, the great Milton Glaser was working on *Esquire*, while *McCall's* had Otto Storch: with a circulation (in 1966) over eight and a half million, they could do things like hiring a Boeing 747 and laying out a panoply of succulent dishes on its wing to make a cover photograph. *The Saturday Evening Post* had Herb Lubalin, another marvellous art director. In Germany, *Twen* was started in 1959 with Willie Fleckhaus as art director. In France, *Elle* became one of the liveliest women's magazines in the world, with a print order of about 800,000 copies weekly by photogravure. It had Peter Knapp as art editor until 1966, and then Roman Cieslewicz. The dazzling graphic displays in all these and other magazines caused changes for the better throughout the periodical industry. An ingenious exception was *Private Eye*, which started in 1962 with William Rushton as art editor. Produced to begin with on a shoe-string, it had no typesetting at all, but was done in a Soho office on an IBM Executive typewriter with Letraset headings.

These magazines were all illustrated in my book. *Magazine Design* was published by Oxford University Press in 1969, and was the first book on the subject, as far as I know, in any language. But in 1970 the period of great magazine design was ending, killed by competition with TV. My book, now long out of print, had quite unintentionally become an elegy for a lost flowering.

In 1960 both the *Sunday Times* and *The Observer*, at that time Britain's two leading Sunday newspapers, decided to follow American precedents and divide their papers into two sections. *The Observer* had won the Newspaper Design Award for three consecutive years, but when Ken Obank, assistant editor and responsible for the paper's looks, tried to design a front page for the new 'Week-End Review', it did not look right. David Astor, the paper's editor and proprietor, called me in on a Saturday, explained the problem, which included making a new masthead for the new section, and asked me to have a go.

I never normally went in to London on a Saturday, but here I was, summoned by the editor of a national newspaper, and being offered a job. When I accepted, I was sent downstairs to see the business manager and discuss terms, more or less of my own choosing. So when I stepped out into the street again I had a large smile on my face and a contract in my pocket. The smile was wiped off my face when I opened my car door and found a note attached to the steering wheel which said 'Come at once to 58 Frith Street. Serious news'. This was signed by my assistant and partner Fianach, who had a key for my car, and who never normally came in to London on a Saturday.

What worries could an intelligent and glamorous blonde of 22, unmarried and unengaged, possibly have? Filled with gloomy forebodings, and assuring myself that it could not possibly have anything to do with me, I drove to our office in Frith Street.

Inside the reception area on the ground floor I found Fianach sitting with something small and furry in her hands, and an expression that she was trying to make look pathetic (but failing).

It appeared that her sister Mel had given her a puppy – a light brown corgi, tiny, and looking very cheerful. It was a present for having looked after Mel on her return to the UK after some seven years working her way round the world. Fianach had tried to decline this new complication but Mel swore that the puppy would enrich all our lives – which he did, in his own way.

What on earth would James Shand, owner of our house and office in Frith Street, say to having a puppy in the building? And if we were keeping the puppy, he had to be given a name.

When next day the subject was broached with James, he showed no dismay and remained calm. Our new friend was christened 'Captain Joshua Slocum, US Navy, Retd', after the circumnavigator about whom I was then reading, or 'Slocum' (long 'o') for short. 'Slocum! Come here! Where's he gone?' Answer was always 'Round the World!'

Our offices were on the tops of buildings without elevators – at Charlotte Street, at Frith Street, and later in Villiers Street. Slocum considered it part of his job to be official welcomer of all our clients, block makers, printers, messengers, and friends. He would stand at the top of the stairs, barking or wagging his stump of a tail, as the exhausted figure finally reached our offices. He *was* the office dog.

Later, he came to Mull with us, and supervised the baiting of the lobster pots in my Shetland boat. He liked to come and bathe in the pool at Broomrigg with Tony and me, but then got in a state when he had convinced himself that we were about to drown. He would put up with almost anything just to be included. He lived happily with us until he was almost 20.

When I started work on *The Observer*'s Week-End Review, I found that it was in fact a magazine rather than a news page, featuring a main article, story, which was normally decided on by the middle of the week; but a news crisis on Saturday might mean something topical having to be substituted at the last moment. The paper went to press on Saturday evening. My preliminary designs were accepted, and for some months the front page look of *The Observer*'s Week-End Review was my work

One week, the front page of the Review consisted of a selection of new poems. I decided to set them in Monotype Grot 216 and 217, a sanserif that in those days before Univers was the most legible sans available. I had a hunch that more people would actually notice the poems if they were set in something relatively unfamiliar; and sanserif would certainly print better, at speed on newsprint, than a more conventional elegant 'literary' face like Perpetua.

I thought it worked, and so did the editor; but the typographer Hans Schmoller at Penguins was outraged and took the trouble to write to David Astor saying that poetry should *never* be set in sanserif!

It was exciting to find oneself plunged into a world I had not set foot in before. David Astor was kindness itself, but I did not see much of him. He listened seriously to any advice that was given to him, including from the office-boy. The witticism, 'the editor's indecision is final' may or may not have been fair comment. Ken Obank accepted me as a member of the team, and I began to re-design *The Observer* itself; but it became clear that to do the job properly I would have to give up my Saturdays, and I had a young family. My work had persuaded *The Observer* that a designer was required on the staff, and suddenly a journalist–designer appeared: Clive Irving, then 27 and Features Editor of the Week-End Review. I had commissioned Edward Bawden to re-draw the Royal Arms: his drawing was reproduced across a whole page of *The Observer* and looked splendid. Years later it was incorporated, much reduced, for the 'ears' on each side of the front page's masthead, and remained there at least until 1988.

Clive also accepted, or maybe had to accept, the new mastheads I had drawn for the Week-End Review and for *The Observer* itself. The lettering was then painted, from my enlarged and retouched drawings, on the fascia of the paper's office in Tudor Street, (see p. 145), just south of Fleet Street. When *The Observer* moved into a lavish new building off Fleet Street, the architect had my lettering incised on the stainless steel

Masthead lettering drawn by the author for *The Observer* newspaper, 1960, used for *The Observer*'s London office in Tudor Street.

façade of the office. The paper soon adopted a new masthead, but my lettering (in steel) had to remain there for years.

Book-designing was usually a typographer's least well-paid activity. Advertising was much better paid, but experience had shown me that I couldn't get seriously interested in it. Magazines, however, sometimes paid well and were highly enjoyable. Robert Harling had once propounded to me that the only way to design a magazine was to become its editor; over the years I found this true, if often impractical.

In my early days, while still at Penguins, I was asked by Jim Richards at the Architectural Association if I would redesign the *Architectural Review*. I wrote a report saying that under the editorship of De Cronin Hastings its pages were brilliantly visual and should not be interfered with. It was so unlike any other magazine, so admirably eccentric, that it could sometimes get away without even having its title on the cover. Jim's other magazine, the *Architect's Journal*, however, could certainly be improved. But in getting from Penguins out at Harmondsworth to Jim's office in Westminster, I was once so late that Jim was furious and sacked me. I am glad to say that later we became friends.

A bit later, *The Economist* found that its circulation was falling, and asked both me and my friend Vivian Ridler to tell them how to redesign it – without telling either of us that they were consulting both. Designers were then forbidden to compete with each other, except in proper competitions, but we were friends, we both wanted the job, and we found that we both intended to make nearly identical suggestions, so we agreed (privately) to reply. *The Economist*'s chief fault was that its article titles were far too clever, too witty, and quite obscure. It was, and is, a magazine for busy people, who have to look rapidly through it to see which articles they should read: but the titles didn't tell what the article was about. It was an important example of editing being required before typography. Vivian's layouts were far better presented than mine and he got the job. But I never saw that *The Economist* ever actually took his advice.

Then I had a job on the *New Scientist*, a paper which started in 1956. In 1961 the paper's management, whom I had known in Hulton Press days, asked me to talk to the editor, Percy Cudlipp, a died-in-the-wool Fleet Street journalist. The *New Scientist* was in fact conceived as a newspaper, not a magazine. I was warned that Cudlipp didn't believe in design or designers and did not want to meet me. This was perhaps partly due to the fact that the paper's first designer, the eminent Hans Schleger, had not been a great success. He had designed the cover with blue and black strips that required alignments with type which had to be made for each issue, on the stone, by compositors, which was far too complicated: the comps soon gave up trying. The result was a nonsense: the paper looked dowdy, provincial, inefficient.

I met Mr Cudlipp in El Vino's, and apart from making a howling gaffe – I asked him if he'd been editing anything before, to which the answer was the famous *Evening Standard* newspaper – we seemed to get on all right. I had to explain that the last thing I wanted to do was to have his paper 'tarted up'. I wanted it to look like what in fact it was: an efficient up-to-date plain weekly documentation of science news. As soon as he realised that I was actually on his side he became quite affable. My new layouts were simple and direct, including a new title on the cover in sanserif drawn by young Matthew Carter, and were accepted. The *New Scientist* was at that time printed by rotary letterpress on newsprint, so the reproduction of photographs was no better than in any other newspaper, a serious drawback. I knew the paper should be printed by offset-litho, but they decided they couldn't afford it. I ought to have said 'You can't afford not to' ... but I didn't. By the time the circulation had risen high enough, and the costs of offset-litho had come down, Percy Cudlipp had died, and the new editor had his own designer friends: the *New Scientist* was excellently redesigned for litho by my friend Germano Facetti.

Another magazine association for me went on longer and was more fun, because the editor was a woman who was a born hostess and held a monthly editorial dinner. This was the *Twentieth Century* magazine, which had begun life as the *Nineteenth Century*, edited by James Knowles from 1877, and had been profitable and influential. In the twentieth century, facing new and varied competition, it remained a forum for serious and independent political and literary criticism, but was making a loss. It was saved by the generosity and idealism of David Astor, editor and proprietor of the Sunday *Observer*. It was now a monthly, set in single column like a book, without any illustrations (no concessions to 'popularity') and about the only periodical in Britain in the 1950s able to print long and serious articles. The editor was Eirene Skilbeck, a granddaughter of James Knowles. She had trained as an actress and her passion was the stage. The monthly dinner was held in her flat, where she cooked economically, and then put away her apron and presided, more than holding her own, over twelve loquacious men. These included John Beavan (political editor of the *Evening Standard* and later Lord Ardwick), Guy Wint, John Weightman, William Clark (Anthony Eden's private secretary, who resigned over Suez and joined the World Bank), Anthony Sampson, Sir Richard Rees, and my old friend Allen Sanderson, at whose instigation I had been invited to join the editorial board and look after production and design. At the monthly dinners John Weightman did the carving, I handed round the plates, and the others talked, usually simultaneously. We drank a lot of Spanish wine and dissected world affairs, often unprintably and from detailed inside knowledge.

We changed the cover of the magazine from a sober mauve to an eye-catching daffodil yellow, and commissioned cover drawings from Edward Bawden at £10 a cover. He continually amazed me and the board by the wit and scope of his inventions. There were two special numbers planned, one on Africa and the other on Youth, then giving noticeable trouble both in Britain and elsewhere in Europe. I thought both subjects might be outside Bawden's true scope. But I forgot that he had been a war artist in Africa and had marched with Colonel Athill's column from Khartoum to Abyssinia, and he had taught teenage art students in South Kensington for years, besides having two of his own. His cover designs were possibly the best things in either issue.

The happy time ended with Eirene's death and a complete change in ownership, style and organisation of the magazine.

In 1965 I was asked to redesign the *Journal* of the Royal Microscopical

Society (for a microscopical fee? murmured Fianach). When I was sent a copy to peruse, I could not find a single word in it that I could understand – there seemed to be no short words until I found the word 'hairdryer' embedded among the polysyllables, where the author was recommending the use of an electric hair-dryer to dry slides before placing them in the microscope. In the same issue an article was entitled 'Preputial skin and glands in *Ceratotherium* and *Diceros*', illustrated with a photograph of the penis of a rhinoceros which was not at all microscopic. I made the design, and sat waiting for a letter from the Society. Still waiting.

By coincidence at the same time we received a letter from the 'London Society Against Obscenity', inviting us to design a letterheading for them. I am not normally against obscenity; it is a fact of life which I accept. I agreed to see their secretary, because I valued the friendship of the person who had given them my name. As a precaution, I arranged on my desk an open copy of *Playboy* magazine, vol. 2 of the paperback edition of *Lolita* just obtained from Paris, which I was reading, and a colour photo of a mandrill's rear end. When the Society's secretary arrived, he did not attract me. He had shifty eyes, did not appear to look either at me or the material on my desk, but gave me the impression of being more interested in what he could see of the obscenities of Soho outside our windows. However, some of the names of the Society's sponsors to be printed on the letterheading were known to me and respected, and we produced his letterheading. I doubt if it won any prizes. We certainly didn't charge for it; we had already had our quiet fun.

Jobs came to us in various ways – and were also lost in various ways. After Vivian Ridler had become Printer to Oxford University, he telephoned me one day to ask if I would like to design the journal and literature published by the Women's Institutes of Great Britain. He had been consulted by the Lady President, and had put forward my name. I said yes, of course, thank you. 'Good', Vivian replied, 'she will take us out to lunch, probably at the University Women's Club in Audley Square, do you know it?' I did, because I had been taken there by my wife's Somervillian mother. I remembered it as being spartan and I thought that it did not even have a bar. 'In that case', I said to Vivian, 'will you promise me that we have a gin somewhere beforehand?' – to which he agreed.

When the invitation came, it was to Pruniers in St James's Street, still one of the most luxurious restaurants in London. The last time I had been there was with two parsons of the Church of England.

The lunch party was extremely pleasant. There was at first an empty seat beside me, because our hostess, it was revealed, was about to retire as President of the W.I., and the incoming President was on a train returning from Aberdeen, where she had been on a Royal Commission investigating poisoned meat. I wasn't told who she was. When she arrived, she turned out to be the sister of Janet, the wife of my dear friend Reynolds Stone. She was also extremely beautiful. We got on very well. I was made welcome as the new designer for the National Federation of Women's Institutes. Many congratulations. The first job I had to tackle was their Annual Report for 1964.

It was also the last. The third lady at the lunch was the lady who actually ran their office and publications. I went back to her office with her and soon realized that no way was she going to have me interfering with her routines. If I insisted, she would resign, and that would make far too much trouble for the President and everybody else concerned. I did design the Annual Report, with a cover bearing a wood-engraving by Reynolds Stone and printed in pink, pale terra cotta, and black. It looked good. End, as far as I was concerned, of story.

Then there was *Punch*. I had known and loved *Punch* all my life. Its back numbers had been an essential part of my childhood. I could recognize the work of, and usually name, nearly every artist who had drawn for it since I had begun reading it in the 1920s. *Punch* had even once accepted an article by me and reprinted it (without additional fee or telling me) in *The Pick of Punch*. Now, *Punch* had been bought by United Newspapers, owners of the prestigious *Yorkshire Post*, and had appointed a new editor to succeed Malcolm Muggeridge, who, it was well known, had lost interest in it and never saw what was in the paper until a printed copy arrived on his desk.

I was asked by the management (important point: not by the editor) to advise on its design. This was the assignment, I thought, to which my whole career had been leading. I should have known better.

I was taken out to lunch by the editor, the assistant editor, the deputy assistant editor, the art editor, and the assistant art editor. It was hilarious and very expensive. I was put on the payroll and invited to join the Monday morning planning meetings, presided over by the editor, who slept, leaving it to Alan Coren and Miles Kington, sitting at opposite ends of the room, to spark each other off: it was like the Goon show. I even attended a Round Table lunch, at which the guest of honour was the Prime Minister, Harold Wilson himself. He was a great humorist in

Lettering designed by the author for Hulton Press office in Fleet Street. Reproduced in
Nicolete Gray's *Lettering on Buildings*, 1960.

his own right. But no way did the editor want anything from me. The
sales of *Punch* appeared at last to be going up. I prepared layouts, and
made a new design (of which I was inordinately proud) for a new title
logo. I wonder where they are now. A pity I couldn't follow Robert Harling's advice (to design a magazine, you have to become the editor). My
time with *Punch* ended, and so, a bit later, did *Punch*.

The famous magazines make news, and sometimes the fortunes of
designers. But there are many other magazines which exist for specialized
publics, all reflecting human needs and passions. In a list published by
one of the Press Guides I found no fewer than fifty whose titles ended in
the word 'world' – for example, *Bee World*, *Cordage World*, *Dog World*, *Hockey
World*, *Psychic World*, *Woman's World*, and *Yachting World*. Among other
intriguing titles I found *The Abstainer*, *Accordian Digest*, *The Anti-Slavery
Reporter and Aborigine's Friend*, *Band of Hope Chronicle*, *The Bartender*, *Brass Band
News*, *British Journal of Inebriety*, *Cheap Steam*, *Fish Friers Review*, *Leprosy Review*,
Pig Breeders Gazette, *Poor Souls Friend and St Joseph's Monitor*, *Sewage Purification*,
Vegetarian Messenger, and *Woman's Hockey Field*, to name but a few. Where are
they all now? How many of them ever employed designers?

16. Jan Tschichold

WHEN he left Penguins in 1949, Jan Tschichold returned to Switzerland, but we kept in touch, and saw him and Edith on their occasional visits to London. No English translation of any of his books had yet appeared; I had translated his little book on how to draw layouts, *Typografische Entwurfstechnik*, 1932, of only 24 pages, because I thought it so useful, but had never found a publisher for it. (It was eventually published as *How to Draw Layouts* in a limited edition of 150 copies by Merchiston Publishing, of Napier University in Edinburgh, in 1991.) Now he asked me to translate his *Typographische Gestaltung* (Typographic Design) which had been published in Basle in 1935. It was a more measured and persuasive account of his views than his first and epoch-making *Die neue Typographie* of 1928. This proposed new translation was to be really a new edition: Jan wanted to omit some passages which he considered had been of interest only to Swiss and German readers, and he had also found several new and better illustrations. We called the new version *Asymmetric Typography*, and it was published, i.e. financed, not by a conventional publisher, but by a highly intelligent firm of typesetters in Toronto called Cooper & Beatty. The distribution was done in Britain by Faber & Faber, and in USA by Reinhold. One of the Cooper & Beatty directors, W.E. Trevitt, wrote a short introduction in which he said of Tschichold 'He fascinates us. His seeming rejection of the ideas put forward in this present book caused a turbulence among designers that has yet to settle. How *could* he? And how *could* he then do those classical solutions so maddeningly well?... Among the campfires of typographers *Typographische Gestaltung* has become the great underground book of the century.' His introduction ended 'If you are asking yourself why it took four years to reach publication date, then you are obviously neither a practising typographer nor an expert in transoceanic correspondence. I now happen to be both for which I will remain eternally grateful.' The book was published in 1967, and we were eternally grateful to Cooper & Beatty. It was the first ever of Jan Tschichold's books to be published in English, and the only one until the 1990s.

Our next collaboration was a translation of *Die neue Typographie*, 1928. Jan decided that it too should be planned for contemporary use; there

Jan Tschichold at Penguin Books, 1948.

were pages that had no usefulness for modern English readers, he could find some better illustrations, and there were certain statements which he now found were wrong or needed modifying. He left them in but wrote comments in English on them to be printed as footnotes, such as 'What a mistake!' or 'Here, the baby is thrown out with the bath water!'

For me, the translation had to be done in the evenings whenever I could find the time. It was quite a labour. My friend the poster artist Hans Unger gave me enormous help by making rough translations which I could put into better English. At last it was finished, but then Jan could find no publisher interested. Eventually, after Jan's death in 1974, I placed my typewritten translation in the St Bride Printing Library in London where any student could look at it. But Jan's reputation was growing all the time, especially in the United States. At last the University of California Press decided that it was time to publish a translation of this famous book, of which a new facsimile edition had been published in Berlin in 1987. California, however, decided that they should publish it as an exact and complete translation of the original text; not the new edition Jan had had in mind, but as a work of historical scholarship. This meant that I had to make a virtually new translation, word for word, but we included Jan's priceless comments on himself as notes. *The New Typography* was published in 1995.

In 1970 the City of Leipzig invited Jan to address their prestigious printing conference in May 1971, and for some reason I was also invited, not to speak, but as an 'Ehrengast' (honoured guest), which meant that I was given expenses and a visa. As Tony and I had just bought a new car, and Jan and Edith had no car, we offered to drive them to Leipzig, which they gladly accepted. We drove across Europe to Berzona where Jan and Edith now lived, in a house previously reserved for their holidays. It had a small but beautiful garden, terraced on the mountainside looking south to Locarno. The road to Berzona consisted mostly of hairpin bends, so that during the day there tended to be a continuous music of motor-car horns coming up from below. We stayed in a guest apartment above the garage; in the house itself, Jan had three different studies to work in, each, I believe, with a bottle of sherry tucked away somewhere as Edith did not allow him to drink very often. After a few days we set out for Leipzig. It was something of an adventure for Jan to go back to where he had been born, now in Russian-controlled East Germany – the first time he had been back since leaving his country before the war. It was also our first visit to behind the 'iron curtain'. It did not help when

Antonia McLean with Jan and Edith Tschichold, on the way to Leipzig, 1971. (Photo by the author.)

I discovered, as we were approaching Leipzig in trepidation, that I had left my visa in London. Jan remained calm: he smiled and said, 'That will be interesting'. In fact all that happened was a long delay while endless telephone calls were made, and I had to pay for another visa.

Apart from listening to Jan's talk, and looking at the exhibition of book design, I had nothing to do at the conference. Tony and I made several visits to Bach's St Thomas Kirche, where on each occasion we listened to Bach being played on the organ, to an empty church, and there was a fresh bunch of flowers each day on his gravestone. On another day we drove along the Elbe to Dresden: a hundred miles of beautiful country, not unlike the Thames Valley in England, and not a single café or wine bar or restaurant open along the whole route. Dresden had been scrupulously rebuilt after the bombing, and the only restaurant we could find was like a giant Lyons, full of Russian soldiers on leave, both in and out of uniform. It was not enjoyable. But on the way back we visited Meissen, which seemed to be undamaged and unchanged, and found in the cathedral three gravestones in black slate engraved by Albrecht Dürer, which we had not known existed.

We left Jan and Edith in Leipzig – he found relatives still alive and well – and drove homewards. It was only when we had left East Germany that we began to see examples of 'civilisation' that we had been missing: for example, it was a pleasant shock to see a shop selling deck-chairs and garden tools. Nothing like that in Leipzig. And we began to realize that all the time we had been in East Germany we had seen no men of middle age, only very young or very old. Buses, shops, museums and offices were all run by women. Where were the men?

I never saw Jan Tschichold again. We corresponded, and he knew that I was working on an introductory book about his work. He gave me material and help on this, and it was published in 1975; but Jan never saw it, for he died of cancer in Locarno Hospital in August 1974. I later wrote a second short account of Tschichold's work, *Jan Tschichold: a Life in Typography,* which was published by Lund Humphries in 1997, containing new illustrations, and translations of many of his ideas.

Jan Tschichold was single-minded in his devotion to the truths about design as he saw them, and a man of absolute integrity.

Jan Tschichold's *Ex Libris, c.* 1925,
in black and red, actual size.

17. 'Every tenth drink'

I settled into a swivelling armchair in the parlour car as the train moved out of Boston, and watched the scenery slide past: first fields and woods in deep snow and bright sunshine, and then along the coast, past estuaries and marshes and deserted shoreline and shacks and cabins on stilts with boats beneath.

A black conductor walked solicitously up and down the empty coach, and when I asked, about twelve noon, if I could have a drink, he replied, 'Sho, sah, and every tenth drink is on da house'.

I only got up to two, but I felt marvellous sipping them and watching sea and snow and sunshine slipping past.

No one ever goes by train from Boston to New York if they can fly; but Boston airport was closed by the heavy snow, and I had to lecture in New York that evening, so I was booked into a parlour car and enjoyed the only period of four hours complete rest and relaxation on my entire trip.

New York's fantastic skyline came into view at 2:30. At Gallery 303, where I had to lecture, my host Doc Leslie kissed me on both cheeks: he had never thought I would get there. Within minutes I was loading my slides in the carousel.

The trip had begun in Toronto. In 1967 I was asked to lecture on Victorian colour printing to the Friends of the Osborne Collection of Early Children's Books, housed in Boys and Girls House in Toronto Public Libraries. In order to make the trip financially possible (as opposed to actually profitable) I had to ask friends to organize a series of lectures whose fees might possibly add up to something like my main expenses. This resulted in a programme of three talks in Toronto, two in Boston, two in New York, and one each in Charlottesville, Yale, and Princeton. I prepared three different talks and took 215 slides, mostly of nineteenth-century colour printing never before put on slide. As I had just become Hon. Typographic Advisor to Her Majesty's Stationery Office in London, I also arranged a visit to Washington, armed with a letter of introduction from the Controller of the Stationery Office, to see how they did things in the Government Printing Office in America.

The Osborne Collection is housed in a well-designed modern building with glass-fronted shelves and display cases all round a large room where serious students can work. Next door is a normal Public Library for children, in which they come and go freely in hordes. After being shown around, I joined a tea-party at which I was introduced to a professor of Sanskrit, wearing a kilt, who said he had picnicked with me in Oxfordshire when we were both ten; also some Toronto publishers and Miss Sybille Pantazzi, a high-pressure talker of mixed Romanian and Scottish parentage, who collected Victorian books and with whom I was already corresponding.

The occasion at which I had to talk, the next evening, was the first Annual Meeting of the Friends of the Osborne Collection. It therefore began with protracted official business, through which I had to sit, on the platform, metaphorically biting my nails. It was presided over by a lady who was so funny that I soon relaxed. She walked with a steel crutch, but was hilarious and courageous. When the evening ended she refused to be seen home with the words, 'I'm not young, or beautiful, or rich, so I'm safe!'

My second talk in Toronto was to students in the Ontario College of Art. The third was to a combined meeting of three Toronto societies interested in printing. It was a social occasion attended by gentlemen and their wives, who had come through a blizzard of snow to enjoy themselves whatever the entertainment provided by the speaker. My last slides showed a story called 'The Dog's Dinner Party' (c. 1870) which ends with the disgraceful behaviour of Mr Bulldog, and the words, 'Poor Mrs Blenheim! She was, indeed, much to be pitied, to have her nice dinner party spoiled by so vulgar a creature. This shows how careful we should always be in avoiding low company'. A lady came up afterwards with tears in her eyes: where could she get a copy of that Toy Book, which she had not seen since she was a girl?

I had always been nervous of speaking in public, but in Canada and the States everyone was so friendly that it began to come naturally. I was taken to lunch in the Arts and Letters Club and introduced to a group of elderly clubmen. We discussed Oscar Wilde, Max Beerbohm, the Arts Club in London, and the Charles Rennie Mackintosh exhibition then in Toronto which I never got to see. About thirty people sat down to lunch. In between courses my host asked me to stand up and say a few words. This would have paralysed me in London, but I knew that no one cared in the least what I said; I only had to smile, look relaxed, and be friendly. I ended my few words by instancing, as a hazard of being a freelance designer, the fact that one of my best clients, Shell Chemicals, had just been taken over by themselves (i.e. by Shell Chemicals International) so I had lost them. When I sat down, I found that the man sitting on my right was the head of Shell in Canada. 'Yes, that's typical' he sighed.

From Toronto I flew to Boston, where I stayed with Rollo and Alice Silver. Rollo had made money in the tobacco business and had become a notable collector of Walt Whitman, and now taught bibliography in Simmonds University. They had a beautiful old house in Mount Vernon Street, full of books, no children, no servants, and a kitchen in which neither of them ever cooked.

Rollo wanted to give me 'the best meal in Boston' and took me to Locke-Ober's, to prove that it was not as good as Rules in Covent Garden, to which I had taken him on his last visit to London. Of course, I could not agree.

My first Boston lecture was another social affair, preceded by a dinner without alcohol, because that is against the (Methodist) University rules. After the lecture, suffering from nervous exhaustion and a dry throat, I never succeeded in getting anywhere near the buns and coffee. I had to chat to kind Bostonians, and remembered my old typographer friend John Lewis's dictum that après-lecture is more tiring than après-ski. He himself, in America, had once stood for two hours answering questions after giving a lecture, and had then fainted.

I was taken to lunch at the Club of Odd Volumes, to hear Samuel Eliot Morison. During the war the U. S. Navy had appointed Morison to write the history of its naval operations while they were actually happening and to take part in as many of them as he could. By the end of the war he had served in eleven different ships and become a Captain with seven battle stars on his service ribbons. His series of fourteen volumes were extremely good reading and remarkable for the fact that from time to time they contained pungent criticism of senior U.S. naval officers. He arrived late, a massive white-haired figure, spoke after lunch briefly about his recent visit to Tokyo while researching on Commodore Parry, and made an immediate getaway afterwards.

The most important new friend I made on this visit to Boston was Dorothy Abbe, the friend and colleague of W. A. Dwiggins, who had died in 1956. I had been corresponding with Dorothy about Dwiggins' work as typographer and illustrator for seven or eight years but had never yet met her. She was a trim, smart, sweet-looking woman, looking 50, but I was told she was 60. On Sunday she drove me in a large and fast grey Buick to the sea coast at Cohasset, to a restaurant where we waited for a very long time for martinis, only to be told that we couldn't have them until the church came out. After a lunch of lobster platter, ice cream, and coffee, we drove to Hingham to see the studio Dwiggins had himself built in his garden.

His workroom was upstairs, with a puppet theatre seating thirty or forty people downstairs. Dorothy told me that when Dwiggins died, she had seriously thought of setting fire to the whole place and throwing herself on the flames. But she converted the theatre into a large sitting-room, with all his books, and closets, bathroom, kitchen, and a work-shop with a power-operated printing platen and photographic enlarging equipment. She had a bedroom upstairs next door to his workroom. Since his death, she told me, she had nothing to do in the evenings so she decided to go to bed early and get up every morning at 3am and work for twelve hours a day on a book about the marionettes and the theatre Dwiggins had made. Already a professional typographer, she now taught herself to become a fine photographer.

In 1964 she had written, 'It is now a long while since those first days when, as one of the family, I could, at will, open the "cage" back of the miniature stage not only to look at, but actually to handle, the delicate little creatures that hung there – the marionettes that Bill had so lovingly contrived in the "spare time" of a dozen years ago. Even now, I cannot forget the emotion which filled me then as I first perceived the beauty, skill, and imagination with which they were made ... As I observed everything in place, just as it had been left after the last rehearsal; as I heard of the delight of working with Bill from those who were the puppeteers, it was a sorrow to me that all of this happy activity should disappear without any record. And besides, I delighted in various mechanical devices, not only for their efficiency, but especially for their beauty of construction. These needed to be pointed out, for they were not intended to be seen.

And so, I thought, I shall take a few photographs, and make a small book...'

But the material proved to be so rich that the 'small book became very large, and the edition very small' – in fact, five volumes, in an edition of four copies, printed from hand-set type, with black-and-white photographs mounted on the pages, and the colour photographs incorporated as transparencies. She had worked on it over a period of ten years and made the record she felt was needed. Then the New York publisher Harry N. Abrams saw one of the four copies and was inspired to have Dorothy turn it into a printed book, which was published by Abrams in 1970.

Dorothy professed to be disappointed in the commercial printing of her book; but by the highest standards it is a very remarkable achievement. It is a large book (350 × 275 mm and 30 mm thick) devoted to showing the Dwiggins marionettes (which are beautiful in themselves), how they were made, how they and the theatre were operated, including details of the mechanical devices all made by Dwiggins, (sometimes helped by friends like the well-known engraver Rudolph Ruzicka), with examples of the accompanying Dwiggins typography, and illustrating the settings, works of art in themselves. I was lucky enough to be given a copy, and I have always thought it was one of the most beautifully designed and illustrated books of the twentieth century.

The proscenium of the theatre, painted by Dwiggins, the marionettes, a collection of all the books designed by Dwiggins and his worktable, with the tools on it which he made himself, are all now, thanks to Dorothy, housed in two rooms in Boston Public Library. Dorothy also made a collection of Dwiggins' books for England, and asked me where they should go. We sent the books concerned with typography to the St Bride Printing Library off Fleet Street, and the illustrated works to the Victoria & Albert Museum Library.

My last visit in Boston was to meet the 'Lowell House hand printers', a group of eight or nine undergraduates who were setting type and pulling proofs on a hand press under the supervision of a craftsman. It was embarrassing to find that they knew nothing about typography, did not want criticism, had never heard of Dwiggins, and knew only Updike the novelist (as opposed to the famous Boston printer D. B. Updike).

I stayed for my last few days in New York with Jim and Maria Barnett, who became, with Harold Hugo, the people I got to love most in America. Jim was Harold's representative in New York; Maria, an expert print-colourer, had been previously married to Herbert Bittner, the German New York publisher and friend of George Grosz, the great anti-Nazi caricaturist. Bittner had published a book of Grosz's drawings when Grosz was in New York during the war, but the savagery with which Grosz drew the horrors he had watched in Nazi Germany disappeared from his work in America.

Jim took me book-hunting among the secondhand bookshops on

Opposite: Title-page opening for *Kim*, Limited Editions Club of New York, 1962. The illustration by Robin Jacques printed in full colour, the title lettering, drawn by the author, printed in red. Reduced from 255 × 180mm.

KIM

By Rudyard Kipling

With an Introduction by
Charles Edmund Carrington
and Illustrations by
Robin Jacques

New York
For the Members of
The Limited Editions Club
1962

Harold Hugo in the Meriden Gravure printing office, Meriden, Connecticut (1970s).

Fourth Avenue, and took the precaution of not shaving (which made him look like a hobo) in order to keep the prices down. In fact I don't remember buying anything except a few martinis. Jim told me how he had joined the Meriden Gravure Company. A job there was advertised as assistant to the New York salesman, for which Jim, with no experience of printing or any other work, applied. There was one other

162

applicant, who did have printing experience. When Parker Allen, the owner of the firm, was asked which one he'd take on, he replied, 'We don't know much about printing ourselves. Pick the one who knows nothing, the other might come and try to teach me how to run the place'. That was Jim's first job, and he stayed with Meriden until his retirement.

I had a few typographic jobs for American clients. It may be asked, what could I do that American designers couldn't do? The answer was of course nothing – but three things no doubt helped. First, it sounds good to go to an expert in another country. Second, it provided an excuse for the client to have a trip to England; and third, there was so much more money to be made in advertising that very few American designers were bothering with books. So I had several books to design for the Limited Editions Club of New York and the Imprint Society of Barre, Massachusetts; and through a friend I was asked to design the annual calendar/prospectus for Bryn Mawr College, and was briefed in New York by the lady who edited it.

Kim, which I was asked to design for the Limited Editions Club, was another interesting experience. I was not asked to choose the illustrator, and when I heard it was to be Robin Jacques in London (whom I very much admired) and that Robin had never been in India, I was horrified. I myself had been in India for a year and a half during the war and to attempt to illustrate *Kim* without having been in India seemed to me ludicrous. Robin's illustrations, in colour and black-and-white are I suppose the best illustrations for *Kim* that have ever been made or ever will be made.

After all, actresses who play Lady Macbeth do not have to have committed murder.

After New York, Washington. The Public Printer (head of the Government Printing Office) was a political appointment, it had to be remembered. I was first welcomed by the Head of Design. When he took me to his office and I saw an enormous desk without a single piece of paper on it, I knew that he never did any design. He was, however, charming. He had once, I think, been a designer, but design was not a serious function in the Government Printing Office, much to the chagrin of the American designers I knew, and who greatly envied the excellent graphic design in our Stationery Office. The Head of Design conducted me to shake hands with the Government Printer. I still remember a very large room, with at one end of it a desk and above it the Stars and Stripes, with a man curled up underneath listening on the radio to a football match. He too made me welcome, and explained that if someone brought in, one evening, a book the length of *Gone with the Wind*, a million copies could be printed and bound in that building during the night and delivered the next day. The whole place existed to get Government printing done very fast indeed and at rock bottom prices. There was a virtual embargo, I was told, on any colour printing in the G.P.O., in case of accusations of extravagance. Any printing in more than two colours had to be put out to outside firms. As a result, colour was hardly used at all in government leaflets or booklets, which increased their drabness. Design (I was naturally interested to observe) was something they neither knew nor cared much about. It was very different from the Stationery Office in London.

I had to give two more lectures and then retired to rest, exhausted and without a voice, in the care of Harold Hugo in Meriden, Connecticut. I collected letters from home ('Dear Daddy, I'm sorry I haven't written before, I keep forgetting'), and wandered peacefully through the rooms of the Press talking to Parker Allen, Johnny Peckham, and Harold. When I returned to London, the first thing I had to do was to make a 'Martini Map of London' showing Harold, on his next visit, where he could get a decent dry Martini, not weak and not warm. The second was to write a large number of letters saying thank you.

18. Nelson's Prayer, and some other clients

ONE sunny morning, sitting in my office in London, I suddenly thought that I would like to have, framed and hanging above my desk, a photograph of Nelson's prayer before Trafalgar. I had just been reading Carola Oman's 750-page *Nelson*, but it was not illustrated there, nor could I find it shown in any other book. Strange.

I looked up the prayer as quoted by Oman, found a British Museum reference, and wrote to the BM asking for a photograph. In a few days it arrived, but the prayer was not in Nelson's hand: Oman had not quoted from the original manuscript. So I made an appointment to see the Keeper of Manuscripts in the BM, and a few days later went in to see him.

I was greeted in the Department of Manuscripts by a British Museum warder, a short stoutish man in the regulation blue uniform, but wearing the three ribbons of the First World War preceded by the CBE ('Commander of the British Empire'), obviously awarded, I thought, for long service in the Museum. He told me that I would have to wait for a few minutes as the keeper on duty was engaged, but could he help me? I showed him the photo of the prayer and he immediately said, 'Oh, no, that's not Nelson's handwriting, is it!' He turned to an adjacent case, pulled back the curtain and showed me a collection of Nelson's letters – written of course with his left hand – with which I was in any case already familiar. He gave me a chair, and came back every few minutes to show me other trifles in the room, like Magna Carta and Domesday Book. When I was ushered in to see the keeper, the first thing I had to say was, 'Who is that man?' 'Oh, don't you know, he is a Captain Royal Navy, retired, the President of the Irish Archaeological Society. When he retired from the Navy he wrote to the Director of the Museum asking for a job. The Director wrote back to say he was very sorry, the only job in the whole place was that of a messenger in the Dept of Manuscripts. The Captain was over the next day to ask for it.'

The ribbons he was wearing were obviously only a few of those to which he was entitled. His service had included witnessing the surrender of the Japanese Fleet in Tokyo Bay, on board HMS *King George* V, a fact he mentioned with some hauteur to a Japanese visitor who had tactlessly asked 'And what do those ribbons mean, my man?' His name was Captain Donal Bernard O'Connell, RN, CBE.

The keeper told me that Nelson's last diary, including the prayer, was in fact lodged in Somerset House, and I would have to go there to look at it.

More time, more trouble. But once the chase was started, it must be finished. I went to Somerset House, and learned, for the first time, how to look for a will. It involved looking up catalogues, filling in forms, paying a trifling fee, and then going to a numbered room down a corridor and waiting.

What then happened was again unpredictable. A man arrived and handed me three large volumes, and hurried off. My heart sank. What he had actually brought me, when I looked at the volumes, was the will of every man who died in HMS *Victory* at Trafalgar with Nelson, but not that of Nelson. I sat bemused.

Some time later, a man came in with long white cuffs on his sleeves. I told him what had happened, or rather, not happened. 'Oh, I see. Yes. No, it's not there. I can show you – will you come with me?'

He set off down a corridor, then down several flights of iron staircases just like in an old ship. We ended up in Somerset House's basement, beside a little mahogany cupboard, the kind that stands beside beds. 'Oh, damn, I've left the key behind, so sorry!' he muttered, 'Will you wait here?'

In a few minutes he was back, unlocked the cupboard – which I could now see had three shelves – and brought out a small wooden box marked 'Shakespeare'. 'Just like my office,' I said, 'we'd file Nelson's will in a box marked Shakespeare!' 'Oh dear!' he said, but before he took the box back I said, 'If that contains Shakespeare's will, may I please see it before it goes back?' So he opened it, and I found myself looking at – and touching – a five-page document containing three of the five known (at that time) signatures of William Shakespeare. Fairly awe-inspiring. He then put it back in its box, replaced it, and took out a box marked 'Nelson'. There was the last private diary kept by Lord Nelson, beginning 'Friday night at half past ten drove from dear dear Merton...' and ending with the prayer and a codicil to his will. The prayer itself occupied three pages. 'You know,' said my friend, 'there is a second copy of this in the National Maritime Museum in Greenwich?' I didn't, if for no other reason than that no life of Nelson that I was aware of had ever said so.

Before I left the small cupboard, I asked my guide if Shakespeare and Nelson were the only Englishmen who rated a box to themselves. It was an assessment with which I agreed. What was in the cardboard box? He kindly opened it, and for a few minutes we looked at the wills of the hoi polloi, such as Sir Francis Drake, Sir Thomas Bodley, Handel, the Duke of Wellington, William Penn, Shelley, and Thomas Hardy, lying heaped together like the Autumnal leaves in Vallombrosa. I refrained from asking what was in the paper bag.

For the only two wills of Englishmen preserved in Somerset House in their own named boxes to be those of Shakespeare and Nelson was a pleasing discovery.

At that time one of my friends was Oliver Warner, who had been my editor for the very first work I had ever been commissioned to write, a booklet on *Modern Book Design* for the British Council, in 1951. Oliver was now a leading authority on Nelson. It was news to him too that Nelson had written his Prayer out twice, with the enemy fleet in view before Trafalgar. I took him to look at the document in Somerset House, and we then went to the Maritime Museum and looked at their copy and had proper photographs made of each manuscript. A comparison made it quite clear that neither was a 'mechanical' copy. Each must have been written separately, but they were identical in wording and in Nelson's erratic use of capitals and punctuation.

Since apparently no facsimile of the diary and prayer existed, we decided to make one. Oliver agreed to edit it. There were 36 pages, and a transcription was necessary: every published text of the prayer, for example, had been given capitals and punctuation that were not in what Nelson himself had written, and in the diary even some words could be deciphered in different ways.

When I got Oliver's edited transcript and found that in one or two cases I did not agree with his decipherment, I had no compunction in altering it to what my eyes told me I could see. Oliver wrote an erudite introduction and was able to contribute, for the frontispiece, a portrait of Nelson by Friedrich Heinrich Füger which had never before been reproduced. He also most generously dedicated the book to me.

There was one final coincidence. In 1917, Gilbert Hudson, better known as an elocutionist, had printed his own transcript of the diary with an introduction and notes – a little book that had been long out of print and was now scarce. While our book was in proof, Oliver found a copy of Hudson's book in a secondhand bookshop with corrections, in Hudson's own hand, for a second edition which had never appeared. The corrections appear as a postscript on p. 80 of our book.

It was published in 1971 by Seeley, Service & Co. in London and the Kent State University Press in Ohio. I don't think anyone noticed. The three photographs which make up the prayer are still in an envelope. I must find a framer.

I had already designed several books for the Kent State University Press. I had visited them in 1970 and lunched at the Country Club with the publishing board of the University. At this lunch there was a discussion between members of the board that became so heated that I thought they might actually come to blows: it was about youth, the police, and so on. The tragic shootings on Kent State University campus occurred the very next day.

I had spent my summer holiday in 1968 reading a new life of Keats by Robert Gittings, and then the equally absorbing earlier biographies by two Americans, Aileen Ward and W. J. Bate. I wanted to see the five great Odes in Keats' own handwriting. I asked Robert Gittings if they had ever been produced in a book. He said no, and it would be worth doing, and what was more, it would fit in well with his immediate programme. He would set about it. The Ode to a Nightingale was in the Fitzwilliam in Cambridge; the Grecian Urn manuscript was the only one that had disappeared, but the earliest copy, in the hand of Keats' brother George, was in the British Museum; the Ode to Psyche was in the Pierpont Morgan Library in New York; and of the Ode to Melancholy, the first two stanzas were in Princeton in the collection of Robert H. Taylor (where as it happened I had already seen them), but the third and last stanza, on a separate sheet, had been sold by Sothebys in 1932 and had disappeared. In due course Robert found this missing stanza was safe and sound in the Berg Collection in the New York Public Library, a fact hitherto apparently unrecorded until by us.

The Odes of Keats and their Manuscripts, edited by Robert Gittings, was published in 1970 by Heinemann Educational Books in London and by Kent State in the USA. I had the text printed in London by the Curwen Press, and the plates of Keats' manuscripts by Meriden, in Connecticut, in 300-line screen offset. When I got the bill from Meriden, it was the first – and so far, the only – time I have ever seen a printer's invoice that was lower than his estimate.

In 1963 the University of Newcastle was founded, having separated from the University of Durham. The Vice-Chancellor, C. I. C. Bosanquet, employed a leading firm of public relations consultants to advise on the opening. One of the firm's executives, Harry Bawden, told the Vice-Chancellor that the university must employ a designer for its prospectuses and literature, and recommended me. We had already worked together on two occasions. The Vice-Chancellor said there wasn't time, they would need the prospectuses in a few weeks. Harry said it's now or never, and you must. At that moment I was on holiday on the Island of Mull. The requirements were read out to me on the telephone. It was agreed that the prospectuses of the new university should be in A5 size and the design simple. Pencil layouts went off to them in the next post. They were approved, Fianach in London organized the production, and they got their prospectuses on time.

After that, I was allowed to call myself Typographical Adviser to the University of Newcastle, and for many years we designed and produced every prospectus, faculty booklet, inaugural lecture and other literature for the university. Publications were supervised, in theory, by a committee of professors, at least half of whom did not agree with having a typographical adviser. I was never allowed a retainer, which would have saved them money and been more convenient for my office: every job had to be invoiced separately. It was, however, fun to get to know some lively people and also the City of Newcastle, where two of my favourite artists, Thomas Bewick and Joseph Crawhall, had been born.

As our freelance practice was increasing and James Shand's interest in *Motif* decreased, Fianach and I and Slocum decided to move out of the Shenval Press offices and the doubtful joys of Soho. We needed more room, and we found it in four rooms on the fourth floor of a house in Villiers Street, which runs from Charing Cross station down to the River Thames embankment.

Typography for book and magazine publishers is exacting work, requiring attention to every kind of minute detail; it was never, in itself, particularly well paid. Advertising paid better, but was not my field. Fianach, now my partner, had no art school training, but had shown herself to be a born 'art director'. A creative designer must be able to think of at least ten solutions to every problem, but it is a different gift, which even brilliant designers often don't have, to know which is the right solution in given circumstances. Fianach had this gift. She was an ideal partner.

We found we were working more and more for people like universities, foundations, and professional bodies who required to publish, but for whom it would not make financial sense to set up their own publishing office and pay the necessary full-time salaries. It was far cheaper to employ people like us, and, we ventured to think, they got a better result. And whereas it would have been difficult for us to survive on design fees alone, which in this field were not high, we also undertook the task of print production and charged a percentage on the total cost. We obtained estimates from suitable printers, discussed them with the client, selected the most sensible (not always the cheapest), placed the order, corrected proofs, checked deliveries, paid the bills, and invoiced the client. Our clients, publishers in practice but not by profession, included the Nuffield Foundation, the Gulbenkian Foundation, the Science Research Council, the Ray Society, and other important bodies already mentioned.

Clients who knew what they wanted were best. If, knowing what they wanted they also told me *how* to do my work, they were less loved. It was, for example, a privilege to design the 'Cadet' edition of the Hornblower novels for Michael Joseph Ltd; but when the books were delivered and I found that my typographic instructions had been altered without consulting me (by Joseph's Managing Director, Bob Lusty) I could not believe it. Norah Smallwood, the Managing Director of Chatto & Windus, was a friend for years: a charming and beautiful lady whom I loved whatever she did. But she was hell to work for. She so loved typography that she hired typographers, and was then unable to resist teaching them what to do, often after they had finished – which was perhaps why I had avoided working for her. Her partner, Ian Parsons, was as generous as Norah, but more gentle. He and I were walking one evening toward the car park, after a Double Crown Club dinner at Kettners, shortly after our move to Villiers Street, which was a stone's throw away from the Chatto offices in William IV Street. Realizing that we needed at that moment all the work we could get, Ian in his generosity said that it was a long time since I had designed anything for them, and he had a book that was just the job; would I like to tackle it? He would send the typescript down to our office immediately. It was, he said, all about lemmings. I was grateful.

The typescript never arrived. After various phone calls, I walked to his office, picked it up from the floor beside his desk, and took it away without his blessing. I was intrigued to think that this powerful man, co-head of a thriving business, could not organize a small packet of paper to be moved from Place A to Place B, five minutes distant.

When I looked at the book, I think I understood why. It was by quite a long way the most boring book I had ever read. It contained far, far more about lemmings than even lemming-lovers could want to know. I think that in his heart, Ian was ashamed of offering it to me. I think he felt exactly the same way about it as I did. It is the only book I have ever designed of which I did not want to keep a copy when it was printed.

We now called ourselves 'Ruari McLean Associates'. In Villiers Street the Player's Theatre (the only theatre in London where you could take a glass of beer to your seat) was nearly opposite us, and Kipling's first home in London was a few doors down. Next door we had an Angus Steak House carpeted in Stewart tartan and wallpapered with, surprisingly, a photographic panorama of fine bookbindings. A few months after we had got used to all this, it became a Kentucky Deep South Fried Chicken Restaurant, but the face-lift went only as far as the front room: beyond that, the tartan carpet and the books remained.

In Frith Street we had taken on a young designer to help with menial jobs, recommended to us by no less a person than Ashley Havinden, then the leading graphic designer in London. I soon understood why. In everything our young designer did there was a mistake, sometimes a crucial one. He was not careless: I think he was trying to prove, probably to himself as much as to us, that he was really an artist, not a typographer. He had to depart. We then got a prize-winning student from one of the leading art schools. The trouble with him was that he resented working for other people, and tried to do everything his way, not ours. He too departed. Now we had Terence Ridley-Ellis, a calm, easy-going young man, gifted as a designer but content to do what he was asked and get on with it. We liked him very much. We also now had a secretary, Anne, who, I discovered, was the daughter of an old friend at Penguins. She was married to John Porter, an architect who should have been a typographer (he was an authority on Victorian publishing) who became one of my closest friends.

Our corgi dog, Slocum, belonging to Fianach, became an endearing companion, but he tended to be nervous of sudden noises. A bottle of champagne opened in his presence had caused a torrent of barking, and from that moment, any bottle was assumed to be a provocation, and made him bark. He also barked at men who came to see us wearing hats. He usually lay on the floor between my desk and Fianach's; I once trod on him when getting up, and he bit me. 'Poor Slocum, he's bitten Ruari!' was Fianach's only comment.

Fianach's grandfather had been Sir Harry Peat, senior partner in Peat, Marwick & Mitchell, Chartered Accountants. We were apprised that the Institute of Chartered Accountants in England and Wales had at last realized that they needed a designer; they were publishers in a big way, since every change in any law affecting fiscal matters had to be communicated and explained to their thousands of members; in addition, all training and examinations for chartered accountancy in

England and Wales was administered by them. The first thing they required was a new letterheading, and we were invited to submit proposals. It also became known that we were not the only designers involved: a firm of printers had been invited, and also, as might have been guessed, the niece of one of the partners.

To design a new letterheading was not at all difficult, but Fianach, with some knowledge of the Institute, said that the quality of the design would be irrelevant; what would sway the committee of chartered accountants would be the degree of finish. We decided to swamp the opposition. I drew twelve different designs, some in traditional centred style, some asymmetrical (which for business headings may be more practical). Having made the designs, we had them all drawn by a calligrapher in exquisite penmanship. They predictably chose the worst of my designs and we got the job. It kept us gainfully employed for some years, and design was only a small part of what we did for them. The main part of the work was to obtain estimates from printers, take responsibility for corrections, alterations, and delivery dates, and look after all the normal production office work, which we could certainly do more efficiently than they could.

We also designed and produced the official History of the Institute. It had been written by a tall, charming, and highly distinguished gentleman with a DSO and MC, Sir Harold Howitt, who had lately retired from being senior partner of Peat, Marwick. He had been captured by the Germans in Flanders in 1915, and escaped. He had then become a prototype for John Buchan's Richard Hannay. I would much rather have read his autobiography, if he had written that.

After we had been working for the Institute for three years, the committee decided that their printers, to whom we had introduced them, could now follow the styles we had laid down, and there was no further need to employ us. We were fired.

Jobs came and went. A pleasant surprise came when in the early 1970s my old friend and contemporary, Richard Blackwell, now Chairman of Blackwells in Oxford, decided to revive the former glories of the Shakespeare Head Press as a publisher of fine books, and asked the antiquarian bookseller Colin Franklin and me to join a new board of directors. Colin lived near Oxford, and had previously been a director of the publishing firm of Routledge, which his family owned.

We had a series of lunches at Richard's favourite French restaurant in Oxford and discussed a publishing programme. Richard's father, known as 'The Gaffer', and now eighty-five, was usually present at these lunches, appearing to be asleep but every now and then sitting up and asking a pertinent question. We published only two books: *Frank Sidgewick's Diary, and other material relating to A. H. Bullen and the Shakespeare Head Press*, an act of piety which I suppose sold very few copies; and a more lavish affair, an edition of Max Beerbohm's *Zuleika Dobson* with reproductions in colour of the twelve paintings by Osbert Lancaster (illustrating *Zuleika*) hanging in Oxford's Randolph Hotel. The book also included collotype reproductions of five drawings by Beerbohm of the story's characters, made as friendly guides for Lancaster.

Richard wanted to celebrate publication with a party and re-enactment of the book, with my Fianach acting as Zuleika. Fianach modestly (and wisely) declined. We did have a party, rather riotous, in the Randolph; and Nigel Nicolson, reviewing the book in the *Spectator*, wrote 'To read Zuleika in this edition is like eating strawberries off gold plate...'

There were plans to follow *Zuleika* with other ambitious projects, but nothing else happened. I was by this time living in Scotland, and could not travel to Oxford unless summoned. I do not know when Richard's illness started, nor did I ever know that he was dying. He had been for me like a brother, and I had for long been treated almost as a member of the Blackwell family. Richard died just after his sixty-second birthday in 1980.

During the 1970s in Villiers Street, our business was expanding, but I was determined to remain small, with a staff not exceeding four. When you get bigger than that, you tend to stop designing and start administering. I didn't want that. I once compared notes with a designer friend and asked him how many clients he had. He replied 'four'. At that time we had around forty. But his four were four of the largest companies in Britain. Ours were nearly all small. One of them was the Australia and New Zealand Bank. We produced their Annual Report for fifteen years, and then were asked to redesign and rationalize their whole enormous range of stationery. They were extremely good people to work for. I bought some shares in the company, and when the company secretary discovered that I was a shareholder, he had me propose the vote of thanks at the annual general meeting and join the lunch afterwards. The bank grew bigger, and was then swallowed up by a bigger bank and became a group. New executives took the places of our friends. Big firms at that time wanted big firms of designers: it would be beneath their dignity to deal with only two or three people. So we lost the job. I doubt if the new group got better service or better design, but they certainly paid a lot more for it.

We had an interesting time with a well-known textile company,

Edinburgh Weavers. Their Managing Director was Alastair Morton, who I used to meet in the London Arts Club. His family were the inventors of Sundour, the first book cloth to be fast to light, and washable. One day Edinburgh Weavers were awarded the Royal Warrant, which gave Alastair a problem. He now had to print the royal arms on his letter heading, where they already had a fine monogram or device, the letters e and w in lower case, designed by Hans Tisdall. Hans was at this time most famous for his masterly series of calligraphic book jackets for Jonathan Cape; he had been a pupil in Germany of Anna Simons, herself a pupil of Edward Johnston. The Edinburgh Weavers symbol was strongly calligraphic and extremely simple. Alastair's designer could not see how to combine it on the letterheading with the royal coat of arms, and to omit the firm's own symbol was unthinkable.

Alastair finally asked me to try. The royal arms were supposed to go at the top, but this did not work. I put the e w symbol at the top and the arms as far away as possible at the foot. The symbol was in black, the address and the arms were in grey. It seemed to work, and Alastair accepted it. From then on we designed most of his literature.

Alastair was a patron of modern art, and bought a lot of paintings with the intention of using them for fabric designs. It was enjoyable to work with him. I believe he was a Quaker, and I certainly thought of him as ascetic, somewhat austere, and possibly a teetotaller. He visited us one day at our fourth-floor offices in Villiers Street, and having climbed all those stairs he was offered a drink. I was astonished when he asked for a vodka-and-brandy. We didn't have either.

When he died, the firm was found to be in some difficulties, and sadly ceased to exist.

A client with whom we often had drinks was E. P. Tuddenham, known to us affectionately as 'Tuddy'. He was actually a psychiatrist, but he came to us because he was acting (in some kind of mysterious freelance capacity) as adviser and production manager for the quarterly house magazine of Schweppes, manufacturers of soda-water, tonic, and other soft drinks. One evening when we had agreed to go together to an art exhibition, I called for him in a taxi. He lived on the top floor of a building in Lincoln's Inn Fields. He endeared himself to me by coming down the stairs with a glass of whisky in his hands. He proceeded to enter the taxi with the whisky, and, when finished, he bestowed the glass on the kindly driver.

The Schweppes house magazine, called *The Marble Archer,* was printed by letterpress on art paper by Delittle, Fenwick & Co. in York, and judging by the amount of colour we were allowed to use, expense was no object. It was a genuine house magazine, as opposed to a glossy public relations magazines designed to impress the world at large: it was designed purely for the people who worked in Schweppes. It was therefore full of unmemorable material; but looking back at the issues we designed, the Summer and Autumn issue in 1959, entitled 'Schweppes in Belgium', had drawings on the cover by Berthold Wolpe and an article which I suppose I must have written about the typefaces Plantin and Albertus which we were using for the magazine. Berthold had just been made 'Royal Designer for Industry' (RDI) and the photo of him inside makes him look so smooth that it is quite unlike him.

Schweppes made only soft drinks. I had always longed for a wine account, and at last one came. The firm was Lovibonds, who had once been brewers in Salisbury and Greenwich, but who now owned a chain of excellent wine shops all over the south-west of England. The chairman and managing director, Tony Lovibond, lived close to us in Blackheath, and a mutual friend introduced us. The friend had told him that his wine list needed redesigning, which it certainly did. Tony Lovibond was not particularly interested in design, but was interested in what it cost. We got our friends at Shenval to estimate for it and found that we could save Lovibonds a considerable sum and pay ourselves a design fee as well, so we got the job.

Tony Lovibond was one of the old school, to whom publishing and the wine trade were the only businesses suitable for a gentleman. He had been given control of the family business too late in life to be a dynamic salesman; in fact the first thing you read in his Christmas wine list was a series of cautions about breaking wine glasses hired from the firm. I persuaded him to change this, and introduced attractive cover drawings by John Griffiths, Robin Jacques, and Leonard Rosoman. I doubt if the sales went up, but the lists certainly looked better. Then we embarked on the design of labels for their wines and their own brand of vodka – which I much enjoyed. I had hoped that we would be paid in wine, but Tony Lovibond did not think this was proper. Then the blow fell. A cut-price war developed in the sale of spirits, which, it now turned out, had for long been subsidizing the price of Lovibond's and other wine merchants' wines. The old-fashioned firm of Lovibonds tottered and was then sold to, of all people, the London Rubber Company, makers of condoms, who wanted their valuable corner-shop sites. The Lovibond cellars, full of valuable wines, were sold, and everyone who drank wine and had any money available rushed in and found bargains. Our tiny share disappeared too quickly.

In the 1960s, a job came to us from John Bell, an old friend in Oxford University Press now working in London, in charge of their general publishing programme.

OUP produced, at that time, many different series (e.g. The World Classics, the Oxford English Novels, the Oxford Standard Authors) all in different formats and typographic styles. They now decided to draw on them all for one same-size series to be called 'Oxford Paperbacks', with a standard outward-looking style for the covers, but keeping where feasible their existing text settings. I was asked to submit a design for the new covers, and a symbol to say 'OUP', I think the first symbol I had ever tried to design. My designs were accepted, and appeared on various books over the next few years. Eventually the new series was abandoned, but while it lasted it did look good. Edward Bawden was commissioned to provide linocut illustrations for twenty titles between 1969 and 1973, making splendid designs, fifteen of which are illustrated in *Edward Bawden: a Book of Cuts*, Scolar Press, 1979.

Through another Blackheath friend and neighbour we began working for a firm of city chartered accountants. Fianach and I built up a cordial working relationship with their office manager, and this led to a new kind of work for us. Chartered accountants, like other professional bodies, were not allowed to advertise themselves, but they were allowed to advertise for staff. One of the partners wrote witty and lively copy, which I was asked to illustrate with funny (I hoped) line drawings, and a series of eye-catching advertisements appeared in the accountancy press. Perhaps as a result of these adverts, the firm expanded; my friend who had been senior partner died, there was a multiple take-over, and they ceased to know us. It had been fun while it lasted.

Bad clients were those who did not know what they wanted; who thought they knew what they wanted, but were completely wrong; who knew what they wanted, but told us something different; who tried to bully; who let us work for them and then told us they were charities and did not expect us to charge; and those rare ones who were downright dishonest and never intended to pay for the work we had done. We met a few in each category.

There was a Scottish MP who when he tried to shout at Fianach down the phone was surprised to get as good as he gave. The Jardine blood was boiling. Another was a distinguished lady whom we much admired. If she had asked us in the first place if we would work for her cause for

Cover design for *Castle Rackrent*, with linocut illustrations by Edward Bawden, printed in brown and black, blue background, reduced from 203mm deep.

nothing, we would have said yes. But she didn't. She was too arrogant. Another was a well-known actor: the job he gave us, a poster for his new play, was fascinating. It was just a pity that he tried not to pay for it . The theatre is glamorous but also an uncertain business, and designers have to be cautious in that exciting environment of make-believe.

There were other clients, neither good nor bad, with whom I failed to deal happily or competently, either through failure in my own temperament, or because I could not get on their wavelength, or, in at least one case, because I could not understand their broken English. That was when a partnership such as I had with Fianach proved its worth; she was nearly always able to cope when I couldn't.

A curious job came to me in 1971. A friend of mine (a contributor to *Motif*) was commissioned to write a history of erotic art, to be fully illustrated. The publisher had decided that the climate of opinion had changed so much that it would now be possible to publish a book on this interesting subject properly illustrated, in a way that would not have been permitted a few years earlier. I had my doubts.

The author had to find collections of erotic art from which he could borrow examples for reproduction. It was known that the British Museum had several large collections but was not anxious to show them or allow them to be photographed. Did I know any private collectors who would co-operate?

I didn't, but I had a friend in Holland, Sem Hartz, to whom I wrote. He had told me about a certain famous collection rumoured to exist in a certain famous library, but admission to it was rarely granted. However, Holland is a small country, and those who move in the right circles know 'everybody'. He wrote back: 'Never joke again about this matter. A private room is being reserved for you, a private curator will be in attendance, and you may bring your private parts in with you – a Hollander would have to leave them outside.'

As my friend was no linguist and did not know Holland, my expenses were paid for me to accompany him. We crossed the Channel. The private room was available, but the private curator was rather busy on other things. We had to select what we wanted to see from the catalogue – in Dutch. We didn't do too badly. In a morning, we saw a cross-section of all that any collection of erotic/pornographic art could contain. What is the difference between erotic art and pornography? One definition says that 'erotic art is art that is not good enough to be pornography'; but it really hinges on the motives of the artist.

There are only a certain number of things that two people can do to-gether: the range can be extended by having several people doing them all together, and then you can put the people in different costumes.

The phrase 'love-in' is too poetic for most of the pictures we looked at. So many drawings and prints depicted nuns that it really unnerved us when at lunch-time we went out into the streets and met real nuns. Another regular peg for pornography was Napoleon's marshals – Soult in Siberia, Ney in Naples, and so on – the same activities in all sorts of costumes. It became terribly boring. I discovered that Morland, a painter well-known in Britain as a painter of sheep and shepherds, had been prolific in this vein. Two erotic drawings by Rembrandt were not boring. Rembrandt, Rodin, Matisse, Modigliani could not be 'porno-graphic' if they tried. They drew too well, too tenderly.

Another visit had been arranged for us to see a private collection be-longing to a diamond merchant. Even to possess such a collection is against the law in most countries on the continent, I was told, so dis-cretion had to be observed. The diamond merchant lived in the country, and was to collect us from our hotel and drive us out to his home. I hoped for a giant Mercedes, would accept a Rolls. In the event, a hand-some youngish man in a shabby raincoat appeared and led us out to the one really beaten-up Volkswagen Beetle in the street. My friend the author sat in front, I squeezed in behind, and picked up a paperback

Sem Hartz, Dutch
stamp and type
designer.

novel in English lying on the seat. It taught me one thing. This was a manufactured and deliberately filthy book, yet it intrigued me to find that although my brain rejected it, my body rose to the bait like a rocket, which it had never done to any drawings. It told me something about the way my body worked, but I was not sure what. The diamond merchant, driving, had left the book there deliberately, perhaps hoping that we could tell him more titles in that style than he knew about. He told us that his wife had a hair appointment in Amsterdam that afternoon, which was a good thing since it might have embarrassed her if we looked at these books of his in her presence. (It turned out that she was not remotely embarrassed by anyone looking at these books in her presence.)

The house we were taken to was one of the most interesting private houses I have ever been in, completely ordinary suburban outside, lavishly beautiful inside. It was full of works of art as well as a fabulous collection of books. The collection we had come to see was a minute fraction of the whole, but superb in quality. It was also unique, since it consisted almost entirely of seventeenth- and eighteenth-century French literature, poetry and novels, with original paintings in the margins. They were all unsigned, but of such consummate skill that I felt that an expert in French book illustration of that period must be able to identify the artists – they could not have been amateurs. The activities portrayed were the same old activities, the same old variations, but drawn with such loving and delicate detail and colouring that we were spellbound – so engrossed that we never noticed Madame return from her hairdressing until she interrupted us with a smile and a cup of tea. Embarrassed? Not her. My friend the author had a merry time making notes of the pages he wanted to be photographed, including two facing frontispiece portraits in full colour entitled 'His Grace the Duke' and 'Her Grace the Duchess' (but not of their faces). I could not imagine them being published in England, and they were not.

Later, we saw another private collection of erotica. Again, it was a small part of a magnificent library of leather-bound folios in a luxurious flat. The owner, a retired surgeon, showed us the highlights while his elderly wife brought us cups of coffee and asked if we took sugar. While muttering 'two lumps, please', I gazed at a flight of winged phalluses by Felicien de Rops. Erotic? Pornographic? They did nothing for me. But love is as good a subject for drawing as for poetry – why not? Only drawings of love are not so easy to publish, even now.

19. Paperclips

IN September 1966 I was invited to lunch in the Athenaeum by Sir Norman Scorgie, the Controller of Her Majesty's Stationery Office. To my considerable surprise, after some preliminary chat, he invited me to succeed Sir Francis Meynell as Hon. Typographic Adviser to HMSO. I was not sure about the 'Honorary' part of it, but I was of course honoured to accept. When I later pointed out that unlike Sir Francis I had to earn a living as a freelance designer, I was allowed a modest retainer.

Sir Francis Meynell was appointed in 1946 to advise on the setting up of a design department in the Stationery Office. Design as a serious and important element in Government printing had never before been taken seriously. It may be remembered that Sir Francis, the originator of the Nonesuch Press, was himself a distinguished designer, but had been knighted for services as a Civil Servant in the Ministry of Food during the war. He had selected Harry Carter to be the new design department's first head, and he asked me to join the new office under Harry. But after five years of serving under other people in the Navy, I was determined to be my own boss and said no – despite greatly admiring both Harry Carter and Francis Meynell. Meynell and Harry were each totally unpedantic, and gave the layout department a sound start. They laid down that its job was not to standardize design, but to achieve consistency where desirable, to ensure that public time and money were not being continually wasted by treating old design problems as new ones every time they arose, and to see that paper was not being spoiled on a lavish scale by either printing too few words on it, or too many, or too unattractively.

Almost the first thing that happened when I returned to my humble office was that a proof of the Prime Minister's new letterheading for 10 Downing Street, set in gothic type, arrived on my desk on the fourth floor of 29 Villiers Street for my approval. Mr Harold Wilson was having some changes made and asked for it to be shown to his old friend Francis Meynell, who he thought was still at HMSO. I kept quiet and approved it.

The head of HMSO's design and typography unit was now John Westwood, a friend I knew well. He had some twenty men and women working under his direction in a well-equipped office in Atlantic House on Holborn Viaduct in London. My function was, in theory, to be the Controller's informant on how they were doing. An outside 'expert' was needed because the job of 'Controller', or head of the Stationery Office, was not given to anyone who knew anything about printing or what the Stationery Office did. The post was regarded, at that time, as a retirement job in which an eminent and/or amiable senior civil servant could see out his time.

The announcement in the *Times* of my appointment had two immediate effects. I was sent a form to fill in for inclusion in *Who's Who*, and I was invited to go to a leading West End photographer and have my photograph taken, free. The photographs were taken, but were so awful that I did not order any.

During my fourteen years as adviser, I served under five Controllers: every one was a civil servant from outside HMSO, with little or no experience of printing or publishing and less of typography.

It was clear that John Westwood's department was competently organized, but it was also clear that I could be of some help to his staff of young designers, for example by giving them praise for work well done: no senior officer in HMSO was qualified to do so.

Another example of how the Typographic Adviser could be used occurred quite soon.

Britain was almost the last country in the world whose passports were still filled in by hand. The Foreign Office had long wanted to redesign and modernize their production, and, incidentally, make them harder to forge.

Now this was being done: passports were redesigned in modern style, and no longer looked like Sainsbury's or Lipton's account books. The Foreign Secretary, Mr Michael Stewart, had to approve, and wanted to know the whys and wherefores. John Westwood knew all the answers, but it was not possible for him to speak to a Minister because he, John, was only a junior civil servant. The Controller could speak to a Minister, but wouldn't have known what to say. The only person supposed to be capable of explaining, and permitted to meet the Foreign Secretary as an equal, was me.

So I was briefed by John Westwood and sent round to the Foreign Office to wait on the Minister. To reach his office, I was escorted through rooms papered in rich Owen Jones wallpapers which must have been hung in the 1860s and which I never knew existed except in drawers in the Victoria & Albert Museum.

The Minister wasted no time, was affable and interested, and once the situation was explained in words he could understand, he agreed to everything that HMSO wanted.

I gained some kudos from this success. It may have been for this that they made me CBE. (Commander of the British Empire, and not 'Companion', as is often assumed).

HMSO was a very large business. It consisted in 1966 of three divisions: in brief, Publishing, Printing, and Supplying. Publishing included Graphic Design, the publishing of *Hansard*, secret and confidential printing, and the massive production of telephone directories. The third large division was Supplies, which supplied items in millions, from paperclips and rubber bands to briefcases and pencils. But HMSO, although such a large business, was not run like a commercial business. The big fault from my point of view was that Graphic Design and Print Production were under different managements and in different buildings. (In April 1980, HMSO was differently organized under the Government Trading Funds Act; and again, radically changed in 1996.)

I was not employed to design things myself, but Graphic Design was sometimes overloaded, and then John Westwood was empowered to farm work out to freelance designers. On two occasions he gave work to me, which provided a useful insight into how things worked – or did not work.

The first job was a booklet for the National Maritime Museum. The illustrations were glossy photographs of fine quality. That was still in the days of letterpress printing for short-run jobs, and the photos had to be reproduced by half-tone blocks. Obviously these excellent photographs had to be sent, not to any old blockmaker, who would probably return them torn, finger-printed and stained with tea, but to the best blockmaker in the country, at that time V. Siviter Smith & Co.Ltd in Birmingham. To establish this, we had to call a meeting with the production people, unbelievably in a different building and under different management. They completely agreed. In due course, the photographs were returned to us, torn, finger-printed, and stained with tea. The meeting had been a complete waste of everybody's time: the usual routine had been followed by the clerk to whom the photographs had been passed, and they had been sent to the cheapest blockmaker on their list. Apologies, of course; can't think how it happened.

The second job was an important book, *English Sculpture 1720–1830*, for the Victoria & Albert Museum. It included over fifty full-page photographs, each of which, being different in size and shape, had to be individually squared up, and a pencil layout made to show its position on the page. The photographs and layouts were then passed to the girls and boys in the production department. A few weeks later my layouts were reported to all have been lost. Again, apologies; no one could be found responsible. The Civil Service protects its own. Every layout had to be redrawn, at the country's expense. Too bad. What a pity. The book was eventually chosen for the National Book League's annual exhibition of the best designed and produced books of the year.

That was in 1971, when letterpress on art paper was still the normal process for such work in Britain. A few years later, letterpress printing was virtually dead, and photo-litho-offset had taken over. When I organized a small exhibition, actually inside HMSO, with the approval of the Controller, to show the advanced 300-line screen offset litho then being done in the United States, I was roundly snubbed by HMSO's Director of Printing. He did not want to know – or be told by me.

As part of my education in HMSO affairs, I was taken to visit their main printing establishments. The biggest factory I was taken to see in 1970 was a newly-opened works at Gateshead, on Tyneside, where most of the country's telephone directories were printed, using the latest computer-assisted technology. Paper went in on enormous reels at one end and came out as finished directories at the other. At the end of a long sort of chute, on which the printed sheets were folded and then bound, finished directories were being unloaded and stacked on trolleys by men with rolled-up sleeves. The books were heavy, and they came off fast. I observed to my guide that these men were obviously picked as being particularly brawny. Oh no, he replied, actually they are all fully trained bookbinders. As bookbinders, they earn about £40 a week, but as labourers, about £80. (Figures quoted from memory, but facts basically accurate).

Whether printed telephone directories were actually the best way to provide information on telephone numbers had been debated for some time. Each directory, for example, gave the numbers for only one area. London required four volumes, excluding trade directories. An obvious alternative was some button-pressing process on a TV screen, perhaps on the telephone itself. This was certainly technically possible at that time. HMSO had invested millions in the Gateshead works, and had to obtain promises from British Telecom that they would be given plenty of warning before their out-of-date technology was discarded.

In the late nineteen-sixties, HMSO's main offices, including Graphic

Design, were moved out of London to Norwich. A day in Norwich every now and then was a pleasant experience for me. It is a lovely city, with several good secondhand bookshops, a cathedral, and a statue of Nelson.

In 1973 the ten-year lease of our office in Villiers Street expired, and we had to renew it for another ten years, or move. I knew that I did not want to spend another ten years in that interesting but increasingly noisy street: massive alterations were just beginning at Charing Cross Station. Several friends said that we didn't need an office in the West End of London at all. Our clients, as they pointed out in over-flattering tones, were all over the place, including abroad. We thought of a move into the country – near Oxford, perhaps? Terribly expensive. At that moment a house was advertised in Scotland called Broomrigg, with five acres of garden and enough outhouses to provide all the office space we wanted. We bought it.

In 1973 we moved up to Scotland. This made regular visits to Norwich rather difficult. There was no air service that could fly people from Edinburgh to Norwich and back in a day. It meant that I had to spend nights in Norwich, and that meant giving more of my time to HMSO than I owed, or it needed. And I was now, in 1977, trying to get to know the fifth Controller since I had started being HMSO's adviser on typography. The main subject the new Controller tried to discuss with me was the choice of a new racing bicycle he wished to buy. He actually took me into a Norwich bicycle shop and for a ghastly moment I thought he was going to insist that we both had a trial ride. I decided that it was time to disengage from HMSO.

Broomrigg, in the Ochils between Stirling and St Andrews, Scotland, June 1973.

20. Art education

IN 1951 I had had to leave my teaching job at the Royal College of Art, after three years, with much regret. It was only for three days a week, but I had just become George Rainbird's partner, and setting up the new firm required all the days of the week and a bit more.

I never had another actual teaching job, but from the early 1960s I was much involved in visits to art schools all over the country. This was first of all through being an external assessor in graphic design, which was usually an appointment for three years and involved one or two days at the end of the students' last term. Later, it was stipulated that external assessors should see the students they were assessing at least once in the previous year as well.

Then there was involvement in the NCDAD (National Council for Diplomas in Art and Design) and the CNAA (Council for National Academic Awards). This was most enjoyable, and I was lucky in being around when the whole system of art education in Britain was being comprehensively upgraded. It is well described in Robert Strand's *A good deal of freedom: Art & Design in the public sector of higher education, 1960–1982*, published by the CNAA in 1987. Basically, it was decided that artists and designers, before entering art school, should have at least some general education – which had not previously been a requirement – and that all art schools in the country should be invited to award a new Diploma in Art and Design. Before they could do so, they had themselves to be examined and approved by an NCDAD-approved visiting committee composed of artists and designers in the areas taught by the school. These visits usually took two or three days. The committee stayed in a convenient hotel and dined together, discussing the school, the people being examined, and life in general. The committee chairman then had to write a report after the visit which, even if it was approving, often also contained conditions, e.g. that the school, or department, had to be re-visited in one, two or three years time before gaining final permission to award the Diploma. Academic quality was the criterion to be applied all the time.

These visits enabled one to see old friends or make new ones among the committee members or the school's teaching staff. But often the best part was meeting the students and seeing what they were up to.

The visits always began in the office of the art school's principal. There was often what one must not call bribery but perhaps willingness to please. If one of the committee had just published a book, it was often seen lying casually on the principal's desk, as if he were reading it. I often saw a new book by my typographer friend John Lewis and was less than pleased when I was congratulated on having written it. On one occasion, when we strolled into the very large office of an important principal, I was beside Lucienne Day, then the country's leading designer of textiles and wallpapers. Entering the room, Lucienne said 'Gosh, this is my latest wallpaper'. She touched the wall: it was still wet ...

The same school (it became a polytechnic and then a university) had a film-making section, which was part of the school of graphic design, so that was on my programme. Watching bad films is one of the most painful things assessors have to do, and I was alarmed to hear the tutors in charge apologising in advance, in a sort of shame-faced way, for the film I was about to be shown. It was a film made by a boy and a girl, and the subject was transvestites.

I sat down in the greatest gloom, and the lights went out. It turned out to be one of the best and most moving films I have ever seen, illustrating and explaining the condition with the greatest sympathy and kindness. It was informative in the most intelligent way. I was not sure what this film was doing in a graphic design course, but I thanked the two students warmly for making and showing it: the tutors had nothing to apologise for. I wonder where the two students who made it are now.

On another visit, I happened to be wearing in my breast pocket a silk handkerchief I had just been given, printed in lurid blues and yellows. It was pleasing to discover that the girl I was sitting next to at lunch, Pat Albeck, had just designed it. I was not always so lucky. On another visit, sitting in the foyer of a motel waiting to be picked up by our hosts, I remarked to a colleague sitting beside me 'Not a bad example of modern design, don't you think, but they've spoiled it with that life-sized plastic figure at the door soliciting funds for something, haven't they?' He replied, 'Um, yes, well, I designed that!'

The principal of Chelsea School of Art on our first validating visit was Lawrence Gowing (later Sir Lawrence), famous for a particularly bad stammer. He had to spend the day under verbal fire, defending his case and answering a barrage of questions. Yet within half an hour he charmed and dominated us. He was so totally oblivious of his handicap that we ceased to notice it ourselves. Sitting next to him at lunch, I have rarely enjoyed a man's conversation so much, although I was sprayed.

Not long after that visit, from which Chelsea not surprisingly emerged triumphant, he and I were members of the team visiting another school. We shared a breakfast table in the hotel and Lawrence wanted some more toast. I watched paralysed as he beckoned a grey-haired waitress and terrified her by mouthing with a violent contorted face. It never occurred to him to ask anyone for help.

I think the first school at which I was an external assessor was Glasgow, in the 1950s. The department of graphic design was competent in a traditional way. After I had examined it, I asked if I could be shown around the rest of the school, which I had never been in before. It was then the only art school in the country, I suppose, whose architecture, by Charles Rennie Mackintosh, was itself fascinating. In the department of printed textiles on the floor below graphic design, I was astonished to find posters, even book jackets and stationery, which were lively and indeed brilliant. This was due, as I discovered, to the head of the department, Robert Stewart. I had to record this in my final report. Sadly, the school at that time could not accept my observations, and a very black mark was put against my name. When I next visited the place as a member of a team assessing all four of the Scottish art schools (Edinburgh, Glasgow, Dundee, and Aberdeen) in one week, I was not allowed to assess Glasgow's graphic design.

Robert Stewart became a friend and a designer I much admired: he never confined himself only to textiles. As mentioned in Chapter 13, he designed lovely silk squares for Liberty in London, and then went on to superb pottery, and then pictures which were a combination of painting and sculpture. In the school, he taught the philosophy that a design school must not *follow* industry's requirements. At school, students *must* experiment and explore their art – and their own abilities – to the utmost, and not concern themselves at that stage with conventional or stated requirements of the big textile manufacturers.

From time to time I bought a drawing or painting from a student whose work I admired, and put it on our walls at home. There was always the hope that my new acquisition would become immensely valuable because the student had become world-famous. That never happened, but I still like the pictures, and they are still on our walls. I now realize that students often reach the peak of their creativity and ability at art school, especially when there is a brilliant tutor and the right sort of atmosphere in the school, due to the principal and the staff as a whole. Newport, Monmouthshire, in Wales, was a good example of this. It had several brilliant staff, especially in illustration, and the principal, John Wright, was outstanding. I particularly enjoyed visiting Newport because the annual exhibition of students' work was held in a public gallery in the town, which meant that the town itself could become aware of, and enjoy, its own art school. Students' work was roped off while being assessed, but the assessment could be seen happening by the public, which was no bad thing, even when it included the student's mum and dad.

There was one student there, a large young man, unshaven, with a peculiar haircut and wearing outrageous clothes, whose passion was rock music and motorbikes, either racing or repairing them. This student actually frightened me the first time I assessed him, because I felt that he utterly despised and even hated me, and might demonstrate it with violence. He was much bigger than me. But when I came to assess him the second time, for his final (and his graphic work was so poor that I did not expect to pass him) I found he was now dressed in a suit – and what was more, he was already earning a comfortable income by personalizing motor cars in a local garage: so much for a wing, double for the bonnet, and naked girls always a lot extra.

In Newport I looked at book illustration by two students which in any other country would have made them famous: it was masterly. I later heard that those two students had married each other. I hope they are happy, but I have not heard of them again as illustrators. Curiously, it was often the apparently far less talented students who went on later to become successful.

Whenever I finished my graphic design assessment, I always asked permission, if there was time, to see the work of the other departments. Sculpture was often the most worth seeing, to a non-expert: it was an area where you could expect amazing experiments and ingenuity. I have always remembered with affection a student who designed a table whose fourth leg wandered across the floor and away into the corner – and perhaps up the wall.

At the same school, many years ago, a sculpture student showed three large crates, the size of railway trucks. One held a miscellaneous collection of shoes, some painted silver and none in pairs; the second was a mass of cotton waste stained red; the third, nothing but rags. It puzzled all who saw it, until we heard that the student had just seen a film of Belsen.

For a student's final assessment (first internal, by the student's own tutors, then by external assessors) each student had to mount an exhibition of work in an allotted space, representing his or her work of three years. It had to be supported by sketch books, portfolios, and roughs, which were very important as it was vital for us to see how a student had arrived at a final solution to a problem. Was it after appropriate research and hard work, or by luck? We often found a better possible solution lurking in a pile of roughs, which the student, through inexperience, had discarded. The way they tackled their problems mattered more to a good assessor than the final result.

Graphic design could include, even in those early days, typography, calligraphy, lettering of all kinds, including 'signing' – (e.g. lettering for motorways or buildings in a family style), book, advertising and general graphics, illustration, print-making, photography, film and TV graphics. The computer revolution came later and altered the way things were done; but not so much the principles of design. Design was still an undeveloped and unfamiliar profession, and many students thought it would be safer to teach, which required another year at a centre approved for art teacher training. As a professional designer myself, I wanted most to help those who intended to become designers. In that case, the sort of diploma (1st, 2.1, 2.2, or pass) they obtained was not vital: what interested – or should interest – an employer was the student's character and the portfolio of work. If they wanted to teach, then their grade would affect their salary.

I had to walk carefully in areas such as photography and film, where I was non-expert. If I felt a student's work was beyond my competence to judge, I said so, and a specialist assessor could be called in. At Corsham (Bath Academy of Art) where everything tended to be unconventional, a girl in graphic design spent the last two years of her course writing a book on mushrooms. A professor of mycology from Bristol University was called in and praised the scientific side of her work very highly. The graphic design part was less good. The Corsham staff would have killed me if I had tried to fail her. She passed.

From time to time a design cliché would sweep through the art schools, usually started by some brilliantly successful national poster or advertising campaign. One year, at every place I visited, half the students' designs contained Union Jacks; another year it was rainbows. In 1972, my diary tells me, I assessed at nine colleges, starting in Belfast. We were escorted into the college by three armed Scottish soldiers. The view from the college windows was of a gutted department store recently bombed by the IRA. The staff and students, Protestant or Catholic, contrived to work on, apparently oblivious of what was happening in the streets outside. The College of Art seemed to be the only sane place in that trouble-torn city. From there I went to Manchester, Leicester, Brighton and Canterbury, all for the first time; then Camberwell and Bristol for the second time; and finally Corsham for the fourth. The visits must have occupied most of June and July, and completely disrupted my own work; but it was helpful for a few assessors to visit several schools, because it tended to rationalise marking standards across the whole country.

Things changed. Many art schools were compulsorily merged with polytechnics, which caused some agonising at first, but which later proved to be beneficial. I observed this at Kingston, where my daughter Catriona was studying fashion design. When it merged with the polytechnic, she suddenly found herself meeting men who were very different, as men, from her fashion designer colleagues. The polytechnic had a bar whose walls were decorated with paintings of cows in all shapes, sizes, and positions, whose udders lit up when the lights were switched on. The art students apparently abhorred this; but I believe it was better for them than the bare concrete walls of some newly built art schools, like Norwich. It became clear that the design of an art school was something that architects had not thought about for years; but that is another story.

Gradually the burden of committee work and administration increased. Teachers in art colleges were becoming administrators: teaching art and design became a minor activity. Practising designers played less and less part in art education. When a new Head of Graphic Design was appointed at Newport who seemed not to approve of either typography or illustration, I felt we were moving into a world for which I did not care. Neither did my friends on the staff: they resigned en masse. I went back to my own desk.

21. Progress North

IN 1973 we moved from London to Dollar, in Scotland, buying a large house called 'Broomrigg' and turning it into two flats, for Tony and myself downstairs and for Fianach and her newly-married husband Pete upstairs. There was a courtyard behind the house with a four-room cottage embowered with flowers, which became the office. Our designer Terence and his wife had a flat above the office reached by an outside stair. Now, every morning, instead of catching a crowded train from Blackheath into London, descending from Charing Cross Station into noisy Villiers Street and then climbing four flights of stairs, I walked across the courtyard and saved about four hours of travelling per day. Fianach, who had been driving in from near Ascot, saved six hours, and Terence about two. Tony, Pete, and Terence's wife all had to find new jobs, and had splendid ones in no time.

Most of the work we were doing in London we could do equally well in Scotland: but the one job we couldn't take up to Scotland was the monthly make-up of the *Connoisseur* magazine, and that was a more serious loss than we at first realized. It was replaced by the bi-monthly magazine of the Scottish Sub-Aqua Club, *Scottish Diver*, to which we subscribed when Pete and I took up diving. It was so poorly produced that I offered to make it look more professional. The offer was accepted, so it became a job for the office, but we could not make a charge. After some years a grant was awarded by the Scottish Sports Council: the magazine was then able to use more colour, and we got paid a little. This led us to meet Adam Curtis, then the president of the Scottish Sub-Aqua Club. He was Professor of Cell Biology in the University of Glasgow, with snow-white hair, although still under fifty. It was a great privilege to be able occasionally to dive with him, although this often meant hanging about in the Sound of Mull at fifty feet, getting cold, while Adam took photographs of sponges, in which he was specially concerned as part of cell biology. He so much enjoyed diving that any week in which he could not dive at least twice was considered as a lost week. The Scottish Sub-Aqua Club owed Adam a very great deal, and so did I.

Dollar is on a road running across Scotland from Stirling in the West to St Andrews in the East. The village of Tillicoultry is two miles to the west, and four miles further on is Alva. I had heard in London of a printer called Cunningham of Alva, and looked forward to meeting him: he printed books for Chatto & Windus and other London publishers, was himself a scholar and translator, and had written manuals on radar for the RAF during the war. But he died just before we moved north. The firm was sold and the employees looked for jobs. The composing-room overseer was offered a small run-down printing business in Tillicoultry, found two partners, and took it over. In due course he called on us, looking for work. We asked him to print a visiting card. He did that well and quickly and we gave him a letterheading. He was very soon buying in typefaces which he knew we wanted. Within a month his competitive estimates enabled us to place the printing of the Calouste Gulbenkian Foundation's annual report with him, and other work for our London clients. He had brought from Cunninghams not only a Monotype keyboard and caster but also the best Monotype operator in Scotland. At first he could print only letterpress, but he soon had enough work, mostly from us, to install offset litho and filmsetting. His name was Ian Cooper. I got to know him slowly on the golf course. He was a master printer but luckily not a master golfer. It was enormous luck for us to find him on our doorstep, and not bad for him. We saw him every day, as he had to pass our house to get to his works. His value to us was immense, because he had that rare gift of knowing, without being told, the difference between good and bad printing. And our work was more interesting to him than his other main job, which was 'swing tickets', the little labels attached to knitwear produced by the local mills – for which the usual order was a million tickets at a time.

When we left London in 1973, one of my good friends there was Stuart Rose, then design director of the Post Office. Devolution and the setting up of a Scottish Parliament in Edinburgh suddenly became a distinct possibility. That would have to be celebrated by the issue of special Scottish stamps, and Stuart realized that design advice on this and similar matters would be needed in Scotland, not in London, and there was no one appointed in Scotland to do this. He recommended that I be appointed as design adviser to the Scottish Postal Board, and happily for me this was agreed. I found, first in the late Trevor Carpenter, and then in Henry Tilling, very sympathetic chairmen to work for.

The building proposed for the new Scottish Assembly or Parliament was on the Calton Hill above Edinburgh. I commissioned a good artist, Willie Rodger, to draw it for the new stamps. We got a handsome design, but the new Parliament did not happen. When it does, will they remember, and be able to find, the stamp design in the files? I doubt it.

The Scottish Postal Board published two pictorial airletters each year, and these came to me to commission. I enjoyed finding Scottish artists, as often as possible young artists whose first important commission it was. I was allowed to draw three myself, one of Oban and the West coast, one of Scottish castles and one of the Royal Navy (the Scottish regiments had already had three). I think we produced about sixteen airletters, before the rules changed.

In the midst of accustoming myself to living in Scotland (where I had been born) I had to go again to America. My friend Richard Blackwell in Oxford had been invited to give a lecture to the Graduate School of Librarianship in the University of Denver. He could not make it and asked them to ask me, which they very kindly did. Flying from New York to Denver is about as far as from London to New York, with a time-change of some two hours. Denver is at an altitude of 7,000 feet. I was advised about drinking alcohol when I got there: it was either more potent at that height and you had to drink less, or it was less potent and you had to drink more – I could never remember which, and I think the people who advised me were not sure either.

When I arrived at the university I was put to bed to rest for three hours and then told to prepare for the 'cocktail hour' and dinner with the Chancellor; after that, I had to deliver the 'Fifth Annual Isabel Nichol Lecture' at eight o'clock in the Lindsay Lecture Hall. When I heard that the Chancellor was a scientist, my heart sank, and I was sure his would also: what on earth would we have in common? But when I was introduced to Chancellor Maurice Mitchell, I found that he had been on the board of the Encyclopaedia Britannica in Chicago with Stanley Morison, and was himself an amateur printer and a most congenial host. We had an extremely good dinner with delightful wine. I never did discover whether I should be drinking more or less, so I followed my usual habits of acceptance – drink all that's offered. In a halo of bonhomie and devoid of all nerves, I enjoyed myself on the platform and the young librarians in the audience responded warmly. My talk had been entitled (not by me) 'A Book is not a Book', and its intention was to say something about those 'three-dimensional physical objects with corners' to students so preoccupied with information-storage and retrieval systems that they might have forgotten, or never known, what it was like to hold a book in their hands for pleasure. As a final kindness the university had my talk printed, with illustrations from my slides, by my friends at the Meriden Gravure Company.

194

Our move to Scotland coincided with the growth of inflation. Business-wise it was not a happy time. We began to lose our London clients, owing to distance, deaths of partners or friends, take-overs, and the growth of new London design businesses.

However we found friends ready to employ us in Edinburgh publishing. An intriguing invitation came from *Blackwood's Magazine*. Its editor, David Fletcher, was the first editor of that famous Scottish monthly who was not a Blackwood, and he was having problems – or rather the paper was. He asked me to redesign the cover – 'but don't change it very much'. I prepared my suggestions and took them in to David, who took me and them up to be presented to Douglas Blackwood, the Managing Director, from whom the brief had originated. His office was a room of history: all the bound volumes of 'Maga' from 1817 lined its walls. Douglas Blackwood had been a distinguished fighter pilot, led the Czech wing of Hurricanes in the last war, and then, reluctantly, it was said, returned to head the family firm. He sat at a big old desk; his son sat beside him at a smaller desk.

My design was accepted – it was just a tidy-up – but of course that was not the way to save the declining fortunes of the paper, as David well knew. A totally new publishing initiative was needed, and he was planning how to do it, but Blackwood and his son (whose passion was fast cars) could not bring themselves to agree. David was dismissed, and set up as an independent publisher and consultant, where he thrived. Blackwoods went out of business in 1980.

One of my oldest friends in Edinburgh was Robin Lorimer. He was a hair-raising car driver ('I learned in a tank') and an authority on pipe music: he composed a pibroch for the launching of my boat *Piaf*. By profession he was a book editor with the Edinburgh publishers Oliver & Boyd. He had asked me to design a picture book of Edinburgh, edited by himself, planned to be grand enough for the Lord Provost of Edinburgh to present to the City's more distinguished visitors. It was beset by contretemps. First, the commissioned text, when it was delivered (a year late) was so poor that it had to be turned down. A much better text, nobly and anonymously produced in a month by Moray McLaren, was contemptuously turned down by an official deputed to act for the Lord Provost 'because it contained so many Scotch words'. Finally, a third and excellent text was written in Robin's office by Janet Rose, his American assistant editor, and was allowed to be printed. The next problem was with the illustrations. After looking at hundreds of the best available photographs of Edinburgh, of which those few taken by Eric de Maré made all the others look inferior, Robin decided he must have completely new ones taken. He and his assistant walked over a hundred miles through Edinburgh choosing subjects, which were then commissioned from local photographers who charged half their usual rates to make the book possible. The result was the best collection of pictures of Edinburgh that I know. One of the photographs we chose showed dustbins off the pavement in the High Street (the 'Royal Mile'). 'You can't use that', we were told, 'The Lord Provost won't like it!' Robin insisted that if the dustbins went, so did he, and they stayed, as did a few other views of the City's less pretty but characteristic aspects.

Poverty hath one name with Pride / in my land

wrote Rachel Annand Taylor.

After more than twenty years, I still admire the portrait of Edinburgh in the mid-1960s that Robin managed to create.

When we moved to Scotland, Robin had already left Oliver & Boyd and set up his own publishing firm, Southside, which was then taken over by Canongate Publishers to allow Robin to concentrate on a greater task. His father, latterly Professor of Greek in the University of St Andrews, had left Robin some money and his manuscripts, and Robin wished to complete and publish the translation of the New Testament into Scots on which his father had been working for the last twenty years of his life. In Robin's editorial introduction he says that his father 'read through 72 different versions of Jude, Hebrews and James, in 14 languages' – which are listed, and include Faroese, Occitanian, Catalan, and Esperanto.

When the manuscript was nearly ready, Robin invited me to help with the design and production. We agreed that Bembo would be a suitable typeface, and Robin set up a charitable trust to invite subscriptions to help finance this inevitably expensive project. I was impressed by the number of Cabinet ministers he wrote to who had been at Balliol with him before the war. The book was published for the Trustees by Canongate under his own imprint Southside. The Trustees decided on an initial printing of 2,500 copies, but had no idea if they would sell *even* a hundred copies. The whole edition was sold in less than two weeks, a second impression was issued less than a month later, and sold out in three weeks. In fact, Lorimer's *New Testament in Scots* became a best-seller, was published in paperback by Penguin in 1985, and is still in print.

Robin Lorimer involved me in another Scottish publishing venture, *The Concise Scots Dictionary*. This came from the Scottish National Dictionary Association, compilers of *The Scottish National Dictionary*, which covers the Scots language from 1700 to the present day in ten volumes.

The *Concise Scots Dictionary* appeared in 1985, consisting of over 800 pages in double column. It could never have appeared without considerable financial help from someone; it was provided by Robert Maxwell, who agreed to underwrite its production and publish it over the imprint of Aberdeen University Press which he owned.

The dictionary text was highly complicated, consisting of a mass of historical and etymological information which had to be compressed in a series of abbreviations, using every typographical resource available: type, size, roman, italic, bold, phonetic symbols and so on. As each passage was finalized by the editors in type script, it was keyed on a wordprocessor in the Association's office by a skilled secretary, and the discs were sent to Aberdeen, where they were converted, without further keyboarding, into printed proofs. The range of typefaces available to us was far less than it would be today. We finally selected Baskerville, which in the small sizes we were forced to use had a far more noticeable bold than Times New Roman. The problem was to achieve maximum legibility within the constraints imposed by having to fit so much difficult copy into a reasonable number of pages.

The Scotsman reviewed it on 10 August 1985 and said, 'If you are looking only for a definition, you will find that very readily. But you will also find alternative spellings, distribution of the word by area and time and its etymology. Much of this is conveyed by an ingenious use of typography, punctuation and abbreviation in a system which is described very lucidly in the introduction. The Dictionary is a model of clarity for a work of this kind.' I ought to have bought that reviewer a drink. The book has now been reprinted several times, but after Maxwell's demise the Dictionary was taken over by Cassels, who dropped my jacket design to follow their own house style.

I often wondered how we got through so much work when we had so many distractions. The garden of Broomrigg, with two pools and avenues of wonderful azaleas and rhododendrons, was big enough for me to practise golf shots in, over the trees. We had hens. Then Fianach installed two kinds of ducks and some geese, and began to breed rare and beautiful pheasants. The main distraction came after we had been in Dollar for four years. Pete and Fianach had been trying to start a family, without success. Everything the doctors could think of was tried, to no avail. Then one evening, when Fianach in her Lancia was about to turn across the main road to enter our drive, a car came round the corner behind her at 60 m.p.h. and crashed into her. The driver, a young local garage mechanic with his wife sitting beside him, sober, and apparently looking for a cigarette in his glove compartment, needed 40 stitches and a new car. Fianach was unhurt and so, surprisingly, was Slocum on the back seat. Her car was heavily damaged.

A few weeks later Fianach found herself pregnant. Had the crash unlocked something? Her daughter Isla was born ('she's gorgeous' said the nurse on the phone) in 1978. Chickens and pheasants took second place and were soon phased out.

Slocum lived two more years. In the office, he lay at Fianach's feet and did not mind when three goslings came and sat at mine. At last he died peacefully and we buried him under a fir tree on the edge of our policies.

Around this time (c.1978), the publishers Thames & Hudson in London invited me to write a book 'Typography' to appear in a new series of manuals 'for the use of students and staff in art colleges, polytechnics, colleges of education and other institutes of higher education, for craft teachers in schools, and for extra-mural students'. This was indeed a challenge, and I settled down to tackle it in my Broomrigg library of beautiful glass-fronted book-cases which might have been designed by a pupil of Charles Rennie Mackintosh – which when we first saw it contained no books, but one double-barrelled shotgun.

I had to collect (or re-think) my thoughts, and write down all I had discovered (or thought I had discovered) over a period of some forty years. Apart from the writing, I had the greatest pleasure in assembling a collection of exciting illustrations, some of which I had to draw myself, but were mostly from the historic past or from living friends.

I was lucky in having had what was probably a wider experience of typographic design than most of my contemporaries since it had started immediately after the end of the war in 1945, when everything needed re-designing and there were very few designers around to do it. My work had ranged from letter headings for friends, and then companies, parish magazines, children's books for Penguin, then the comics *Eagle*, *Girl*, *Swift* and *Robin*, to magazines like *Picture Post* and the *New Scientist*, and then a wide range of books (including the Bible) produced by Rainbird, McLean and other publishers.

The *Manual of Typography* apparently did what it was intended to do: it

The office at Broomrigg often contained ducks, goslings, a hen, a cat, and a dog.

has been reprinted many times, and is still in print, and has been translated into Spanish, for the South American market;* and I still am happy in receiving letters from students in art schools who (to my intense pleasure) say they have enjoyed it – as well as learning something from it!

The new technology began to impinge. If we had been younger we would have installed a word processor and keyboarded our own books. But it was too late. Fianach and I were not motivated to become rich, and our lives were full enough. Tony had now retired from teaching history, and having discovered that I was 65 we decided that we had been maintaining two houses and two gardens for long enough; we would now concentrate on one and it would be on the island of Mull.

Why live on Mull? About a mile from our front door at Carsaig, away to the right, is a line of majestic, thousand-foot cliffs, which always look different, presenting facets, details, shadows, colours, scars, movements of light, falls of water, which we think we have never seen before. Across the sea in front of us are the Paps of Jura, mountains made of the same stone as the Allegheny Mountains north of New York. Closer in is a long reef on which the gulls, cormorants and seals lie, and when the breeze is right and the sun is shining, the sea breaks in white explosions like shouts of laughter.

There were some 10,000 books to bring from Dollar to Carsaig on Mull, all packed in whisky-bottle cartons. The move had to be made in winter. Pickfords required two vans, one of which was too big for MacBrayne's winter steamer, so they had to bring up another steamer from Glasgow. The first van nearly got to the cottage but was then bogged down in snow. The second van thoughtfully broke down beside the only pub, some four miles away, and its contents were decanted into an empty hut from which I later had to fetch them across the hill in a series of car trips. Then I had to take every book out of its box and decide where to put it in my new library, a log cabin we had had to build beside the cottage to hold the books, since the cottage was already full of books. The first book I picked up was *Memorable Balls* (containing the full list of guests invited to the Duchess of Richmond's Ball before Waterloo), edited by James Laver. Its place, I decided, was beside some American favourites, *You too can make a Stradivarius Violin*, *Junior Fun in Bed*, and *Three Years in a Man-Trap* (by the author of *Ten Nights in a Bar-*

---

* Translations into Greek and Serbo-Croat are also in hand.

Antonia and Ruari McLean, Carsaig, 1984.

Room). My well-thumbed paperback, *All that Men Know about Women* (100 completely blank pages, published by Pentangle, Wallop, England, n.d.) went on the same shelf. Another book, chosen for its unlikely title, *The Women in Gandhi's Life*, by Eleanor Morton, published by Dodd, Mead New York, 1953, turned out to be serious and very moving. *Liaisons Dangereux* and *Les Femmes d'Amis* could look after themselves.

I went on sorting out my books, like a fussy headmaster arranging next term's pupils. Of course, they didn't all fall into categories. Here they all were, many shapes and sizes, things that I could pick up, put down, stroke, touch: objects, as well as containers of words and ideas. The pages themselves had tactile and visual qualities that could excite. Here was lithography, here etching, here letterpress, denting the paper from type or metal or wood. The paper pages themselves had many different qualities and textures, from smooth machine-made, to rougher hand-made – and it did not even need always to be paper: there was vellum and card.

Not to mention typography and lettering. Here were letters cut by – for example – William Caslon, Bruce Rogers, W. A. Dwiggins, Edward

Johnston; and by people who had been or still were my friends, Reynolds Stone, Hermann Zapf, Berthold Wolpe, Fritz Kredel, Matthew Carter....

I was now an old-fashioned, non-electronic, ex-typographer, but perhaps not entirely useless. The younger generation are intoxicated with the new technical opportunities, but somebody needs to remain sober. Clarity of communication still matters.

Thinking about words and poetry, Frederic Prokosch wrote:

love, music, hurricane
Enter and rush like ghosts through that old cave, the human brain.

I never thought that being a typographer was work.

It was a comfort that in 1981 I was appointed a Trustee of the National Library of Scotland, the year that Tony and I moved to Carsaig on the island of Mull.

Michael Strachan, chairman of the Trustees of the National Library of Scotland, 1980, with Antonia and Ruari McLean.

Postscript: Is typography necessary?

Publishers and even printers have been known to smile indulgently when watching a typographer pondering the proof of a title-page long and earnestly and at last marking a point of space in between two capital letters. What does it matter, they ask, and was it not perfectly legible before?

Legibility is not enough to aim at when one is printing books. True, G. K. Chesterton said that if a thing is worth doing, it is worth doing badly. And a poorly printed copy of a favourite book is better than no copy at all. Probably everybody will agree that a well-produced book is better than a moderately-produced book. The difference between the two is small. Is it worth the extra trouble? Will one point (one seventy-second of an inch) be noticed? Does typography matter?

Assuming that anything matters, then certainly it matters how things are made and what they look like, and typography is responsible for how printed words are made and what they look like. Many books today are printed in good types, on quite good paper, and yet the result is only moderately pleasing. An enormous amount of skill (five hundred years of it, at least) has gone into the design and manufacturing of the types; the brains of engineers and scientists of many generations have gone into the making of the paper and the ink and the printing machinery; and highly skilled craftsmen have done the actual printing. It has lacked one ingredient, the brains of a typographer, and so is by that amount less good than it should have been.

The fact that good types are available at all today is due to typographers' efforts in the past; that work is now done, and a publisher can be sure that every book printer today is stocked with several excellent founts of type. Of what does typography consist when applied to the actual production of a book?

The first and all-important principle is that the type matter should be so arranged that the author's message is transferred to the reader's brain as quickly and smoothly as possible; the mechanism by which this is achieved should not be noticeable. If one is judging a new type face, one looks at a page of it, and if any letter springs to the eye, even as being particularly beautiful, that letter is wrong.

A great many modern books offend by trying hard to be well-designed or 'modern', and there certainly are cases where the contents matter so little that a piece of clever design relieves what would otherwise be boredom; but in all real books, the book is the author, and not the printed page: it is just as annoying when the printer or typographer obtrudes his personality into the author-reader relationship as when some outsider rings a bell for tea or switches on the telly.

But if some books are spoiled by too much typography, more books are spoiled by having too little. One of the first concerns of a typographer in planning a book is to decide on the size of type that will be right for the size of page, and for the length of line, and to determine the amount of leading required. Normally there should be not less than ten words per line on a book reading page, and not more than fifteen: too short a line means turning back too often, and too long a line means losing the right line when you turn back. The amount of leading, or white between the lines, depends partly on the length of the ascenders and descenders of the fount. Most type is easier to read if it is slightly leaded. It is also a rule of good composition that setting should be close, and as even as possible; the space between words should be about the width of the letter 'i', and never much more. The longer the gap between words, the harder the work for the eye, and the greater the risk of a word in the line below being nearer than the next word, in which case the eye will jump to it instead. Also, when spacing between words is too wide, ugly rivers of white appear, and the even grey texture of a well-set page of type is lost.

Margins are also important. They are the frame surrounding a page of type and separating it from the scenery in the background. In the old days, when people read books seriously, they were used for making notes, and they were always as generous as possible because every time a book is re-bound, something more is sliced off all sides. Nowadays the convenience of having books we can slip into the pocket and the exigencies of wartime have made us less sensitive to margins and we find we can, when necessary, do with very narrow ones. Sometimes, modern books are printed with normal margins reversed, *i.e.* with the outside margin narrower than the inside margin. If such books will never need to be re-bound, there seems no technical argument for this. It merely looks awful.

There are a thousand other details in which good typography can improve a book, and one seventy-second of an inch may in fact make a noticeable difference. That all made things should be made as beautiful as possible is one of the details in which civilisation consists. It is no more important that books should be well-made, than that anything else should be well-made; unless, indeed, you happen to regard books as friends. We do not want our friends all to be well-dressed, but we do, I think, want them all to be comfortably and appropriately dressed. Therein lies the pleasure and the skill of book typography.

ANYWAY, what is a typographer?

I am writing this in the UK, where 'typographer' does *not* mean, as it does in the USA, the man, woman or firm who sets the type. I mean the designer.

But today, when there are so many different terms covering so many different activities – layout staff, graphic artists, 'graphikers', visualisers, etc., – let us use the word 'typographer' in its traditional sense of the person who lays out or arranges type in order to be read.

As opposed, for example, to the graphic designers who make 'images', who use not words but symbols, shapes, photographs and other visual ideas. That is something completely different. The two skills are not often found in the same person.

The typographer, then, in the original sense of the word, uses type to communicate an author's message. For many years after the invention of moveable type way back in the 1400s, the typographer was always the printer. In a famous book published in London in 1683—4, called *Mechanick Exercises or the Whole Art of Printing*, the author Joseph Moxon wrote 'by a typographer, I mean such a one, who by his own Judgement, from solid reasoning within himself, can either perform, or direct others to perform from beginning to the end, all the Handy-works and Physical Operations relating to Typographie'. That still does not define the actual job. But Moxon was writing a manual, and went on to describe those 'Handy-works and Physical Operations' in detail.

Putting words together, letter by letter in the composing-stick, was the job of the compositor. 'A good Compositer, [sic]', wrote Moxon, 'is ambitious as well to make the meaning of his *Author* intelligent to the *Reader*, as to make his work show graceful to the eye, and pleasant in Reading'. That says it all. Designing printed matter so that the words 'show graceful to the Eye, and pleasant in Reading' continued to be the work of compositors for centuries. They sometimes worked on their own, but more often under the direction of the Master Printer.

By the end of the nineteenth century, Monotype and Linotype

hot-metal composition systems had both been invented (in the United States). The old days of hand-setting, hand presses and hand-made paper were ended. The Master Printer now had to master a lot of new techniques, including machines run by steam and electricity, not to mention the host of new typefaces made possible by the Benton punch-cutting machine. His hands were full. No wonder that he had to look around for someone else to attend to the finicky details of typographic design.

Since many of these new developments came from America, it is not surprising that the first freelance typographer, Bruce Rogers, and the first freelance type designer, Fred Goudy, were both Americans.

But typography did not become a profession, in which you could be qualified, and be awarded a degree, as in medicine, accountancy and architecture, until much later. In Britain certainly it came only after 1945. But the job remained the same: to make words 'graceful to the Eye, and pleasant in Reading'.

It is a more complicated job than at first may appear. There are many different kinds of book, let alone the modern visual aids, and there are many different kinds of text: some, like dictionaries, that you usually only want to read a few words at a time; some that have to be read very carefully and perhaps re-read several times; others that have to be skimmed through very quickly in order to find a needed reference or fact: and the ideal type and typographical treatment for each may be quite different.

Aren't the author's words sacred?

It depends.

When a typographer is given a work of literature – poems, prose, or whatever – then of course the words, or punctuation? or use of capitals? – may not be changed without the author's permission. Authors, like everyone else, make mistakes – some are very grateful when they are corrected, others less so! But mistakes (e.g. quotations from the Bible, or other words of printed literature) have to be corrected.

But not all typography is book typography, in which the words are usually sacred. Magazine, brochure or newspaper texts, especially headings, often can, and even *must* be changed. In a magazine, the title of an article usually has one main purpose: to tell the reader what the article is about, to give him or her the choice whether it's a 'must' or can be skipped – or in some 'popular' journalism and in advertising, to try to make the reader want to read it. Designers *must* have the freedom to suggest better wording for a title, perhaps to fit a space or an illustration that the original writer did not know about.

All experienced typographers know that in many kinds of work words that come to them are *not* right. In a letterheading for example, it is surprising how often the client supplies the wrong street number or postcode, or leaves out some important wording completely.

I once had to design a poster for the notice-boards of a university, telling graduates and undergraduates how to register for their courses at the beginning of the academic year. The university could not understand why the existing poster was being ignored.

I sat down to read the 'copy' I was given. It took me all of *three hours* to puzzle out what the man who wrote that copy was trying to say. He could not write plain English – a gift, like that of 'common sense' which is not so common as you may think. Having, with many doubts, arrived at what I thought was meant, I re-wrote the copy and returned it to the university saying (apologetically) 'Is this what you mean?' It came back saying 'Thank you, yes'. The 'typography' was then easy. But with a text that did not make sense, it was impossible.

The words have to be right.

(Some of the above was originally printed in *The Folio*, Vol. 1, No. 5, May–June 1948.)

The author in Carsaig library, 1990. (Photo by Colin Banks.)

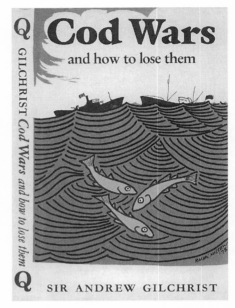

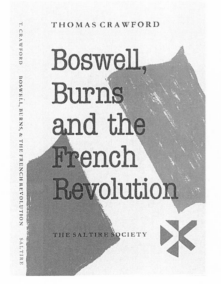

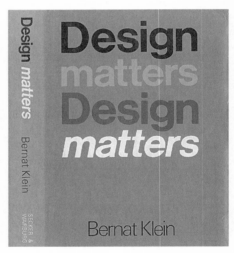

Four jackets designed by the author for different publishers.

Checklist of works by the author

Books written, compiled, or translated by Ruari McLean. All published in Great Britain unless otherwise stated.

1. *George Cruikshank*. Art & Technics, 1948.
2. *Modern Book Design*. British Council, 1951. Translated into Swedish, Gebers, Stockholm, 1956.
3. *Modern Book Design*. Faber & Faber, 1958. Reprinted.
4. *Late Spring*, by Joe Lederer (novel), Cape, 1958. Translated from German by David Hardie (R. McL.).
5. *The Wood Engravings of Joan Hassall*. OUP, 1960. Reprinted.
6. *Victorian Book Design and Colour Printing*. Faber & Faber, 1963. Enlarged new edition, 1972.
7. *The Reminiscences of Edmund Evans*. (Edited) OUP. 1968. Reprinted.
8. *Asymmetric Typography* by Jan Tschichold. Faber & Faber, 1968. Translated from the German *Typographisches Gestaltung*.
9. *Magazine Design*. OUP. 1969.
10. *Pictorial Alphabets*. Studio Vista, 1969.
11. *Victorian Publishers Bookbindings in cloth and leather*. Gordon Fraser, 1973.
12 *A Book is not a Book* (reprinted lecture). University of Denver, USA, 1974.
13. *Jan Tschichold, Typographer*. Lund Humphries, 1975. Reprinted.
14. *Three Stories by Courteline*. Translated from the French. Privately printed in Holland by Sem Hartz, 1975.
15. *Joseph Cundall, Victorian Publisher*. Private Libraries Association, 1976.
16. *The Noah's Ark ABC*, etc. (Edited), Dover, USA, 1976.
17. *A Book of Cuts by Edward Bawden* (Edited). Scolar Press, 1979.
18. *The Thames & Hudson Manual of Typography*. Thames & Hudson, 1980. Reprinted and translated into Spanish, Greek, and Serbo-Croat.
19. *The Frog Prince & other Stories* by Walter Crane (Introduction), Woodward Reprints.
20. *Victorian Publishers Bookbindings in Paper*. Gordon Fraser, 1983.
21. *The Last Cream Bun*. Drawings by Roger Pettiward (Paul Crum). (Edited). Chatto & Windus, 1984.
22. *Detail in Typography* by Jost Hochuli. Translated from German. Compugraphic, USA, 1987.
23. *Benjamin Fawcett, colour printer* (with Antonia McLean). Scolar Press, 1988.
24. *Edward Bawden, War Artist, and his letters home, 1940–45*. (Edited) Scolar Press, 1989.

25. *Nicolas Bentley drew the Pictures.* (Edited) Scolar Press, 1990.
26. *Designing Books* by Jost Hochuli. Translated from German. Agfa Compugraphic, USA, 1990.
27. *How to draw layouts* by Jan Tschichold. Translated from *Typografische Entwurfstechnik.* Merchiston Publishing, Edinburgh, 1991.
28. *The New Typography* by Jan Tschichold, Translated from *Die neue Typographie,* University of California Press, USA, 1995.
29. *Typographers on Type* (Edited). Lund Humphries, 1995.
30. *Jan Tschichold: A Life in Typography.* Lund Humphries, 1997.
31. *How Typography Happens.* The British Library & Oak Knoll Press, 2000
32. *True to Type.* Oak Knoll Press & Werner Shaw, 2000

Booklet illustrated by Ruari McLean
McLean's Silly Diving Signals. Scottish Sub-Aqua Club, 1990.

Periodicals edited by R.McL.
SIA Journal (Society of Industrial Artists, London). Issues 39 to 46, 1954–5.
Motif, nos. 1–13, 1958–67.
The Connoisseur, Art Editor 1962–73.

Index

Heading for *The P. L. R. Bulletin* (catering trade magazine), 1946.